THE
EVERYTHING®
Guide to
Government Jobs

Dear Reader,

In an uncertain economic climate, working for the government is a smart choice. Jobs in government often provide more benefits, better retirement packages, and greater job security than their private-sector counterparts.

If you're interested in finding a government job, you've come to the right place. This book shows you where to look for these jobs, describes them in detail, and explains how to apply for them. You may have to jump through some hoops to get a government job. Most applicants have to take tests, get put on a waiting list, and submit to invasive background checks and credit checks. This is the gauntlet you must pass through if you want a government job. You have to be passionate about your job goals. The most successful people, in or out of government, are those who are passionate about what they do.

And who knows? You may even be enriched and rewarded in more ways than purely financial. The job you find may be an opportunity to serve the greater good and make a difference in the lives of your fellow citizens. Not a bad way to earn a living. Not bad at all.

James Mannion

The EVERYTHING® Series

Editorial

Publisher	Gary M. Krebs
Managing Editor	Laura M. Daly
Associate Copy Chief	Sheila Zwiebel
Acquisitions Editor	Lisa Laing
Development Editor	Jessica LaPointe
Associate Production Editor	Casey Ebert

Production

Director of Manufacturing	Susan Beale
Associate Director of Production	Michelle Roy Kelly
Cover Design	Matt LeBlanc Erick DaCosta
Design and Layout	Heather Barrett Brewster Brownville Colleen Cunningham Jennifer Oliveira

Visit the entire Everything® Series at *www.everything.com*

THE
EVERYTHING®
Guide to
Government
Jobs

A complete handbook to hundreds of
lucrative opportunities across the nation

James Mannion

A
Adams Media
Avon, Massachusetts

Dedication
*This book is dedicated to all those in government service
whose motivation is to serve a cause greater than themselves
and to give something back to the community.*

Acknowledgments
*To the very patient Lisa Laing and any other of the
editorial, development, and production people at Adams Media
who had to put up with this hack writer.*

An Everything® Series Book.
Everything® and everything.com® are registered trademarks of F+W Publications, Inc.

Published by Adams Media, an F+W Publications Company
57 Littlefield Street, Avon, MA 02322 U.S.A.
www.adamsmedia.com

ISBN 10: 1-59869-078-7
ISBN 13: 978-1-59869-078-1

Printed in Canada

J I H G F E D C B A

**Library of Congress Cataloging-in-Publication Data
is available from the publisher.**

This publication is designed to provide accurate and authoritative information with
regard to the subject matter covered. It is sold with the understanding that the publisher is not engaged in rendering legal, accounting, or other professional advice.
If legal advice or other expert assistance is required, the services of a competent
professional person should be sought.
    —From a *Declaration of Principles* jointly adopted by a Committee of the
American Bar Association and a Committee of Publishers and Associations

Many of the designations used by manufacturers and sellers to distinguish their
products are claimed as trademarks. Where those designations appear in this book
and Adams Media was aware of a trademark claim, the designations have been
printed with initial capital letters.

*This book is available at quantity discounts for bulk purchases.
For information, please call 1-800-289-0963.*

Contents

Top Ten Reasons to Consider a Government Job

1. It is an opportunity to serve a cause greater than yourself and be a force for good in the world.
2. It is almost impossible to get fired once you achieve tenure.
3. You can choose from a variety of workplaces, including the traditional office job as well as plenty of jobs in the great outdoors.
4. There are jobs to suit every interest and skill set.
5. The government is not going anywhere—in fact, it is getting bigger every day, giving federal employees great job security.
6. The benefits packages are often better than those in the private sector.
7. In order to attract the best and the brightest, the government is becoming more competitive with the private sector, which means better salaries for many jobs.
8. There is usually some form of tuition reimbursement—for instance, the armed forces will virtually pay for your college education.
9. It is unlikely you will have to relocate, as only one out of six federal employees works in the Washington, D.C., area.
10. You are needed. As a citizen and a taxpayer, you know that you can probably do a better job than those already in government!

Introduction

A government does not run by itself. People run it. It takes a lot of people doing all kinds of jobs to ensure that the wheels of government turn as smoothly as possible. The U.S. government has gotten bigger under every president from George Washington to George W. Bush. While bigger does not necessarily mean better, it does mean that the government will need more than a few good men and women to keep running.

People who hold government jobs come from every walk of life and fill a great range of positions, from working in cubicles to working in the great outdoors, from patrolling the corridors of Washington to patrolling hot spots around the globe. While the federal government is headquartered in Washington, D.C., you can live anywhere and still be a government employee. In fact, most federal government employees live somewhere other than our nation's capital. Keep in mind that a government job does not necessarily mean a federal one. All state and local governments require a reliable workforce. There are plenty of jobs to be filled. You just have to know what the jobs entail, where to look, and how to apply. If you don't have the necessary qualifications for a job you want, you also need to know how to get them.

This book provides all that information and more. Government workers hold jobs as diverse as those in the private sector, ranging from secretaries, scientists, and soldiers to police officers, postal employees, and park rangers. Here you will find overviews of hundreds of jobs and how to apply for them.

The advice provided here can help you land a job that will provide a decent living, job security, and a good benefits package for you and your family. To those who work to live rather than live to work, a government job may be the right career choice. Government jobs offer plenty of vacation days, paid holidays, and sick days so employees have time to stay home when they need to or recharge their batteries with a family vacation. This kind of time off allows workers the leisure to attend to the things that matter most: family and friends.

You can see that there are many reasons to look into the government as a place to work. Many are tangible and practical, such as the salary, benefits, and paid leave. While it may seem corny to some, there is a greater reason to consider a job in the public sector: It is an opportunity to do your part to make this crazy world a better place. It can certainly use all the help it can get.

Chapter 1

So You Want to Work for the Government

Many people today are cynical about the government, often rightly so. They see it as a hindrance to the average citizen rather than a help. It remains a fact, however, that the government is one of the largest employers in the country. The United States needs people with a desire to serve their country unselfishly. Civil servants have a chance to make small differences that can blossom into system-wide changes. As a bonus, there is often a great deal of stability in a government job.

Why Choose a Government Job?

Government jobs offer stability unmatched by most private companies. As long as there is a government, there will be government jobs. Often, people have the perception that these jobs pay little and offer little opportunity for advancement. The private sector thus seems like a better choice to many workers. But it all depends on one's point of view. Government jobs can offer many people the chance to improve their pay and benefits, and for some, government jobs can be the stepping-stone to opportunities in the private sector.

Government jobs also give employees the opportunity to make a difference. Private-sector jobs might offer workers the chance to become wealthy, but civil service jobs offer financial rewards to employees, as well as opportunities to serve their country, state, or community while doing something they love. People who love the outdoors have the opportunity to work as park rangers, for example, protecting America's landmarks while informing visitors of their significance. For those who want to help others more directly, the

1

government offers the chance to become police officers, firefighters, and protectors of homeland security.

E ssential

In the private sector, trade unions are often the engine for employee stability and security. A 2005 transportation workers' union strike in New York City caused a lot of grumbling, but the strike was an effort to ensure that transportation workers were treated equitably. Labor unions have been instrumental in creating humane conditions for workers and ending child labor.

A Short History of the United States

If you are interested in working for the government, it is important to have a basic grounding in the governmental processes and history of the United States. This section provides information that might help you as you consider a career in government service.

The United States of America is a federal democratic republic that was officially formed after the successful conclusion of the American Revolution. Until the United States Constitution was ratified in 1789, the Articles of Confederation formed the basis of America's government. The original thirteen colonies had a loose form of government called a confederation. The colonies were run like independent, sovereign nations, with the federal government providing financial support to all members of the confederation.

After the fledgling country's long, grueling fight for independence was over, America's leaders were eager to form a new type of government in which power was shared. The mother country, England, was a monarchy, which put all power in the hands of the king. The Founding Fathers wanted to ensure that America would not be a monarchy or dictatorship. To that end, they created a government consisting of three branches—judicial, legislative, and executive—and a system of checks and balances.

The three branches of the federal government are designed to work in balance to keep any one branch from gaining too much power or determining the country's policy. The legislative branch has the power to pass laws. The president has the power to sign bills into law or to veto them. The courts have the power to determine whether legislation follows the letter and spirit of the U.S. Constitution. If the actions of any one branch are determined by either of the other branches to be out of step with the needs and will of the country's citizens, the other two branches can use their powers to override, or "check," the branch that is out of step.

The president and his cabinet constitute the executive branch. The legislative branch is comprised of the U.S. Senate and the U.S. House of Representatives. Each of the country's fifty states elects two senators, and the number of each state's congresspersons is based on its population. (At present, there are 435 members of the House of Representatives.) The judicial branch culminates with the U.S. Supreme Court, the country's final arbiter of laws and interpreter of the Constitution. The president appoints justices for lifetime terms to the high court, but Congress must approve these appointments. Below the high court, the judicial branch consists of a system of lower federal courts.

How the President Is Elected

Presidents are elected or re-elected every four years. The major parties nominate their candidates for president, and those names are submitted to the chief election official in each state. These are the candidates whose names will appear on the general election ballot.

On the Tuesday following the first Monday in November, eligible people vote for the president. The candidate who wins the popular vote in a state wins all the votes of that state's electors. (Electors belong to the body known as the Electoral College, described in the following section.) Maine and Nebraska do not subscribe to the winner-take-all method. In these two states, the states are divided into a number of districts. Each district gets one statewide electoral vote.

The state's electors meet in their respective states to cast their electoral votes on the Monday following the second Wednesday of

December. Electors get two votes, one for president and one for vice president. Each elector must cast one of his or her two votes for a candidate outside of the state. This rule ensures that a president and vice president cannot hail from the same state, thus unduly concentrating the influence of the executive branch in one state.

Question

Why do presidential candidates usually choose running mates from other parts of the country?
To increase the likelihood that their party will receive the popular vote. For example, John F. Kennedy of Massachusetts chose Texan Lyndon B. Johnson for his running mate. This isn't always the case, of course. In 1992, Arkansan Bill Clinton chose Al Gore, a senator from neighboring Tennessee, as his running mate.

The electoral votes are sealed and sent to the president of the Senate, and on January 6 the results are read aloud to both houses of Congress. The American voters already know the outcome, since forty-eight of the nation's fifty states grant all of their electoral votes to the popular vote-winning candidate. If no single candidate receives a majority of electoral votes, the House of Representatives votes to choose the winner from among the top three candidates. Then, on January 20, the president and vice president are sworn into office.

The History of the Electoral College

There are several theories to explain the reasons the Founding Fathers may have implemented the electoral system. As a secondary voting body, it is possible that the Electoral College was designed to help balance the interest of different states, especially in cases where candidates from two states had split the vote. It is important to remember that when the Constitution was drafted, the current two-party system had not yet come into existence. With multiple parties, there is no longer any need for an electoral college to balance the interests or votes of the different states.

Even with a two-party system, the electoral college continues to serve one important purpose. It prevents states with concentrated populations from automatically overriding the votes and the interests of less populated states. Each state is permitted the same number of electors as it has representatives in Congress (senators and congresspeople). States with larger populations do have a greater number of electors, but less populated states can combine their electoral votes and contribute to the outcome of an election.

Changes to the Electoral System

Because there were no political parties when the Constitution was drafted and the United States came into being, the electoral system as originally conceived did not take the effects of political party differences into account. Electors were each given two votes, only one of which they were permitted to cast for candidates of their own state. There was no distinction between a vote for president or vice president. The candidate who won the most votes was elected president, and the runner-up was elected vice president. If the candidate with the most votes did not also win the majority, the vote went to the House of Representatives, with each state getting a single vote. The vice presidential candidate was not required to win a majority.

This system became a problem almost immediately, when different political theories divided elected officials along party lines. Federalists believed that the country's power should be consolidated into a central ("federal") government, with state power being subordinate to the interests of the federation. Members of the Democratic-Republican party believed that primary power should reside with the individual states. In 1796, the Federalist John Adams was elected president. His runner-up was Thomas Jefferson, who belonged to the Democratic-Republican Party.

Things got worse in the subsequent presidential election, in which Thomas Jefferson and Aaron Burr both ran as Republicans. There was no way for electors to distinguish their votes for president and vice president, and as a result of some tricky political maneuvering, neither candidate won a majority of votes. As a result, the vote for president went to the House of Representatives. The House voted thirty-five times, finally only breaking the tie and electing Jefferson after more tricky politics. (This long contest sparked the feud already smoldering between Aaron Burr and Alexander Hamilton and ended with their duel, in which Burr killed Hamilton.)

The Twelfth Amendment to the Constitution was drawn up to keep such a tie from recurring. Henceforth, each elector cast only one vote for president and one for vice president. In the event that no one receives an absolute majority of electoral votes, the House of Representatives votes to decide among the three top candidates.

After the famous presidential election of 1800 and the drafting of the Twelfth Amendment, the House of Representatives has voted to elect the president only once. This happened in 1824, when four Republicans—John Quincy Adams, Henry Clay, Andrew Jackson, and William Harris Crawford—split the electoral vote, with none of the candidates receiving a majority. Crawford received the fewest electoral votes and was thus dropped from contention when the vote went to the House, where John Quincy Adams was ultimately elected president.

Pros and Cons

The Electoral College has been controversial since it was created. But it does have some positive points, including these:

- The Electoral College ensures nationwide popular support of presidential candidates.
- Minority groups wield power thanks to the Electoral College. Small minorities within states may shift the balance of the electoral votes in favor of one candidate over another.
- The Electoral College promotes political stability because it promotes a two-party system. Third-party candidates rarely achieve national prominence, which compromises their ability to win electoral votes. As a result, the country's two dominant parties are forced to absorb interests espoused by third-party candidates.

But the electoral system has its share of negatives as well, including these:

- If the country were to become extremely politically divided, it could cause three or more presidential candidates to split the electoral vote. As a result, a third-party candidate could be elected.
- Electors have the potential to vote against their party's candidate, possibly invalidating the will of the state's voters.
- The Electoral College may be a factor in low voter turnout. Since each state only gets a certain number of electoral votes, regardless of voter turnout, individual voters have little impact on the outcome.
- For some, the Electoral College smacks of an oligarchy—a form of government in which a limited number of people have the power to elect a nation's leaders.

One of the most serious complaints about the Electoral College comes from folks who believe that it prevents America from truly being a democracy because it can cause the candidate who wins the most popular votes to lose the election. This happened in 2000, during the race between Al Gore and George W. Bush.

State and Local Governments

The United States has had fifty states since 1959, when Alaska and Hawaii joined the union. Each of these states has its own constitution and laws. Each county and municipality within a state has its own laws as well. Some things that are perfectly legal in one county or town can be illegal in another town or county.

The governor is the state's highest elected official, and each state has its own legislature and court system. The good news for you, government-job seeker, is that you can probably find a good job in your own backyard. Every community, regardless of its size, has government jobs that must be filled. Areas of needed expertise run the gamut from building inspection to law enforcement.

Some Issues to Consider

Most government jobs have set salaries, and they do not always offer great opportunities for upward mobility. In many cases, employees have to take tests or get additional education to advance to a new level. Government jobs have many rules, some of which can seem counterintuitive or even counterproductive. It is possible to become more focused on red tape than on serving others. In addition, depending on your job, you may find yourself at the wrong end of dinner-table conversation. People love to grouse about the government, and you may find yourself on the defensive from time to time.

Fact

"Dry" counties and towns do not sell alcohol, but they may be adjacent to communities that do. Once the site of Methodist camp meetings, the town of Ocean Grove, New Jersey, remains dry despite its location on the Jersey Shore, which is filled with beach towns that sell liquor by the truckload.

Overlapping Duties

Some government agencies have similar functions, and this can cause difficulties. For instance, the FBI and the CIA both seek to quash crime, but they don't always share information with one another. In this case, duplication of effort can be more than an inconvenience; it can actually serve as a threat to national security. Different offices working toward the same ends can also lead to redundancy and what some folks like to call "government waste." Former vice president Al Gore worked to streamline the federal government, and the Bush administration has continued that effort. But rivalry and repetition persist. At best, these problems can cause you to be on the receiving end of anti-government harangues. At worst, they can cause you daily headaches on the job.

Government Shutdowns

The government actually can shut down! It doesn't happen very often, but disagreements over budgets can cause the wheels of government to grind to a halt. New Jersey's government shut down for nearly a week in 2006, for example. Essential services such as the police, fire, and state-run hospitals continued to operate, but all other services were closed. As a result, state government employees were laid off, albeit briefly.

A budget impasse also shut down the federal government for a few hours in 1981. In 1984, a half-million government workers were sent home, but they were back at work the next day. The most serious shutdown took place during President Bill Clinton's administration. The president and Congress were unable to reach an agreement on the budget. As a result, many civil servants were sent home from December 1995 until April 1996.

Government Bureaucracy Versus the Private Sector

A bureaucracy is an organization composed of appointed officials who have managers reporting to them. The American governmental democracy is unique in that politicians control the bureaucracy through the executive, legislative, and judicial branches. One way this is done is through patronage. "Patronage" is the practice of government leaders appointing their friends to positions in the government. In addition, federal agencies often share their functions with counterparts at the state and local level.

A Growing Bureaucracy

The federal bureaucracy expanded eight times between 1816 and 1861, in large part due to the ever-growing United States Postal Service. During the Civil War years of 1861 to 1865, it grew even larger. The Great Depression was a catalyst for the federal bureaucracy's largest growth spurt. With more and more Americans being put out of work, President Franklin Roosevelt did what he could to counteract the loss of income by implementing a policy known as the New Deal. Basically, Roosevelt's goal was to create jobs and establish an economic safety blanket through the Social Security system. The bureaucracy expanded further during the 1960s, with President Lyndon Johnson's implementation of the modern Medicare and welfare systems.

E ssential

People may argue the pros and cons of bureaucracy, but there's little doubt that it is a boon for civil servants. After they are hired, most employees are put on probation for a year, after which they are granted tenure. Unless the person does something illegal or makes an egregious error, a tenured employee's job security is all but ensured.

Some might argue that the government has become a voracious beast that feeds on a steady diet of tax dollars simply to perpetuate its own existence. Others would argue that the United States is a very large and very powerful world power. Though a bureaucracy is not without its drawbacks, it is also necessary to keep the country functional and strong.

Private Privations

It's a fact that there are more opportunities to make greater sums of money in the private sector than in government. Opportunities are not guarantees, however, and with the potential for wealth comes risk. In addition, when you work in the private sector, you work at the company's pleasure. You're there as long as your supervisor needs you there, and you often will face a salaried position with no chance for overtime pay. A government employee, by contrast, punches a clock and leaves at a reasonable hour. Most government offices are closed by 5 P.M. Lunch hours and break times are guaranteed.

In a free-market, capitalist society, private-sector business must produce results to stay in business. Workers are held accountable for their performance, reviewed periodically, and terminated for poor performance. Layoffs are common, whether it's one person or thousands, and workers have no say in the matter of who is let go. Some would argue that this sparks employees' desire to innovate and provides them with the motivation to work harder and become more valuable than their peers. Others would say that it creates instability and fear, which can debilitate workers. At the same time, some would argue that government jobs inspire neither motivation nor innovation because they offer so much job stability. But others would say that stability gives workers the opportunity to be innovative without fear of losing their jobs.

☼ Alert

Bureaucracy may take the phrase "office politics" quite literally. One criticism of the government is that people believe many decisions, such as promotions, are based on politics rather than merit. Of course, private sector office politics can be just as brutal, if not more so. It's a fact of working life.

A Wealth of Opportunities

State and local governments provide citizens with services such as transportation, public safety, health care, education, utilities, and courts. State and local governments employ some 7.9 million workers. This makes the government one of the largest employers in the economy. Seven out of ten government employees work for local governments, such as counties, cities, and towns. In addition to these 7.9 million, a large numbers of state and local workers work in public education. These workers form a large part of the educational services industry.

Citizens are often served by more than one local government unit. Most states are subdivided into counties, which may contain various municipalities, such as cities or towns, as well as unincorporated rural areas. Townships, which do not exist in some states, may or may not contain municipalities and often consist of suburban or rural areas. Some government entities supplement these forms of local government by performing a single function or activity. For example, many special districts manage the use of natural resources. Some provide drainage and flood control, irrigation, and soil and water conservation services.

Fact

In addition to the fifty state governments, there are about 87,500 local governments in the United States. This number includes 3,000 county governments, 19,400 municipal governments, 16,500 townships, 13,500 school districts, and 35,100 special districts. Illinois has the most local government units (more than 6,900); Hawaii has the fewest, a mere twenty.

State and local governments employ people in occupations found in nearly every industry in the economy, including chief executives, managers, engineers, computer specialists, secretaries, and health technicians. Some jobs are unique to the government, such as legislators, tax collectors, urban and regional planners, judges and other judicial workers, police officers, and correctional officers and jailers.

Professional and service occupations account for more than half of all jobs in state and local government. Most new jobs are created by the growing demand for community and social services, health services, and protective services. Increasing demand for services for the elderly, the mentally impaired, and children result in steady growth in the numbers of social workers, registered nurses, and other health professionals. The demand is also high for information technology workers. Jobs in management, business, and financial occupations are expected to grow in state and local government. Office and administrative support jobs are not expected to grow and are likely to be victims of increased outsourcing.

E ssential

The benefits offered with government jobs include health, life insurance, and most likely retirement benefits as well. This is one of the areas in which government jobs excel. Retirement benefits are more common for civil servants than for employees in the private sector.

Chapter 2

An Overview of Federal Jobs

The federal government defends the United States from foreign attacks, represents U.S. interests abroad, enforces laws and regulations, and administers domestic programs and agencies. Employees of the federal government monitor the weather; ensure that food is safe to eat; secure travel by air, land, and sea; and protect banking through federal insurance. The federal government is one of the largest employers in the nation.

Where the Jobs Are

The executive branch of the government employs 96 percent of federal civilian employees, excluding U.S. Postal Service workers. The executive branch is composed of the Office of the President, fifteen executive Cabinet departments—including the newly created Department of Homeland Security—and nearly ninety independent agencies.

⛅ Alert

At all levels of government, there are periods when no new personnel are hired. This often happens because of budgetary issues or because few employees are retiring and no new hires are needed. If you have taken a civil service test and are on a waiting list when a hiring freeze is enacted, you may have a long wait.

The Office of the President is composed of several offices and councils that assist the president in policy decisions. These include the Office of Management and Budget (OMB), which oversees the administration of the federal budget; the National Security Council (NSC), which counsels the president on matters of national defense; and the Council of Economic Advisers, which makes economic policy recommendations.

The Cabinet

The Cabinet consists of the secretaries of the fifteen departments of the executive branch. These departments administer programs with direct influence on basic important aspects of life in the United States, and the secretary is the highest official in each department. Together, the fifteen members of the Cabinet report to the president and act as his personal advisory committee. While the president appoints his Cabinet members, Congress approves these appointments. Here are snapshots of the Cabinet departments:

- The U.S. Department of Defense (DOD) manages the U.S. Armed Forces. The civilian workforce employed by the DOD performs various support activities, such as administering payroll and overseeing public relations.
- The U.S. Department of Veterans Affairs (VA) administers programs to aid U.S. veterans and their families, runs the veterans' hospital system, and operates national cemeteries.
- The U.S. Department of Homeland Security (DHS) works to prevent terrorist attacks within the United States. It also administers the country's immigration policies and oversees the U.S. Coast Guard, which used to be part of the Department of Defense.
- The U.S. Department of the Treasury regulates banks and other financial institutions, administers the public debt, prints currency, and collects federal income taxes.
- The U.S. Department of Justice (DOJ) works with state and local governments to prevent crime and ensure public safety against threats both domestic and foreign. It also enforces federal laws, prosecutes cases in federal courts, and runs federal prisons.

- The U.S. Department of Agriculture promotes U.S. agriculture domestically and internationally, researches new ways to grow crops and conserve natural resources, ensures safe meat and poultry products, and administers programs including food stamps and school lunches.
- The U.S. Department of Interior manages federal lands, including the national parks and forests, manages the Bureau of Indian Affairs, runs hydroelectric power systems, and promotes conservation of natural resources.
- The U.S. Department of Health and Human Services performs health and social science research, assures the safety of drugs and foods other than meat and poultry, and administers Medicare, Medicaid, and other social service programs.
- The U.S. Department of Transportation sets national transportation policy, plans and funds the construction of highways and mass transit systems, and regulates railroad, aviation, and maritime operations.
- The U.S. Department of Commerce forecasts the weather, charts the oceans, regulates patents and trademarks, conducts the census, and compiles statistics.
- The U.S. Department of State oversees the nation's embassies and consulates, issues passports, monitors U.S. interests abroad, and represents the United States before international organizations.
- The U.S. Department of Labor enforces laws guaranteeing fair pay, workplace safety, and equal job opportunity, administers unemployment insurance, and regulates pension funds.
- The U.S. Department of Energy (DOE) coordinates the national use of energy and oversees the production and disposal of nuclear weapons.
- The U.S. Department of Housing and Urban Development (HUD) funds public housing projects and enforces equal housing laws. It is also involved in the Section 8 program that provides government-subsidized housing for low-income people and families.

- The U.S. Department of Education monitors and distributes financial aid to schools and students and prohibits discrimination in education.

Other Agencies

Independent government agencies perform the tasks that fall between the jurisdictions of the executive departments. Some of the better-known agencies include the Peace Corps, the Securities and Exchange Commission (SEC), and the Federal Communications Commission (FCC). The majority of these agencies employ less than 1,000 workers—some have less than 100 employees—but others are pretty big. The largest independent agencies are the following:

- The Social Security Administration issues Social Security numbers, administers the Supplemental Insurance Program, and pays retirement benefits to American workers.
- The National Aeronautics and Space Administration (NASA) oversees aviation research and conducts space exploration.
- The Environmental Protection Agency (EPA) runs programs to control and reduce pollution of the nation's water, air, and land.
- The Tennessee Valley Authority operates the hydroelectric power system in the Tennessee River Valley.
- The General Services Administration (GSA) manages and protects federal government property and records.
- The Federal Deposit Insurance Corporation (FDIC) maintains confidence in the nation's financial system by insuring bank deposits up to $100,000.

Out of the Office

While it's true that many federal employees work in office buildings, hospitals, or laboratories, a large number can be found outdoors at places like border crossings, airports, shipyards, military bases, construction sites, and national parks. Inspectors or compliance officers visit businesses and worksites to ensure that laws and regulations are obeyed.

The majority of federal employees work full time, often on flexible or "flexi-time" schedules that allow them to have more control over their work schedules. An increasing number of agencies offer telecommuting or "flexi-place" programs, which allow workers to perform some job duties at home.

E ssential

Before the FDIC was created in the 1930s, bank runs were a common occurrence in Depression-era America. After the Wall Street crash, banks could run out of money—just like any other business—and depositors could suddenly find that in a matter of minutes, they had lost all of their savings. The FDIC gave people peace of mind and allowed them to once again bank with confidence.

Who Works for the Government?

The federal government employs workers in every major occupational group except sales. The government has very little product available for sale, and as a consequence there is minimal need for people with those skills. A high proportion of federal government occupations are in the professional, management, business, and financial fields.

Professional and related occupations account for a third of federal employment opportunities. The largest group works in the life, physical, and social sciences, including biological scientists, conservation scientists and foresters, environmental scientists and geoscientists, and forest and conservation technicians.

The Partnership for Public Service surveyed federal hiring needs for 2005 to 2006 and found that most of the new hires in the federal government would come from the following areas:

- Security, enforcement, and compliance—positions include inspectors, investigators, police officers, airport screeners, and prison guards

- Medical and public health fields
- Engineering and the sciences—positions include microbiologists, botanists, physicists, chemists, and veterinarians
- Program management and administration
- Accounting, budget, and business—positions include revenue agents and tax examiners needed mainly by the Internal Revenue Service

Many health professionals are employed by the Department of Veterans Affairs in VA hospitals. A large number of federal employees work as engineers, including aerospace, civil, computer hardware, electrical and electronics, environmental, industrial, mechanical, and nuclear engineering. Engineers are found in many departments of the executive branch, but most work in the Department of Defense. Some work in the National Aeronautics and Space Administration and other agencies.

E Fact

According to Paul Light, director of the Center for Public Studies at the Brookings Institution, the "true size" of the federal government workforce was 12.1 million in 2002. That figure includes the more than 8 million jobs the government funds by contracts and grants. Jobs funded that way are not listed on the federal budget as government jobs.

The federal government hires many lawyers, judges, and law clerks to write, administer, and enforce many of the country's laws and regulations. Computer specialists, primarily computer software engineers, computer systems analysts, and network and computer systems administrators, are employed throughout the federal government. They keep computer systems running smoothly.

Management, business, and financial workers make up about 27 percent of federal employment and are responsible for overseeing operations. These employees include officials who, at the highest levels, may head federal agencies or programs. Middle managers oversee one aspect of a program. Other occupations in this category are accountants and auditors. They prepare and analyze financial reports, review and record revenues and expenditures, and investigate operations for fraud and inefficiency.

Administrative and Service Occupations

Administrative support workers in the federal government include information and record clerks, general office clerks, as well as secretaries and administrative assistants.

In the service field, most opportunity lies in the protective services. Seven out of ten federal workers in service occupations are protective service workers, such as correctional officers and jailers, detectives and criminal investigators, and police officers. These workers protect the public from crime and oversee federal prisons.

ᴇ Alert

By law, employees of the federal government are not allowed to go on strike. No-strike clauses are written into employment contracts. In 1955, Congress made strikes by federal employees punishable by stiff fines or jail time. The U.S. Supreme Court upheld this action in 1971, in the case of United Federation of Postal Clerks v. Blount.

Federally employed workers in installation, maintenance, and repair occupations include aircraft mechanics and service technicians, as well as the electrical equipment mechanics who inspect and repair electronic equipment. The federal government employs a small number of workers in transportation, construction, farming, fishing, and forestry.

A Diverse Work Force

The federal government strives to have a work force as diverse as the civilian labor force. It serves as a model for all employers by protecting current and potential employees from discrimination based on race, color, religion, sex, national origin, disability, or age. The federal government also makes an effort to recruit and accommodate persons with disabilities.

The headquarters of most federal departments and agencies are in the Washington, D.C., area, but only one out of six federal employees works in the nation's capital. Federal employees work throughout the United States, and another 93,000 are assigned overseas in embassies or defense installations.

Job Requirements

Applicants for federal jobs must be U.S. citizens. Applicants who are veterans of military service can claim veteran's preference. This gives them preferred status over other candidates with equal qualifications. For jobs requiring access to sensitive or classified materials, applicants have to undergo a background investigation to obtain a security clearance. These investigations look into the applicant's criminal, credit, and employment history.

Requirements for jobs with the federal government are basically the same as those for comparable positions in the private sector. Many jobs in managerial or professional and related occupations require a four-year college degree. Engineers, physicians and surgeons, and biological and physical scientists are required to hold a bachelor's or higher degree in a specific field of study. Registered nurses and many technician occupations may be entered into with two years of training after high school. In general, office and administrative support workers in the government need only a high school diploma.

The Federal System

Each federal department determines the amount of training necessary for its various positions. Each department also offers workers a chance for upward progress through technical or skills training, tuition assistance or reimbursement, and other training programs, seminars, and workshops. The different ranks of government pay levels are referred to as "grades." Typically, new employees start out at a low grade and progress through higher grades as they gain additional experience and training. Some federal departments and agencies have been granted the opportunity to experiment with different pay and promotion strategies in order to make jobs competitive with those of the private sector.

Candidates who do not have a high school diploma and who are hired as clerks start at Grade 1. High school graduates with no additional training hired at the same job start at Grade 2 or 3. Employees with some technical training or experience who are hired as technicians may start at Grade 4. College graduates who hold a bachelor's degree generally are hired in professional occupations. For example, an economist would start at Grade 5 or 7. Applicants with a master's degree or Ph.D. may start at Grade 9. Others with professional degrees may be hired at Grade 11 or 12. See Appendix B for a complete list of pay grades and salaries for 2005.

Fact

The highest demand for workers is and will continue to be in areas such as border and transportation security, emergency preparedness, public health, and information technology.

The General Schedule (see Appendix B) has fifteen pay grades for civilian white-collar and service workers. There are also smaller "within-grade" step increases that occur based on length of service and quality of performance. New employees usually start at the first step of a grade, but if the position is difficult to fill, candidates can receive higher pay or special rates. Physician and engineer positions fall into this category. Federal employees who work in the continental United States receive locality pay. The amount is determined by comparisons of private-sector wages and federal wages in the particular geographic area.

The Federal Wage System

The Federal Wage System (FWS) is used to pay workers in craft, repair, operator, and laborer jobs. This schedule sets federal wages so that they are comparable with regional wage rates for similar types of jobs. Salaries paid under the FWS vary significantly from one locality to another.

Getting Promoted

When most federal workers reach the cap level of their career grade, they have to compete for promotions, which makes advancement more difficult. Promotions may occur as vacancies arise, and they are based on merit.

The top managers in the federal civil service belong to the Senior Executive Service (SES). This is the highest position that federal workers can attain without being specifically nominated by the President and confirmed by the U.S. Senate. Few workers attain SES positions, and competition for these positions is fierce. Most are located in the Washington, D.C., metropolitan area.

Incentives and Benefits

Along with a salary, federal employees also receive incentive awards. These are one-time awards, ranging from $25 to $10,000, and are given for a significant suggestion, a special act or service, or sustained high job performance. Workers are also eligible for premium pay, which is granted when an employee has to put in overtime or work on holidays, weekends, at night, or under hazardous conditions.

Fact

In an effort to compete with private-sector jobs, some government agencies have adopted different pay systems. The two largest departments experimenting with new pay systems are the Departments of Defense and Homeland Security. Pay increases, under these new systems, are based on performance as opposed to length of service.

Benefits are also an important part of federal employee income. Federal employees can choose from numerous health plans and life insurance options, and the premium payments are partially offset by the government. New hires also participate in the Federal Employees Retirement System (FERS), which is a three-pronged retirement plan including Social Security, a pension plan, and an optional thrift savings plan. Participation in the thrift savings plan is voluntary, and contributions made are tax-deferred and matched by the federal government. Some federal agencies also provide public transit subsidies to encourage the use of public transportation.

Federal employees receive both vacation time and sick leave. They earn thirteen days of vacation leave a year for the first three years, twenty days a year for the next twelve years, and twenty-six days a year after fifteen years of service. They also receive thirteen days of sick leave a year, which may be accumulated indefinitely.

Chapter 3

National Security

There are many departments that work together to protect the safety and security of the United States at home and abroad. In addition to the Department of Homeland Security, you can choose from a veritable alphabet soup of career opportunities if your primary goal is to protect your country. These include the Central Intelligence Agency (CIA), Federal Bureau of Investigation (FBI), Bureau of Alcohol, Tobacco, and Firearms (ATF), Drug Enforcement Agency (DEA), and U.S. Department of Justice (DOJ).

U.S. Department of Homeland Security

In the aftermath of the terrorist attacks of September 11, 2001, the Bush administration created the new cabinet-level Department of Homeland Security (DHS). Congress passed the Homeland Security Act in 2002. The goal of this legislation was to streamline government functions, and promote interagency cooperation within and among government agencies that deal with security and the gathering of intelligence. If you are interested in protecting the sovereignty and freedom of the United States, a job with the DHS might be just right for you.

The six-point agenda of this department, in its own words, is to achieve the following:

1. Increase overall preparedness, particularly for catastrophic events
2. Create better transportation security systems to move people and cargo more securely and efficiently
3. Strengthen border security and interior enforcement and reform immigration processes
4. Enhance information sharing with our partners

5. Improve DHS financial management, human resource development, procurement, and information technology
6. Realign the DHS organization to maximize mission performance

You are probably familiar with the FBI, CIA, and other agencies within the security and intelligence arm of the federal government. But you may not be aware of the many other, lesser-known organizations that fall under the umbrella of the DHS, including these:

- The Office of the Secretary and Office of Management: Here you can work in the many offices contributing to the overall DHS mission.
- The Office of Inspector General: You will be working alongside special agents, attorneys, engineers, and information technology experts to prevent and detect fraud, waste, and abuse in DHS programs and operations.
- Border and transportation security, as part of the U.S. Customs and Border Protection (CBP), U.S. Immigration and Customs Enforcement (ICE), and the U.S. Transportation Security Administration (TSA). These brave citizens patrol the country's air, land, and sea borders. They also protect the transportation systems and official ports of entry and enforce the immigration laws.
- Federal Emergency Management Agency (FEMA): This agency prevents losses from disasters wherever possible and assists when they do happen.
- Information analysis and infrastructure protection: Here you can use your talents to help prevent acts of terrorism by "identifying and assessing threats, mapping them against our vulnerabilities, issuing warnings, and supporting the implementation of protective measures to secure the homeland."
- Science and technology: Here you can use your skills in research and development programs in almost all technical fields to ensure that first responders have the scientific resources and technological capabilities they need.

- U.S. Bureau of Citizenship and Immigration Services: These men and women are responsible for overseeing the reams of paperwork involved in the legal immigration process. The President and Congress continue to discuss the future of immigration law, and the result could be a number of new job opportunities.
- U.S. Secret Service: Best known as the bodyguards of the president, the Secret Service is also involved in many other aspects of law enforcement, including the investigation of counterfeiting rings, information technology, communications, administration, intelligence, forensics, and many other areas of law enforcement.

For many Americans, the Department of Homeland Security is linked explicitly with the controversial Patriot Act. The act became law one month after September 11, 2001, and it is designed to improve law-enforcement investigation into possible terrorist attacks. Proponents believe it promotes the safety of the United States and its citizens, while detractors believe it compromises America's civil liberties.

Federal Bureau of Investigation (FBI)

In the old days, the Federal Bureau of Investigation (FBI) was responsible for tackling crime inside the nation's borders, and the Central Intelligence Agency (CIA) operated abroad. There has been a blurring of responsibilities since the terrorist attacks of September 11. The FBI has since stated that it will produce and use intelligence to protect the nation from threats and bring to justice anyone who violates America's laws. This is the FBI's ten-point plan:

1. Protect the United States from terrorist attack.
2. Protect the United States against foreign intelligence operations and espionage.
3. Protect the United States against cyber-based attacks and high-technology crimes.
4. Combat public corruption at all levels.

5. Protect civil rights.
6. Combat transnational and national criminal organizations and enterprises.
7. Combat major white-collar crime.
8. Combat significant violent crime.
9. Support federal, state, county, municipal, and international partners.
10. Upgrade technology to successfully perform the FBI's mission.

There are many opportunities in the FBI, but one job has become more famous and notorious than any other, courtesy of movies and television. That is the position of special agent. In order to become a special agent, you have to be between twenty-three and thirty-seven years of age. You must be a college graduate and have a valid driver's license. You must be in excellent physical condition and prove it by passing a grueling physical, and you must have a clean criminal record and undergo a thorough background check. Successful applicants then attend the FBI Academy, located on the U.S. Marine Corps base at Quantico, Virginia. Those tough and smart enough to graduate from the FBI Academy become special agents at a starting salary of $42,548.

In order to be considered for entry into the FBI Academy, applicants for the job of FBI special agent must possess training and/or education in a critical skill area. Applicants must be able to show a work history including at least two years of relevant work experience. A college degree in the skill area is also acceptable. The FBI has identified the following skill areas as critical:

- Accounting and finance: Certified public accountants (CPAs) are qualified in this skill area
- Computer science and other information technology specialties
- Engineering
- Foreign language fluency
- Intelligence experience
- Legal experience (as an attorney or judge, for instance)

- Law enforcement or other investigative experience
- Military experience
- The sciences, including study and research in applied or pure physics, chemistry, mathematics, biology, nursing, biochemistry, forensics, and the medical specialties

Applicants interested in working for the FBI can work in many other professional capacities, including intelligence analysis, information technology, applied science (engineering and technology), linguistics (including translation and intelligence work), business management, FBI police, and investigative support and surveillance.

Central Intelligence Agency (CIA)

The Central Intelligence Agency (CIA) was born during World War II. Originally known as the Office of Special Services (OSS), it was the espionage wing of the military. OSS agents went behind the lines in secret to collect information to support military operations rather than storming the beaches in uniform. After World War II, differences in politics and theories of government led to the Cold War, which pitted the democratic United States against the communist United Soviet Socialist Republic. There were no military confrontations between America and the USSR. Instead, the two countries used espionage to learn everything they could about the other's military strength and plans in order to prepare for victory in case of another armed conflict. In this war, the spies thrived.

If you are interested in a career at the CIA, you should be aware of what is expected of you. In its own words, the agency demands "an adventurous spirit, a forceful personality, superior intellectual ability, toughness of mind, and a high degree of integrity."

The CIA does not use words like "spy." It prefers euphemisms like "agent" and "operations officer." There are many jobs other than the cloak-and-dagger variety. The CIA also employs secretaries and receptionists, foreign language experts, desk-bound analysts, information technology specialists, and maintenance staff to ensure the restrooms are clean and the garbage is disposed of in its Langley, Virginia headquarters.

Prior to the 1970s, the CIA gathered intelligence using paid informants and spies who worked undercover behind enemy lines. Since then, the agency has shifted its focus to satellite technology. Many find fault with this policy shift and maintain that there is nothing like the personal touch in the spy game. Some even claim that relying on satellites rather than spies on the ground contributed to the terrorist attacks of September 11.

You must be a U.S. citizen over eighteen years of age to join the CIA. A college degree is not mandatory, but it helps, particularly if you are interested in an overseas clandestine job. Men and women in the armed forces cannot transfer to the CIA to fulfill their enlistment obligations. The CIA is not a branch of the military, but the CIA and military often find themselves in the same hotspots around the world.

⚡ Alert

Don't expect to get a job with the CIA overnight. If you want to join the agency, you will be obliged to take a drug test and submit to a thorough background check. The depth of this check will depend on the type of job you are applying for, as there are many levels of security clearance in the CIA.

The CIA describes the background check procedure as follows: "Applicants must undergo a thorough background investigation examining their life history, character, trustworthiness, and soundness of judgment. Also examined is one's freedom from conflicting allegiances, potential to be coerced and willingness and ability to abide by the regulations governing the use, handling and the protection of sensitive information."

A lie-detector test and thorough physical is also part of the CIA screening process, which can take from two months to up to one year.

U.S. Department of Justice

The U.S. Department of Justice (DOJ) is an umbrella organization that shelters many other government agencies and departments. The head of the DOJ is the attorney general of the United States, a position appointed by the president. The DOJ began in 1789 with a staff of one, the attorney general. Originally, the attorney general worked part time, as it was not even a full-time job.

 Fact

The mission statement of the Department of Justice outlines the following departmental goals and objectives: "To enforce the law and defend the interests of the United States according to the law; to ensure public safety against threats foreign and domestic; to provide federal leadership in preventing and controlling crime; to seek just punishment for those guilty of unlawful behavior; and to ensure fair and impartial administration of justice for all Americans."

The first attorney general was Edmund Randolph. He kept precarious peace between bitter rivals Thomas Jefferson and Alexander Hamilton. After he left office, Randolph went back into private practice. His most famous case involved defending Aaron Burr against charges of treason. Burr, most famous now for killing Alexander Hamilton in a duel, supposedly intended to create a rebel army that would have carved a massive new country out of portions of the American Southwest. Burr was acquitted.

While he was attorney general, Randolph's mandate was "to prosecute and conduct all suits in the Supreme Court in which the United States shall be concerned, and to give his advice and opinion upon questions of law when required by the President of the United States, or when requested by the heads of any of the departments, touching any matters that may concern their departments."

Of course, it was only a matter of time before the workload became too much for one person to perform efficiently. Private lawyers were employed to help the attorney general. Then, in 1870, Congress passed the Act to Establish the Department of Justice, setting the new department up as "an executive department of the government of the United States" with the attorney general as the head. Since its establishment more than a century ago, the U.S. Department of Justice has become the world's largest law office and the central agency for enforcement of federal laws.

Drug Enforcement Administration (DEA)

The drug problem in America is a controversial one. The country's prisons include many people who have committed nonviolent drug-related crimes. According to some, such people belong in treatment centers rather than the criminal justice system. Other people believe that the root cause of the nation's drug problem lies in the fact that drug use is illegal in the first place. They argue that legalization would put drug culture in its entirety under government control, making society better able to control and eliminate it.

At the same time, popular culture continues to make drug use seem glamorous, and the underworld teems with violent gangs that earn untold profits in the illicit importation and sale of all kinds of drugs. There was no single branch within the federal government to combat the drug problem until 1973, when Richard Nixon's Reorganization Plan Number 2 proposed that there be one federal agency to coordinate the government's "war on drugs." This consolidated the Bureau of Drug Abuse Control (BDAC) and the Federal Bureau of Narcotics (FBN) into a brand-new federal organization, called the Drug Enforcement Administration (DEA).

According to the mission statement contained on its Web site, the goal of the Drug Enforcement Administration is "to enforce the controlled substances laws and regulations of the United States and bring to the criminal and civil justice system of the United States, or any other competent jurisdiction, those organizations and principal members of organizations, involved in the growing, manufacture, or distribution of controlled substances appearing in or destined for illicit traffic in the United States; and to recommend and support non-enforcement programs aimed at reducing the availability of illicit controlled substances on the domestic and international markets."

According to the agency, the DEA carries out its mission in the following ways:

- Investigation and preparation for the prosecution of major violators of controlled substance laws operating at interstate and international levels
- Investigation and preparation for prosecution of criminals and drug gangs who perpetrate violence in our communities and terrorize citizens through fear and intimidation
- Management of a national drug intelligence program in cooperation with federal, state, local, and foreign officials to collect, analyze, and disseminate strategic and operational drug intelligence information
- Seizure and forfeiture of assets derived from, traceable to, or intended to be used for illicit drug trafficking
- Enforcement of the provisions of the Controlled Substances Act as they pertain to the manufacture, distribution, and dispensing of legally produced controlled substances
- Coordination and cooperation with federal, state, and local law enforcement officials on mutual drug enforcement efforts and enhancement of such efforts through exploitation of potential interstate and international investigations beyond local or limited federal jurisdictions and resources
- Coordination and cooperation with federal, state, and local agencies, and with foreign governments, in programs designed to reduce the availability of illicit abuse-type drugs on the United States market through non-enforcement methods such as crop eradication, crop substitution, and training of foreign officials
- Responsibility, under the policy guidance of the secretary of state and U.S. ambassadors, for all programs associated with drug law-enforcement counterparts in foreign countries
- Liaison with the United Nations, Interpol, and other organizations on matters relating to international drug-control programs

The DEA has many types of positions within its ranks. The most glamorous is the role of special agent. DEA special agents are men and women in the field on the front lines of the war on drugs. They work both within and outside the United States battling the drug dealers. The typical duties of a DEA special agent include the following:

- Conducting surveillance
- Infiltrating drug-trafficking organizations
- Conducting investigations
- Arresting suspects
- Confiscating illegal drugs
- Conducting money-laundering investigations
- Collecting and preparing evidence
- Testifying in criminal court cases

To work for the Drug Enforcement Administration, you must be a U.S. citizen between twenty-one and thirty-six years of age, have a valid driver's license, and be able to obtain a top-secret security clearance. You must be in great shape, with excellent hearing and vision (at least 20/20 in one eye and 20/40 in the other). You cannot be colorblind and must be able to lift and carry a minimum of forty-five pounds.

E ssential

You must be a college grad with a minimum of a 2.95 GPA to join the DEA. Special consideration will be given to candidates with a background in law enforcement, finance, economics, and computer technology. If you are fluent in the following languages you will be especially welcome: Spanish, Russian, Hebrew, Arabic, Nigerian, Chinese, or Japanese.

Of course you have to take a drug test, as well as submit to a verbal written test, a medical exam, a physical task test, a polygraph examination, a psychological assessment, and an exhaustive background investigation.

Besides the position of special agent, the DEA has many other positions available, ranging from lab technicians to administrative assistants, budget analysts, and attorneys.

Bureau of Alcohol, Tobacco, and Firearms (ATF)

The Bureau of Alcohol, Tobacco, and Firearms (ATF) is a lesser-known law enforcement agency, yet it produced one of the most famous lawmen of the twentieth century. Eliot Ness of The Untouchables fame was not an FBI agent, as many assume. Instead of a G-man (as FBI agents are known, short for "government man"), he was a T-man, or treasury agent. This was an earlier version of the agency that was to become the Bureau of Alcohol, Tobacco, and Firearms (ATF).

The ATF continues to act as a law-enforcement entity with unique enforcement skills. It developed the state-of-the-art Integrated Ballistic Identification System, which is a computerized matching program for weapons and the ammunition fired from them. The ATF has an accelerant and explosives/weapons-detection canine program, which trains dogs to sniff out not just explosives but the chemical agents used to construct bombs and other detonated explosives. On the social prevention level, the ATF's Gang Resistance Education and Training (GREAT) program gives young people the tools to resist the peer pressure to join street gangs.

Fact

In 2003, the Bureau of Alcohol, Tobacco and Firearms became part the U.S. Department of Justice under the Homeland Security Act. The agency's name was changed to the Bureau of Alcohol, Tobacco, Firearms and Explosives, though it is still known by the old familiar acronym ATF.

ATF Special Agent

An ATF special agent is responsible for investigating violations of federal law that are related to firearms, explosives, arson, and illegal alcohol and tobacco distribution. This involves conducting surveillance, participating in raids, making arrests, interviewing suspects, and performing a wide range of other potentially hazardous aspects of law enforcement. Applicants must be physically and mentally tough, be ready to travel on a moment's notice, and be ready to relocate to a different part of the country if transferred.

Other ATF Jobs

As with the Federal Bureau of Investigation and the Drug Enforcement Administration, the ATF offers a multitude of career opportunities besides the position of special agent. Other job titles in the ATF that you (or even your dog!) might hold include the following:

- Accelerant- and explosives-detecting canines
- Certified explosives specialist
- Certified fire investigator
- Criminal investigative analyst
- Explosives enforcement officer
- Explosives Industry Programs Branch
- Explosives research and development
- International response team
- National response team
- Relief of explosives disabilities

Starting salaries for these positions with the ATF range from $30,000 to $38,000, based on prior experience and the pay grade an applicant is assigned upon accepting employment. There is an incentive program that awards raises to those who learn a foreign language. You have to be between twenty-one and thirty-seven to be hired. Special agents may retire if they have twenty years of service at age fifty; mandatory retirement is at age fifty-seven. The usual physical exams, drug tests, and background checks apply. And, of course, there are clerical, secretarial, and other non-field positions, as there are in every bureaucracy.

Airport Security

The Transportation Security Administration (TSA) came into being after the terrorist attacks of September 11, 2001. Originally part of the U.S. Department of Transportation, the TSA was shifted to fall under the umbrella of the U.S. Department of Homeland Security in March 2003.

The mission statement of the TSA states the organization's goals and objectives as follows: "The Transportation Security Administration protects the Nation's transportation systems to ensure freedom of movement for people and commerce. The Transportation Security Administration will continuously set the standard for excellence in transportation security through its people, processes and technologies."

More Than Just Screening

If you think that the only job available in the TSA is the job of airport screener, think again. There are plenty of other opportunities within the TSA. For instance, if you're one of those who believes that a dog is man's best friend, you will be interested to hear about opportunities in the TSA National Explosives Detection Canine Program (NEDCP). This program exists to detect explosive devices in the transportation system. It also functions as a deterrent. The bad guys know it exists, and they are consequently a lot less likely to try to smuggle explosives aboard an airplane or into an airport. As almost everyone knows these days, a dog's nose has the power to sniff out almost anything.

Your local airport and modes of mass transit are increasingly going to the dogs. TSA-certified explosives detection canine teams are stationed at each of the nation's largest airports. These highly trained teams are used several times each day to search aircraft and terminals, to check out suspect bags or cargo, and to deter terrorist activities.

The predecessor of this TSA program has been in existence for more than thirty years. On March 9, 1972, officials received a tip that a TWA flight from New York to Los Angeles had been sabotaged and there was a bomb on the plane. The jet returned to JFK International Airport in New York and was evacuated. A heroic pooch named Brandy was brought aboard to do her thing. Brandy found the bomb with only twelve minutes to spare. That very day, President Nixon created the Federal Aviation Administration Explosives Detection Canine Team Program. Similar programs now exist just about everywhere—bomb-sniffing dogs are on almost every law enforcement payroll.

 Fact

The dog breeds used by the TSA are German shepherds, Belgian Malinois, and Labrador retrievers. They are chosen for their agreeable personalities and keen sensory abilities. TSA dogs live with their handlers, and many of them retire to the handlers' homes after ten to twelve years on the job.

A canine team is comprised of a dog and its handler. Both must undergo ten weeks of intensive training at the TSA Explosives Detection Canine Handler Course at Lackland Air Force Base in San Antonio, Texas. Once certified by the TSA, man and beast must have several hours of proficiency training each week in their operational environment. The dog must get used to various odors, both fair and foul, in a well-trafficked environment like an airport, railway terminal, or subway system. Once deployed and on the job, annual recertification is mandatory.

Job Requirements and Training

Increased security is here to stay, which makes it easier to get a job with the TSA. While there are plenty of job opportunities within this agency, the most common is the position of screener, or transportation security officer (TSO). As a TSO, your responsibilities, according to official TSA guidelines, include the following:

- Continuously and effectively interact with the public, giving directions and responding to inquiries in a reasonable tone and manner.
- Maintain focus and awareness within an environment containing numerous distractions, people, and noise.
- Stand and remain standing for periods up to three hours without sitting.
- Lift and/or assist another individual to lift (from the ground) an object weighing at least seventy pounds.
- Work within a stressful environment, which includes noise from alarms, machinery, and people, distractions, time pressure, disruptive and angry passengers, and the requirement to identify and locate potentially life-threatening devices and devices intended on creating massive destruction.
- Make effective decisions in both crisis and routine situations.

There are both full- and part-time positions available at every commercial airport in the United States. Since an airport never sleeps, you may have to work irregular hours, including nights and weekends. Each individual airport determines the hours its TSOs must work.

The usual governmental rules apply. You must be a U.S. citizen or legal immigrant and have your high school diploma or GED. Your eyesight and hearing will be tested, along with the above-mentioned ability to lift seventy pounds. You cannot be color blind. Given that this is a potentially stressful job, you will be obliged to submit to a physical with emphasis placed on the health of your heart and the measurement of your blood pressure. You will also be subjected to both a drug and an alcohol screening.

You will also have to submit to a background check and a credit check. This second requirement is a relatively recent and controversial check in both the public and private sector. People are being denied work for having bad credit. According to the government, this job is "a non-critical sensitive National Security position that requires you to be fingerprinted, photographed, and complete appropriate security paperwork, including a SF-86, Questionnaire for National Security Positions. If your credit check reveals that you have defaulted on $5,000 or more in debt (excluding certain circumstances of bankruptcy), owe any delinquent Federal or State taxes, or owe any past due child support payments, you will not be eligible for this position."

Alert

If you are interested in this kind of work, you should develop a thick skin. You will be inconveniencing people who have paid good money for a ticket and just want to get on the plane. The work you are doing is necessary to ensure safety, but you must do it with respect, even in the face of hostility.

You will also have to complete between fifty-six and seventy-two hours of classroom training, and 112 to 128 hours of on-the-job training, as well as a certification examination.

Chapter 4

The Military

You can be all you can be . . . one of the few and the proud . . . It's not just a job, it's an adventure. These slogans are recruiting catch phrases of different branches of the United States Armed Forces. In this chapter you will learn how you can make a living, get a free education, and serve your country. This much is certain: If you choose a military career in today's geopolitical climate, you will be kept busy.

Selective Service

Upon reaching the age of eighteen, young men are required by federal law to register with Selective Service. The Selective Service System is not part of the Department of Defense. It is a separate, independent government agency whose purpose is to keep track of men between the ages of eighteen and twenty-five in the event they are needed to serve the country in an armed conflict or other crisis. All male residents of the United States, including citizens, immigrants with work visas or green cards, and undocumented aliens are required to register with Selective Service. Forms are available at any post office, and it is also possible to register online by visiting the Selective Service Web site, at ✑*www.sss.gov.*

Qualifying for Service

Once you have spoken with a recruiter and decided to enlist in the army, you have to report to the nearest Military Entrance Processing Station, or MEPS for short.

This procedure applies to everyone entering any branch of the military. All recruits have to pass through an MEPS facility before heading to boot camp. MEPS is a U.S. Department of Defense organization staffed with both military and civilian professionals. They determine your "physical qualifications, aptitude and moral standards as set by each branch of military service."

Fact

You will be required to take a test called the Armed Services Vocational Aptitude Battery (ASVAB). This series of tests measures aptitude in a broad range of career fields. A product of more than fifty years of research, the ASVAB is now available in both computerized (CAT-ASVAB) and traditional written versions. Some young people take the ASVAB in high school for enlistment purposes. Each service combines the test section results to produce its own unique scores for various career fields.

Everyone has to be in good shape to survive the challenges of basic training and military service. The physical examination consists of the following:

- Height and weight measurements
- Hearing and vision examinations
- Urine and blood tests
- Drug and alcohol tests
- Muscle group and joint maneuvers
- Complete physical examination and interview
- Specialized tests, if required

For Women Only

According to the Army, "The MEPS will provide a drape or gown for you during the physical examination. Your visit with the physician will be in a private room. Underclothing is required during your physical. A female attendant will accompany you when you must remove your clothing. You will also be given a pregnancy test." Medical technicians will instruct you on how to complete the questionnaire pertaining to your medical history before the physical examination begins.

Women play a more active role in the armed forces than ever before, but the prospect of women in direct combat remains a controversial subject. In days past, women were relegated to positions behind the lines. The only women who were close to combat were military nurses. These days, women find themselves on the front lines.

☀ Alert

Since the war on terror began, rumors of a draft reinstatement have arisen. Ironically, one of the first efforts to reinstate the draft after September 11 came from two Democrats, both of whom oppose the war. Congressman Charles Rangel of New York and Senator Ernest Hollings of South Carolina introduced separate bills in 2003 that would compel draft-age men and women to perform military or civilian government service. These bills were floated prior to the war in Iraq. Their purpose was to make sure that military service would not fall disproportionately on the poor and on minority groups. The bills did not come to a vote before the Republican-led Congress.

Enlistment

If you have met standards set by the physical and CAT-ASVAB tests for the branch of service you have selected, a service liaison counselor will tell you about job opportunities and the enlistment agreement. There will be a final interview and fingerprinting for an FBI check. You will also complete a briefing before you take the oath of enlistment.

Joining the military is a serious decision and one that should not to be taken lightly. Once you have enlisted, it is next to impossible to back out of your commitment. By joining the military, you are entering a new realm that has different rules and laws than the civilian world. Discuss your plans with your parents, counselors, and any veterans you know. Remember, today's military is not operating in peacetime. Though the war on terror is not as clearly defined as conflicts like World War II, it is a war, and chances are you will deployed into a hotspot somewhere in the world.

Arrive Prepared

Here are a few things you should do before reporting to the MEPS facility:

- Discuss any childhood medical problems with your parents and bring documentation with you.
- Bring your Social Security card, birth certificate, and driver's license.
- Remove any earrings, as they obstruct the headset used for the hearing test.
- Dress conservatively. Profanity and offensive wording or pictures on clothing is not tolerated.
- Leave your hat at home, as headgear is not permitted inside the MEPS.
- If you wear either eyeglasses or contacts, bring them along with your prescription and lens case.
- Bathe or shower the night before your examination.
- Wear underclothes.
- Get a good night's sleep before taking the CAT-ASVAB.
- Wear neat, moderate, comfortable clothing.
- Don't bring stereo headphones, watches, jewelry, excessive cash, or any other valuables.
- Ask your recruiter for a list of recommended personal items to bring to basic training.
- Processing starts early at the MEPS, so get up early. You must report on time.

U.S. Army and U.S. Navy

The U.S. Army encourages potential recruits to "Be all that you can be." The U.S. Navy's public relations department emphasizes that you can get an education, learn a skill you can use in civilian life, and see the world. "It's not just a job—it's an adventure," was the slogan a few years back. The navy's new trademarked slogan is "Accelerate your life."

The processes of enlisting in each of these two branches of service are very similar, as are the opportunities and the benefits that come with this service. This section focuses on the process of enlisting with the navy. For those of you who would prefer to remain on solid land, this information gives a basic idea of what to expect from the recruitment, enlistment, and boot camp experiences.

E ssential

If you do not want to join up right away, you can take advantage of the military's delayed entry program (DEP). This allows you to join your chosen branch of the military but not report for active duty until up to one year later. In the meantime, you can get your affairs in order and start an exercise program in preparation for boot camp.

To find out how to enlist with the army or the navy, go online to the appropriate Web site (either ✑www.army.com or ✑www.navy .com) or visit your local recruiter. Regardless of the branch of service you select, you will have to visit the nearest Military Entrance Processing Station and take the Armed Services Vocational Aptitude Battery (ASVAB).

Boot Camp

Army recruits attend boot camp/basic training at a variety of locations around the country. Navy recruits attend boot camp located at The Great Lakes Naval Training Center, on the western shore of Lake Michigan. In either brand of the service, boot camp consists of eight weeks of rigorous physical and mental training. One interesting difference is that army basic training is primarily conducted outdoors, while in the navy, most boot camp exercises are performed indoors. This may seem counterintuitive—keep in mind, however, that sailors are often confined for long periods onboard their ships, while army troops work outside on land.

Here is a week-by-week look at what you can expect from boot camp as a navy recruit:

- **Week 1:** You will get your uniform, a medical and dental exam, and a haircut if you need one. You will learn the navy way to make your bed. You will begin the tough physical regimen of conditioning, which includes swimming, marching, and drilling. In addition, you will also be attending navy classes.
- **Week 2:** This is a week of confidence building. You will be tested in simulations of shipboard situations. The emphasis is on teamwork.
- **Week 3:** This week involves hands-on training onboard a docked training ship. You will learn everything you need to know about life aboard a naval vessel. There will also be classroom studies that focus on all aspects of basic seamanship. You will be asked to perform a physical test consisting of curl-ups, sit-reaches, push-ups, and a 1.5-mile run. If you fail the first time, you will have a chance to take the test again later.
- **Week 4:** This is the week of weapons training. First you will be checked out on the M-16 and the twelve-gauge shotgun. Later in the week you will graduate to the live-fire range. You will also have your graduation pictures taken and complete a written test on all you have learned thus far.
- **Week 5:** This week is a little bit of a breather. You can assess where you are in the process. As the navy says, "This week is all about you. Where you want to go, what you want to do, and how fast you intend to get there. So you find the shortest distance between where you are and where you want to be. If you're feeling a sense of accomplishment for making it this far—good for you."
- **Week 6:** This week you will learn about shipboard damage control and firefighting. These are two of the most important skills you'll need. Your life and those of your shipmates

depend on mastering these skills. You will also be taking the most challenging test of all: the Confidence Chamber. You and about 100 other recruits will line up inside a chamber and put on a gas mask while a tear-gas tablet is lit. You will be ordered to remove your mask and throw it in a garbage can while reciting your full name and social security number.

- **Week 7:** This is the week when you will take "boot camp's ultimate test." It is an exercise of twelve different scenarios incorporating all that you have learned during the previous weeks. You will be graded on your ability to execute the required tasks.
- **Week 8:** This is the week that you celebrate graduation in your dress uniform.

The navy has a set of swim qualifications as well. You enter the water feet first from a minimum height of five feet. You have to remain afloat for five minutes, and you must swim fifty yards using any stroke or a combination of strokes.

E Fact

Sailors who are married can have their family move with them to their home base. In addition to a steady paycheck, you will also get thirty day's leave time.

First Assignment

Two factors determine where the navy will send you on your first assignments: its needs and your wants. In importance, its needs trump your wants. You will be assigned to a detailer. This is the officer who assigns you and who will work with you when you are eligible to transfer elsewhere. He or she will also advise you about further training opportunities should you wish to seek a specialty during your navy career.

U.S. Air Force

The U.S. Air Force (USAF) became an independent branch of the armed forces after World War II. Prior to that, the army and navy both had their own air corps. It was clear that the future of warfare would involve greater use of air power to shock and awe the enemy, so the National Security Act of 1947 created the Department of the Air Force, headed by a Secretary of the Air Force.

The mission of the USAF is to "deliver sovereign options for the defense of the United States of America and its global interests—to fly and fight in Air, Space, and Cyberspace." To achieve its mission, the USAF has a vision of global vigilance, reach, and power. This vision revolves around three key points: developing airmen, developing the technology to fight wars, and integrating operations. These elements make the USAF's six distinctive capabilities possible:

- **Air and space superiority:** With this, joint forces can dominate enemy operations in all dimensions—land, sea, air, and space.
- **Global attack:** Because of technological advances, the USAF can attack anywhere, anytime—and do so quickly and with greater precision than ever before.
- **Rapid global mobility:** Being able to respond quickly and decisively anywhere in the world is key to maintaining rapid global mobility.
- **Precision engagement:** The essence of this element lies in the ability to apply selective force against specific targets. This is a critical capability, as the nature and variety of future contingencies demand both precise and reliable use of military power with minimal risk and collateral damage.
- **Information superiority:** The ability of joint force commanders to keep pace with information and incorporate it into a campaign plan is crucial.
- **Agile combat support:** Deployment and sustainment are keys to successful operations and cannot be separated. Agile combat support applies to all forces, from those permanently based to contingency buildups to expeditionary forces.

The USAF also places great emphasis on three core values: "integrity first, service before self, and excellence in all we do."

The Department of the Air Force is headquartered in the Pentagon, in Washington, D.C. The service is organized in nine major commands throughout the world that provide combat aircraft, airlift, refueling, reconnaissance, and other support to the Unified Combatant Commands. The USAF also has more than three dozen field operating agencies and direct reporting units that directly support its mission by providing unique services.

Together with Air Force Reserve and Air National Guard forces, the USAF considers itself "the best in the world."

E ssential

The Air Force Personnel Center (AFPC), with headquarters at Randolph Air Force Base, Texas, is a field operating agency of Headquarters U.S. Air Force, the Office of the Deputy Chief of Staff for Personnel. The center has responsibility for managing personnel programs and carrying out policies affecting USAF active-duty and civilian members.

The AFPC mission statement is as follows: "The AFPC mission is to integrate and execute personnel operations to develop Air Force people and meet field commanders' requirements. AFPC supervises and directs the overall management and distribution of military officers, lieutenant colonel and below; enlisted, senior master sergeant and below; and civilian personnel at grades GS-15 (or equivalent) and below. AFPC also conducts military and civilian personnel operations to include overseeing performance evaluations, promotions, retirements, separations, awards, decorations, uniforms, education, personnel procurement, disability processing, and the Air Force's voting program. It plans for contingencies, maintains active-duty personnel records and provides transition assistance and support to Air Force retirees. AFPC serves as the single manager for the military and civilian personnel data systems covering active-duty, Reserve, Guard and civilian personnel under the Total Force Management Concept."

Air Force Academy, Naval Academy, West Point

In order to enter any of these branches of the military as an officer, it is necessary to attend the relevant academy. The U.S. Air Force Academy is located in Colorado; the U.S. Naval Academy is located in Annapolis, Maryland; the army's academy is technically called the U.S. Military Academy, but it is better known as West Point, the name of the town where it is located.

The goals of all the academies are similar. In order to avoid redundancy, this section focuses on the process of applying to the U.S. Air Force Academy.

Here is the mission statement of the Air Force Academy: "The staff and faculty of the U.S. Air Force Academy, in the interest of our future national security, molds our future leaders into outstanding young men and women into Air Force officers with knowledge, character, and discipline; motivated to lead the worlds' greatest aerospace force in service to the nation."

 Fact

Information on admissions procedures can be obtained from the Director of Admissions, 2304 Cadet Drive, U.S. Air Force Academy, CO 80840-5025. You can visit the Air Force Academy online at *www .usafa.af.mil.*

The U.S. Air Force Academy is a four-year course of study with emphasis on academics, military training, athletic conditioning, and spiritual and ethical development. Classes include the basic sciences, engineering, humanities, social sciences, and military art and science. All cadets complete a core curriculum consisting of 112 semester hours and can specialize in any one of thirty academic majors and four minors. Four primary areas are stressed: professional military studies, theoretical and applied leadership experiences, aviation science and airmanship programs, and military training. The honor code is at the center of a cadet's moral and ethical development. The code states the following: "We will not lie, steal, or cheat, nor tolerate among us anyone who does."

To be eligible to enter the U.S. Air Force Academy, you must be all of the following:

- A citizen of the United States. Your citizenship must be finalized prior to entering the academy. You must submit proof of citizenship if you are foreign-born or naturalized. Authorized international students are exempt from this requirement.
- Unmarried with no dependents
- Of good moral character
- At least seventeen, but less than twenty-three years of age by July 1 of the year you would enter. The age requirement is public law and cannot be waived.
- Of high leadership, academic, physical, and medical standards

The U.S. Air Force Academy is one of the most selective colleges in the country. You will need to start preparing long before you apply in order to meet the admission requirements, the intense competition for appointments, and the demands of the academy.

While in high school, you should participate in a well-rounded program of academic, leadership, and athletic preparation. Many apply, but very few will be accepted. The cost of an academy education in 2006 was $35,564 per year. Cadets who fail to complete any period of active duty may have to pay back the U.S. government.

U.S. Marine Corps

The U.S. Marine Corps is an arm of the military within the U.S. Navy. Marines are trained and equipped primarily to fight in combined land, sea, and air operations. In 2003, the corps included about 174,000 active-duty marines, 42,000 reserve marines, and 18,000 civilian support employees.

The marine corps is comprised of three marine expeditionary forces (MEFs) and three air wings. The MEFs are stationed at Camp Lejeune, North Carolina; Camp Pendleton, California; and Okinawa, Japan. The main combat force in each MEF is the marine expeditionary unit (MEU).

U.S. Marines are stationed all over the planet, though most of them are stationed at bases on the East and West Coasts of the United States. Approximately 20,000 marines are stationed in Okinawa, Japan, and 5,000 are onboard U.S. Navy ships at sea.

E ssential

The marines have experience fighting a war on terror that goes back long before September 11, 2001. In 1805, the fledgling navy and marines battled North African Islamic pirates who were interfering with United States ships at sea. The line in the Marines theme song, "To the shores of Tripoli," harks back to those battles. Tripoli is the capital of Libya.

Officers

If you would prefer to enter the Marines as an officer, you will have to attend the U.S. Naval Academy. You can do this by being involved in your college Reserve Officer Training Corps (ROTC), or in Officer Candidate School (OCS). OCS accepts college graduates between twenty and twenty-eight years of age. OCS consists of ten weeks of intensive training at Quantico, Virginia. Enlisted marines can also earn commissions through OCS. Marine officers must have a four-year college degree and must be U.S. citizens.

Enlisted Personnel

Approximately 95 percent of the Marines' enlisted personnel are high school graduates. Marines (and all U.S. Navy personnel) must be at least seventeen years old, and most new recruits must be under twenty-five. New enlisted personnel attend twelve weeks of basic training either at Parris Island, South Carolina, or the Marine Corps Recruit Depot in San Diego, California. This is the toughest boot camp in all the armed forces. The recruits undergo demanding training: formal marching drills, close-quarters combat, rifle and weapons use, swimming and water survival, military courtesy, and the history and traditions of the U.S. Marine Corps. The drill instructor, or DI, supervises the training process. Boot camp culminates with a demanding three-day test of physical endurance and combat tasks that is ominously called "the Crucible." During the Crucible, recruits march with fully loaded packs, crawl through mud, carry heavy ammunition cases across simulated battlefields, and face many other physical challenges, all with little food or rest.

 Fact

Approximately 6 percent of Marine officers and enlisted personnel are women. More than 90 percent of all jobs in the Marine Corps are open to women, including flying helicopters and jet aircraft. However, female marines are prohibited from participating in ground combat.

The few and the proud who make it through boot camp at Parris Island or San Diego go to the School of Infantry at Camp Pendleton in San Diego or at Camp Lejeune in North Carolina. They learn basic infantry tactics and the use of U.S. Marine Corps weapon systems. Upon completion of this course, every marine is considered a rifleman. Some marines go on to additional training in a specialty like infantry, field artillery, armor, logistics, communications, or aircraft maintenance.

Tools of the Trade

The "best friend" of a U.S. marine is his or her M16A2 assault rifle, and every marine is tested on it annually. Marine officers also are required to qualify with the Beretta M9 nine-millimeter pistol.

Marines also learn the use of other infantry weapons, including the M203 grenade launcher, the M60E3 7.62mm machine gun, and M252 81mm mortar. Marines also have M1A1 Abrams tanks and wheeled light-armored vehicles (LAVs) for sustained ground-combat operations. For attacking enemy beaches, marines may use the landing craft air cushion (LCAC), a hovercraft designed to carry troops and equipment into battle from U.S. Navy vessels offshore.

The marine corps is also developing an aircraft called the V-22 Osprey that can take off and land like a helicopter but change its engine configuration in flight and fly like a regular airplane.

U.S. Coast Guard

The U.S. Coast Guard is one of five branches of the U.S. Armed Forces, but after the terrorist attacks of September 11, 2001, it has been adjusted to fall under the jurisdiction of the U.S. Department of Homeland Security. The coast guard is older than the navy, and its responsibilities include search and rescue (SAR), maritime law enforcement (MLE), aids to navigation (ATON), ice breaking, environmental protection, port security, and military readiness. There are 38,000 active-duty men and women, 8,000 reservists, and 35,000 auxiliary personnel in the coast guard. A typical day in the life of the coast guard, from coast to coast, involves the following:

- Conducting 109 search and rescue cases
- Saving ten lives and assisting 192 people in distress
- Protecting $2,791,841 in property
- Launching 396 small boat missions
- Launching 164 aircraft missions
- Boarding 144 vessels
- Seizing 169 pounds of marijuana and 306 pounds of cocaine worth $9,589,000
- Intercepting fourteen illegal immigrants
- Boarding 100 large vessels for port safety checks
- Responding to twenty oil or hazardous chemical spills totaling 2,800 gallons
- Servicing 135 aids to navigation

Basic Requirements

To join the coast guard for active duty, you must be a U.S. citizen or a resident alien between the ages of seventeen and twenty-seven. Reservists must be between seventeen and thirty-nine. You should have a high school diploma, but GEDs are accepted in special circumstances. You can have only two dependents. You must pass the Armed Services Vocational Aptitude Battery (ASVAB) test, a military entrance medical exam, and you must be someone who likes the water.

You get paid twice a month, on the first and fifteenth, in an amount that is based on your pay grade. You are eligible for promotions based on your expertise in your chosen career field, your job performance, and service requirements. You get 2.5 days paid vacation per month, totaling thirty days a year. When on active duty, you receive complete and free medical and dental care, and you are covered for $250,000 in term life insurance for less than $20 a month. The GI Bill helps pay for your college education or vocational technical training.

E ssential

The coast guard is always hiring. Call 1-877-NOW-USCG to speak with the recruiter nearest you to determine eligibility and your pay grade upon entry.

The coast guard is busier than ever now that it falls under the umbrella of the U.S. Department of Homeland Security. For example, a ship is regularly on patrol in the Hudson River near the Indian Point nuclear power plant. The hijacked planes that hit the World Trade Center flew right over this facility on their deadly mission. If one of those aircraft had decided to take a nosedive and slam into the power plant instead of the towers, the entire Northeast would have been devastated.

Coast Guard Boot Camp

Boot camp is located at the U.S. Coast Guard Training Center in Cape May, New Jersey. It is eight weeks long, the length of boot camp in the army, navy, and air force—all branches of the military, that is, except the marines. It is a rigorous period of training, combining classroom study with skills such as first aid, firefighting, weapons handling, practical seamanship, and general coast guard knowledge. There are daily physical fitness classes and time spent in the pool learning water-survival techniques.

The minimum physical requirements for graduation are the following:

- Push-ups (in one minute): male, 29; female, 23
- Sit-ups (in one minute): male, 38; female, 32
- 1.5-mile run: male, 12:51 minutes; female, 15:26 minutes
- Sit and reach: male, 16.50; female, 19.25
- Swim circuit: Jump off a five-foot platform into the pool, swim 100 meters, and tread water for five minutes

Needless to say, the ability to swim is mandatory. If you cannot swim, the coast guard will train you, but it is obligatory that you pass their tests.

U.S. Coast Guard Academy

The U.S. Coast Guard Academy is located in New London, Connecticut. Some 300 high school graduates enroll annually. They graduate four years later with a bachelor of science degree and a commission as an ensign.

Two-thirds of academy recruits graduate in technical majors, including civil engineering, mechanical engineering, naval architecture, marine engineering, electrical engineering, operations research and computer analysis, and marine environmental science. The academy is tuition free. Cadets also earn a small salary. Graduates must serve for five years after graduation.

Does Uncle Sam Want You?

The U.S. Army estimates there are 32 million Americans within recruiting age, and they also estimate about 4.3 million of these young men and women are qualified potential recruits. Those who did not graduate from high school and failed to score in the top half on the military service aptitude test are not likely to be welcomed into military service. Enlistment is way down, but recruiters are still trying to cling to traditional standards. In light of nationwide obesity epidemics, many people between seventeen and twenty-four are not suitable material for military recruitment.

In 2006, the army's recruitment goal was 80,000 people; the combined services goal was about 180,000. Here are the army's concerns about today's young people—out of an estimated pool of 13.6 million citizens:

- 30 percent are high school dropouts and would not be the top choice in today's professional, all-volunteer, and increasingly high-tech Army.
- 30 percent of U.S. adults are considered obese.
- There is a decline in physical fitness; one-third of teenagers are believed to be incapable of passing a treadmill test.
- There is a widespread use of Ritalin and other drugs to treat attention deficit and hyperactivity disorder. Potential recruits are not eligible for military service if they have taken such drugs in the past year.
- Other potential recruits are rejected because they have criminal backgrounds and/or already have too many dependents.

That leaves a total of 6.6 million potential recruits from all people in the eligible age range. If none of the issues above relates to you, then Uncle Sam definitely wants you.

Chapter 5

The Finest and the Bravest

If you have a desire to protect and serve your community and your fellow citizens, you may be interested in a career among the finest and the bravest—those men and women who catch the bad guys, put out the fires, and do the many other things that are necessary to keep the peace and save lives.

Police

Police work is a dangerous business. The pay is decent and the benefits are very good, as is the retirement plan, but you put your life on the line every day, and that day may very well be your last. There are law enforcement jobs at every level of government, from the FBI agent to the small-town sheriff.

Uniformed police officers are the ones you are most likely to encounter in your travels. They are in your community patrolling the streets, responding to calls for help, directing traffic, investigating crimes, and performing many other duties. Police officers also interact with the community to maintain good relations with the people they have sworn to protect and serve.

Most cities are divided into police precincts. There is a neighborhood station house in each precinct, and officers stationed there patrol and serve that part of town. The police force consists of uniformed officers who walk the beat or drive clearly marked cars, and plainclothes detectives. Ideally, the cop on the beat should establish a rapport with the businesses and residents of the community. Some officers work alone, but usually they patrol in pairs, either on foot or in their police cruisers.

Some public school districts have their own armed police force, as do modes of mass transit, including subways, railroads, and airports. Some officers specialize in fields of criminology, as is the case with crime scene investigators. You can see how people in this particular specialty solve crimes on no fewer than three top-rated television shows. There are also special units like motorcycle cops, mounted police, harbor patrols, Special Weapons and Tactics (SWAT), and more. Despite what you see in movies and on television, cops spend more time struggling with paperwork than engaging in gunplay.

ⱻ Alert

Cop shows are very popular, but they often give a false impression of what police work entails. Although the job is fraught with danger, most days are monotonous, and the people who do this job are required to churn out paperwork by the ream.

Country Cops

Sheriffs and their deputies enforce the law in small towns and rural communities. Unlike their urban counterparts, sheriffs are also politicians who have to run for office. They oversee departments much smaller than the typical big-city force. For example, there are about 30,000 New York City cops, far greater than the number of residents in many of the towns and counties in a sheriff's jurisdiction.

Every state has a state police force whose members are known as state troopers. They are the men and women you want to avoid on the highway. They catch the speeders and enforce motor vehicle laws. State troopers are also often the first responders at highway accidents, where, if necessary, they are responsible for administering first aid until an ambulance arrives.

In order to keep an extra eye on things, most police cars today are wired for sound and video. So watch what you say and what gestures you make the next time you're pulled over for speeding!

Detectives

Plainclothes investigators, also known as detectives, are officers who have risen within the ranks through promotion. They are the ones who want "just the facts" as they investigate everything from robbery to murder. These investigators scour the crime scene for evidence, interrogate suspects, and make arrests when enough evidence is gathered to make a case. In most urban police forces, investigators are divided up by specialty, with each division working on a specific kind of crime, such as robbery, homicide, vice, and so on.

On the Job

Police work is potentially dangerous and stressful. A cop must always be ready for the unexpected, and this can take its toll on the body and the mind. Police officers also witness things most of us are never exposed to—real-life violence and death, not the stuff of television and movies. Daily interaction with the unsavory underbelly of society can sour a cop's view of his fellow men and women. Divorce and suicide rates among police are high. Unfortunately, a few have their souls corrupted by this constant exposure to negative forces and become racist or crooked cops. Still, it must be stressed that these bad apples are in the minority. They do not represent the overwhelming majority of honest, decent, hardworking cops.

 **Question**

What's an average work week for a police officer?
Most cops work a forty-hour week, but overtime is required. For example, after the terrorist attacks of September 11, the Port Authority Police Department, which oversees the bridges, tunnels, airports, and the World Trade Center buildings, went to mandatory twelve-hour shifts for all personnel for the next couple of years.

Cops are in essence on the job around the clock, seven days a week, 365 days a year. Most carry their guns even when off duty and are expected to respond to a crime or a crisis regardless of whether they're on the clock. Police work is not the kind of job that lets you punch the clock at day's end and forget about it until the next morning. It becomes part of your identity, an integral component of your life.

Becoming a Police Officer

Circumstances may vary slightly in different cities and states, but most people become cops by first applying for and taking a civil service test. All applicants for police work must be U.S. citizens. After taking the civil service test, applicants are placed on a waiting list based on their scores, and they are called in as the need for new officers arises. As the old guard retires, new blood is called.

The next phase involves a physical exam, psychological screening, and background check. Applicants also undergo a drug test and possibly a lie-detector test. Random drug testing may be ongoing throughout your career. The age requirements vary, averaging from twenty or so through the late thirties. All require a high school diploma, and certain jobs may require some college or a degree.

Once the applicant has successfully jumped through all these hoops, the next step is a period of training in the police academy. In big cities, this can be a twelve- to fourteen-week program. Training includes the use of firearms, physical training, self-defense, first aid, and supervised experience on the streets. There is also classroom study in the letter of the law—both criminal and civil.

E ssential

In most police academies, recruits who are attending class wear a uniform that is slightly different from the police force uniform to distinguish them from active-duty cops. At the same time, they are expected to adopt the police officer's code of conduct and public responsibility from day one, and that often includes making arrests if they come upon a crime in progress.

When rookies graduate from the academy, they are placed on probation for a period ranging from six months to three years. Over time, uniformed officers can apply for promotion based on a written test and work history. Again, they are placed on a waiting list and are promoted as veterans retire based on their scores and the available openings.

Many police officers continue their education to improve their performance as well as their potential for advancement. Many colleges offer criminal-justice courses, and the police forces themselves make sure that their officers are kept up to date on the latest law-enforcement technology and weaponry. Cops are also often obliged to take sensitivity training courses to reduce the incidence of police brutality.

The Job Market

There are about 842,000 law enforcement officers on the job. Only 6 percent of these have job with the various federal agencies. State police agencies employ another 12 percent, and local government employs the remaining 80 percent.

Fact

According to statistics compiled by the U.S. Bureau of Justice, "police and detectives employed by local governments primarily worked in cities with more than 25,000 inhabitants. Some cities have very large police forces, while thousands of small communities employ fewer than twenty-five officers each."

Law enforcement is an attractive career for a variety of reasons, not the least of which is the retirement plan. Most officers can retire after twenty years of service and earn half pay for the rest of their lives. Depending on when they joined the force, it is entirely possible and even common for officers to retire while still in their forties. They can start a second career or live frugally and enjoy a long retirement. Like most civil service jobs, cops also have excellent job security. Layoffs are rare, and if you keep your nose clean and do not abuse your authority, you will probably have the job until you retire.

Police and sheriff's patrol officers earn a median salary of $45,210, with the range extending from $26,910 at the low end to $68,880. The median for police and detective supervisors is $64,430, with the high and low salaries being $36,690 and $96,950. Detectives and criminal investigators average $53,990 and the range is $32,180 to $86,010.

The table below shows the average salaries for sworn full-time positions, according to the International City-County Management Association's Annual Police and Fire Personnel, Salaries, and Expenditures Survey.

Police Department Salaries

Position	Minimum Annual Base Salary	Maximum Annual Base Salary
Police chief	$72,924	$92,983
Deputy chief	$61,110	$76,994
Police captain	$60,908	$75,497
Police lieutenant	$56,115	$67,580
Police sergeant	$49,895	$59,454
Police corporal	$41,793	$51,661

These figures do not include overtime, which can greatly increase a police officer's annual income.

Contact your local government or go online to your city or town's Web site to find out the specifics of a law enforcement career in your community.

Fire Department

Firefighters protect people and their property by responding to fires in their community, putting them out, and rescuing those trapped within burning buildings. Thousands of people die in fires every year, and billions of dollars in property is destroyed, but the numbers would be much higher if not for your friendly neighborhood firefighter. These selfless public servants also often double as emergency first responders, since they are trained in first aid and often are the first on the scene of an accident or other medical emergency.

Government-run fire departments did not exist in the United States until after the Civil War. Volunteer-run fire brigades did the job prior to that, but they did not always do the job very well. A brigade, eager to have the honor of saving the day, would try to prevent rival brigades from fighting fires. Sometimes this bizarre competition would continue until the burning building was completely destroyed.

⚡ Alert

When you consider a career in the firefighting field, bear in mind that it is more than a steady civil service job with a decent salary and good benefits. You are obliged to run into buildings that everyone else is running out of. You earn your pension by being a hero day in and day out.

Firefighters get to the scene as quickly as possible, and each one has a particular task in extinguishing the fire. Some connect high-pressure hoses to the nearest fire hydrants and pump the water to where it is needed. Some climb ladders to get into structures and rescue people, while others ventilate smoke-filled areas and provide medical attention to the fire's victims.

Firefighters work in all kinds of environments, from big cities to small towns. Some firefighters specialize in fighting wildfires in national parks and other uninhabited areas. Forest fire inspectors are positioned in watchtowers, ever on the lookout for a fire. Many fires begin naturally, but others are caused by camper neglect. If you are camping, exercise extreme care in extinguishing your campfire. Much damage has been done by careless campers, and heavy fines and possible jail time face those who are caught and convicted.

Between Fires

There is a lot of down time for firefighters. Hours and sometimes days go by between alarms. During these lulls firefighters maintain equipment, write reports, and also take it easy. Fire stations are equipped with sleeping quarters, showers, kitchens, and television rooms. Firemen usually work for a few days in a row, followed by a couple of days off. They live in the station for days at a time.

Unlike some men, male firefighters often become good cooks because they have to fend for themselves. Some firemen have even written cookbooks and appeared on television, where the television hosts sample their delectable dishes.

It is not all relaxation, for firefighters are forever aware that the alarm can sound at any moment, day or night. It is like living in a constant "fight or flight" mode. It takes its toll on the body and mind, and firefighters have been known to die of heart attacks after a lifetime of stress.

Getting the Job

Like police officers, firefighters have to take a written civil service test. Those who pass are then placed on a waiting list. Candidates who are chosen to proceed past that phase have to endure numerous tests of stamina and agility. They must learn to swing like Tarzan on ropes and to carry heavy dummies up and down stairs and ladders. Firefighters must be in top physical condition, and unlike most police officers, they are regularly tested in rigorous physicals throughout their careers. The cliché of the cops who hang out in the doughnut shop does not apply to firefighters.

E Fact

Even though the term "fireman" is still routinely used, firefighting is a job for men and women. There are more than 6,000 female firefighters in the United States, according to Women in the Fire Service, a nonprofit group whose mission is the promotion of women's involvement in firefighting. Of those 6,000 women, more than 150 are fire chiefs.

Potential firefighters must be over eighteen years of age to apply for positions with a fire department, and most fire departments require that applicants hold a high school diploma before they are allowed to sit for the initial test. And of course the usual drug tests apply.

There is also a training period in larger fire departments. Firefighters study fire-fighting techniques and also learn how to use equipment, how to handle hazardous materials, and how to perform first aid and other emergency medical procedures, including CPR.

There are opportunities for advancement in most fire departments. Promotions are earned through written exams, performance, and seniority. You can rise within the ranks to engineer, lieutenant, captain, battalion chief, assistant chief, deputy chief, and chief.

The following table shows average salaries for full-time positions, according to the International City-County Management Association.

Fire Department Salaries

Position	Minimum Annual Base Salary	Maximum Annual Base Salary
Fire chief	$68,701	$89,928
Deputy chief	$63,899	$79,803
Assistant fire chief	$57,860	$73,713
Battalion chief	$58,338	$73,487
Fire captain	$49,108	$59,374
Fire lieutenant	$44,963	$53,179
Fire prevention/code inspector	$43,297	$54,712
Engineer	$41,294	$52,461

Another advantage that comes with being a firefighter is that layoffs are rare. Firefighting is a necessary service, and those who perform it will always be in demand. And like the police, job security, benefits, and retirement plans are excellent, as is overtime pay, which can increase the base salary dramatically.

Emergency Medical Services (EMS)

Emergency medical services, better known by the acronym EMS, is a subcategory of the medical field. The men and women who provide these emergency services are called emergency medical technicians or EMTs. At higher levels of experience and expertise, they are also known as paramedics. Today, EMTs are still the first responders at tragedies such as car crashes, heart attacks, violent crime, and other events where immediate medical attention is required. Sometimes they are also there for happier moments, like childbirth. EMTs provide first aid at the scene of an accident and also transport the victims to the nearest hospital for further treatment.

≡Ê≡Alert

EMTs must deal with human suffering and sometimes a preponderance of blood and gore. You had better be stout of heart and not afraid of viewing the horrors of an accident. This is a job where the thin of skin, weak of stomach, and faint of heart need not apply. Bear these job responsibilities in mind before you consider applying for a position as an EMT.

EMS Certifications

The National Registry of Emergency Medical Technicians (NREMT) registers EMTs at four levels: First Responder, EMT-Basic, EMT-Intermediate, and EMT-Paramedic. Some states have their own certifications and use a numerical rating system of 1 to 4. Here is a breakdown of the four levels:

- **First Responders** are so named because they are the first at the scene. They provide basic emergency care. Firefighters, police officers, and other emergency workers have this level of training.

- At the second level, called **EMT-Basic** or EMT-1, EMTs are trained to treat patients at the scene of an accident and during transportation by ambulance to the hospital.
- The **EMT-Intermediate** (EMT-2 and EMT-3) has advanced training in the use of defibrillators that give shocks to restart a stopped heart. They are also trained in applying airway techniques and equipment to help people with breathing difficulties.
- **EMT-Paramedics** (EMT-4) are certified to provide extensive care. In addition to carrying out the above-named treatments, these paramedics also administer drugs orally and intravenously and can administer and read the results of electrocardiograms (EKGs) as well as other equipment.

The Risks

EMTs take certain risks. It is a physically demanding job involving much bending, kneeling, and heavy lifting. This can result in back injuries. There is also the risk of hearing damage due to the daily exposure to ambulance sirens. EMTs have to deal with the occasional mentally unbalanced and/or violent individual, and they can be exposed to the blood and other bodily fluids of people with AIDS, hepatitis, and other diseases.

 Fact

EMTs work different shifts since someone is on call twenty-four hours a day. They work between forty- and sixty-hour weeks, with periodic overtime. As described above, training is required to be an EMT. All fifty states have their own programs for certification. EMTs have to renew their certification every two years.

The job outlook is good for this profession. It is expected to grow faster than most over the next few years. There will always be a need for emergency service personnel in communities large and small.

Opportunities are expected to be greater in private ambulance companies, though salaries will be higher for EMTs in state and local government. Despite the nature of the work and the responsibility entrusted to EMT personnel, the average salary is not all that great. The median for local government personnel is $27,710. You have to have a sense of dedication and a desire to serve to successfully hold a job like this, lest resentment over the low salary in comparison to what some of your friends are making cloud your judgment and blunt your incentive to give it your all. And give it your all you must, because lives literally depend on you.

911 Operations

911 operators receive calls from citizens and dispatch the appropriate emergency services, whether it is the police, fire department, or EMS. It can be a very stressful job. Dispatchers provide the link between the public and the safety agency. Since 911 dispatchers are hired by their local governments, job requirements and salaries may vary slightly. You can learn about the particulars in your community by visiting the Web site of your city, county, or state government.

For an example, new hires in Santa Barbara, California, are kept on probation for one year, during which they undergo on-the-job training and are obliged to attend a training program at the local college. There they learn federal, state, and local laws and codes, fire prevention, and other services provided by the county. They are trained on how to deal with callers who are often hysterical, angry, and possibly even suicidal. They learn how to keep cool under stress.

If you successfully complete the probationary period, you will be promoted and receive the job title Communications Dispatcher, Level II. In 2006, the salary for that level ranged between $44,422 and $54,232. The dispatch center is, of course, open for business around the clock, seven days a week, 365 days a year, and is administered by the Santa Barbara county sheriff's department. It receives more than 325 calls a day on its 911 emergency lines, for a total of more than 200,000 calls per year.

You must be a high school graduate with one year of experience in a job where you have dealt with people over the phone. You must be able to type thirty-five words per minute. The shifts are ten hours long, and you must be willing to rotate through all of them. You will not have a set shift during your employment.

☀ Alert

As a 911 dispatcher, you may receive calls from unusual sources. In 2006, a dog, trained to hit the 911 speed-dial button with its nose, called 911 when its owner had an epileptic seizure. It also opened the door when help arrived. So do not ignore a summons from anyone, including man's best friend.

After filing your initial application, you will have to submit to a written and oral test. You must get at least a 70 percent score on the written test to be considered. The oral test will be conducted in the sheriff's office. There will also be a background check and lie detector test. If you pass all of the above, next are physical and psychological exams. If hired, you will work a four-days-on, three-days-off schedule, rotating shifts.

Animal Control

Different communities vary somewhat in the way they administer this office's duties, so this section uses as an example the Los Angeles County Department of Animal Care and Control, which is representative of most big-city operations. Los Angeles County has six animal shelters that serve more than 3,200 miles of city, desert, beach, and mountain area. This county service provides animal control and rescue around the clock, every day of the year.

The shelters house lost or unwanted animals available for adoption. The benefits of adopting from a county shelter include receiving free veterinary care, low-cost spaying/neutering, and the assurance that the pet you adopt has had all the necessary vaccinations. And that's not to mention the joy in the fact that you are saving a life that will forever be your devoted and faithful little friend.

Some animal-control employees work exclusively in the shelters, while others work in the field, on the lookout for lost, injured, or abandoned animals. They rescue animals from dangerous situations, investigate reports of cruelty to animals, and enforce all state and local animal-control laws. They are also called on the scene when wild animals have close encounters with human beings.

Fact

The mission statement of the Los Angeles Department of Animal Care and Control states that it "promotes and protects public safety and animal care through sheltering, pet placement programs, education and animal law enforcement." The department's purpose is to "provide responsive, efficient and high quality animal care and control services that preserve and protect public and animal safety."

Many communities have occasional problems with wild cats, coyotes, or bears venturing into populated areas. Animal control, in conjunction with other authorities, tries to humanely remove such animals from the area.

The challenges and rewards of a job in animal control are vast and varied. The days of the dogcatcher and the pound are quickly disappearing. Animal control officers and other employees in the field of animal control strive to serve the public as the front line of defense to protect the health and safety of humans and animals.

The five-point focus of an animal control program covers the following:

1. Public health
2. Public safety
3. Law enforcement
4. Protection of pets and people with the use of education and intervention
5. Agency interaction in communication and cooperative endeavors

The National Animal Control Association sums it up as follows: "Animal Control is a program that effectively treats the symptoms while seeking to eliminate the causes by compassionately using the tools of education and enforcement."

Job opportunities in the animal control field include the following:

Field Operations

- Animal control officers
- Humane officers
- Cruelty investigators
- Livestock officers
- Field supervisors
- Rabies control/bite investigators

Shelter Operations

- Kennel master
- Operations manager
- Shelter manager
- Animal care technicians

Animal Care Attendants

- Euthanasia technicians
- Veterinary technicians
- Animal groomers

Community/Office Operations

- Clerks I & II
- Secretaries I - II - III
- Executive secretaries
- Data processing clerks
- Dispatchers
- Receptionists
- Adoption counselors
- Executive directors/managers
- Public relations
- Humane educators

Salary Ranges

The lowest salary is the lowest allowed by law: minimum wage. Wage increases are based on specialized training, and they vary by geographical area. Salaries paid also depend upon the size of the community and its commitment to modern animal-control programs. Another factor that determines pay rates is whether the department is privately run as a humane society with joint service contracts for animal control or whether it is a governmentally operated department.

The greatest earning opportunities can be found in upper-level, trained positions. Management and investigator levels can earn potentially $50,000 to $85,000 in metropolitan areas; $30,000 to $45,000 in mid-sized communities; and $12,000 to $24,000 in small communities.

Educational/Training Requirements

Careers in the area of animal control involve public health and safety (in terms of the hazards of rabies and other diseases, animal bites, and so on) and law enforcement (local, state, and national laws pertaining to animals). At a minimum, a high school diploma or GED is required for entry-level positions. A college degree in a field of study related to the nature of the job is preferred. You may be able to substitute comparable experience for a degree. Most positions require ongoing specialized training. For instance, you must continue your studies in order to hold the position of certified euthanasia technician, and other positions may require you to be certified in chemical capture or to hold National Animal Control Association certification. Employment requirements usually include mandatory drug screening, background checks, and a valid driver's license.

Advancement Opportunities

Smaller communities are usually limited in positions and advancement opportunities. Small cities sometimes operate as one or two-person departments. Mid-sized and larger cities offer the most variety and opportunities for advancement within the animal control structure.

Pros and Cons of Working in the Field of Animal Control

Some of the many positive aspects of working in animal control include the following:

- Protecting pets and people
- Helping animals find homes with loving, responsible people who are prepared for their lifetime commitment to a pet
- Rescuing animals from cruelty and prosecuting the individuals who torture and abuse animals
- Assuring that impounded animals are being provided with proper and humane care at the shelter, until the pet owner reclaims them or until they are adopted
- Knowing that if no one will care for the surplus unwanted, diseased, and even vicious animals, your concern will guarantee they are provided a humane and dignified death when there are no other alternatives
- Work that is never dull, and challenges that are never-ending
- Unusual animal calls that offer a variety of work and provide opportunities to meet unexpected challenges

Some drawbacks of working in animal control are the following:

- Making pet owners angry when you are only trying to do your job
- The fact that most people do not understand the need for animal-control enforcement until it is their children who are bitten by a dog or their pet that is attacked
- The chance that you will observe otherwise decent people at their very worst, especially when you have to impound a pet or issue a citation

- Blame in the public eye for killing animals, on the part of people who still do not believe, or won't accept, the realities of pet overpopulation
- Having to deal with people who want to own animals but often don't want to accept the personal and financial responsibility of pet ownership
- Stress from the verbal and physical abuse from citizens, depression from animal euthanasia, and exposure to communicable diseases and serious injuries from both animals and humans

Remember that a long-term job commitment in the area of animal control requires tremendous dedication to animals and the public. Some positions require working long hours and being on call at night, on weekends, and even on holidays to answer emergency calls. Check with your local community animal control center about job opportunities.

Other Enforcers

U.S. marshals and deputy marshals protect federal courts and see that nothing happens to disrupt trials. They also protect federal judges, transport prisoners, protect federal witnesses, and perform other duties related to the judiciary. In addition, marshals arrest and track down fugitives from justice.

The U.S. Department of Diplomatic Security special agents fight the war on terror. They protect American embassies and ambassadors overseas. In the United States, they investigate passport fraud, authorize security clearances, and engage in counterterrorism efforts.

U.S. Secret Service special agents protect the president, the vice president, and their families. They also protect presidential candidates, former presidents, and foreign dignitaries visiting the United States. Secret Service agents also investigate counterfeiting, forgery, and fraudulent use of credit cards.

E ssential

Immigration inspectors interview people seeking legal entry into the country. Customs inspectors check cargo coming into the country through seaports, airports, and across the borders. They confiscate prohibited items and arrest smugglers, money launderers, and other criminals.

Most of these positions will put you at the GS-10 grade level. GS-10 employees start at a base salary of $42,548. They can advance to the GS-13 grade level in field nonsupervisory assignments at a base salary of $64,478. Grades GS-14 and GS-15 are paid a base salary of about $76,193 and $89,625.

Chapter 6

The U.S. Postal Service (USPS)

Neither rain nor snow nor sleet nor dark of night will keep you from learning all you need to know about the U.S. Postal Service (USPS) and how you can go to work for this organization, which was founded by none other than Benjamin Franklin himself.

A Little History

On July 26, 1775, members of the Second Continental Congress met in Philadelphia and made the following agreement:

> That a Postmaster General be appointed for the United Colonies, who shall hold his office at Philadelphia, and shall be allowed a salary of 1000 dollars per [year] for himself, and 340 dollars per [year] for a secretary and Comptroller, with power to appoint such, and so many deputies as to him may seem proper and necessary. That a line of posts be appointed under the direction of the Postmaster General, from Falmouth in New England to Savannah in Georgia, with as many cross posts as he shall think fit.

Postal Beginnings

This is how the Post Office Department, the predecessor of the USPS, was born. Prior to this, delivery of mail was a haphazard affair. People from all walks of life became unofficial mailpersons as they crisscrossed the new colonies. Overseas delivery service began in a bar. In 1639, the General Court of Massachusetts designated Richard Fairbanks's Boston tavern as the official drop site for mail arriving from or being sent to England.

Individual colonies created and maintained their own postal routes. For example, Governor Francis Lovelace of New York set up a monthly route between New York City and Boston in 1673. In our day of instantaneous communication, it's hard to imagine waiting a month for a reply to a missive from dear Aunt Sally or good old Uncle George. The New-York-to-Boston service did not last long, but it gained historical significance. The route came to be known as the Old Boston Post Road, and it was later incorporated into the national highway U.S. 1. In the South, private messengers—sometimes slaves—delivered the mail.

 Fact

Two former postmasters became U.S. presidents later in their careers: Abraham Lincoln and Harry Truman. Truman held the title and signed papers but immediately turned the position and its pay over to an assistant. Lincoln was the only president who actually served in the role of postmaster.

Enter Benjamin Franklin

Centralized postal service in the American colonies arose thanks to a man who never set foot in North America. In 1691, Thomas Neale received a twenty-one-year grant from the Crown to create a postal system among the British colonies. Rather than visit the New World himself, he appointed Governor Andrew Hamilton of New Jersey as his deputy postmaster general. Neale's franchise cost the equivalent of eighty cents per year, but the burgeoning service wound up putting him heavily in debt. He died in 1699 after assigning his North American interests to Hamilton and to Englishman Robert West.

The British government bought the rights to the colonies' postal service in 1707 and appointed Andrew Hamilton's son, John, as deputy postmaster general of America. One of Hamilton's successors, Alexander Spotswood, appointed Benjamin Franklin as postmaster of Philadelphia in 1737. At this time, Franklin was only thirty-one years old and just beginning his long and distinguished career in public service. Franklin became a living folk hero. He was an inventor: Bifocals, the lightning rod, the odometer, and the wood-burning stove that bears his name are all his inventions. He was a statesman besides, a member of the Continental Congress, ambassador to France, member of the Constitutional Convention, an abolitionist, and—much earlier—postmaster general for the American colonies.

Franklin took this post in 1753. The keen-minded Franklin made some important and lasting improvements in the colonial postal system. One of the first things he did was to inspect things up close. He set out on a long tour of post offices that took him throughout the North and as far South as Virginia. He surveyed routes, placing milestones on principal roads, and formulating shorter routes whenever possible. Franklin instituted nighttime delivery between Philadelphia and New York. Riders were able to take advantage of nearly deserted roads, and delivery time was cut. Franklin's efforts helped the colonial postal service achieve profitability for the first time. By the time he left the office, postal routes interlaced American soil from Maine to Florida, New York to Canada. Mail was delivered on a regular schedule using posted times.

The American Revolution

Franklin's revolutionary sympathies led the Crown to fire him in 1774. His successor, William Goddard, was no Benjamin Franklin, but he was no slouch as postmaster, either. He set up the Constitutional Post mail service within and among the colonies. The service was funded by subscription, and profits were put back into the enterprise. By the time the Continental Congress met in 1775 in Philadelphia, Goddard's Constitutional Post was flourishing. There were thirty post offices to be found from Williamsburg, Virginia, to Portsmouth, New Hampshire. Goddard required each office to hire post riders with immaculate reputations who would swear to keep the mail under lock and key.

As for the Crown's service, Goddard warned:

> Letters are liable to be stopped & opened by ministerial mandates, & their Contents construed into

treasonable Conspiracies; and News Papers, those necessary and important vehicles, especially in Times of public Danger, may be rendered of little avail for want of Circulation.

The Constitutional Post afforded security to colonial messages and provided a communication line that played a vital role in bringing about American independence.

Soon after the Revolutionary War began, the Second Continental Congress met in Philadelphia. Its goal was twofold: planning for colonial defense against the British army and discussing the state of the colonies themselves. What did the colonies need that they did not have to ensure that the cause of liberty would prevail? The Continental Congress quickly determined that the ability to deliver letters and intelligence was crucial. A committee, chaired by Benjamin Franklin and including Samuel Adams, Richard Henry Lee, Philip Livingston, Thomas Lynch, and Thomas Willing, was named to consider the creation of a postal system.

 Fact

Some people who were postal workers before achieving stardom include Bing Crosby, Walt Disney, William Faulkner, Sherman Hemsley, Rock Hudson, Charles Lindbergh, and Adlai E. Stevenson. Underground author and poet Charles Bukowski worked for the postal service until he managed to make a living solely from writing. His first novel, titled *Post Office*, is a fictional account of his days as a mailman.

The committee reported its findings on July 25, 1775. The Continental Congress wasted no time in creating the position of postmaster general, and Benjamin Franklin was given the job. He served for a little more than a year. During that time, postal service mostly carried letters between Congress and the Revolutionary army. Postmasters and post riders were exempt from military service so that the crucial mail delivery would not be interrupted. The postal service of today stretches back in an unbroken line to Franklin himself. It's no wonder that he has received major credit for establishing a thriving postal service that continues to serve the needs of the United States.

Today's Postal Service

The USPS delivers literally billions of pieces of mail per week. And, amazingly, the vast majority of these missives reach their destinations in a timely manner. There are currently about 619,000 people employed by the postal service, most of whom are window clerks, mail sorters and processors, machine operators, and letter carriers. Clerks are the folks at the window who deal with the general public, while sorters, processors, and machine operators are behind the scenes. Letter carriers are the ones who brave the weather and the occasional cranky canine to deliver letters and packages to your door or mailbox.

In the Office

Postal service clerks, also known as window clerks, sell stamps, money orders, and mailing envelopes and boxes. They weigh packages to determine postage and check that packages conform to acceptable conditions for mailing. They register, certify, and insure mail and answer customer inquiries pertaining to postage rates, post office boxes, mailing restrictions, and other issues. They help customers fill out forms for damaged packages.

The mail sorters, processors, and processing machine operators prep incoming mail for outgoing distribution. These workers are called mail handlers, distribution clerks, mail processors, or mail-processing clerks. They load and unload postal trucks and move mail around the mail-processing center with forklifts and hand trucks. They load and operate mail-processing, sorting, and stamp-canceling machinery.

The USPS employed 75,000 clerks, 335,000 mail carriers, and 209,000 mail sorters, processors, and processing-machine operators in 2004.

Even though technology has advanced to make the process of delivering the mail easier, mail sorters, processors, and processing-machine operators still engage in physically laborious work. They must move heavy bags of mail throughout the mail-processing center. There is a lot of bending, lifting, and lugging. It can be tedious and tiring work. Many sorters, processors, and machine operators in large post offices often work at night or on weekends because the bigger facilities are open around the clock.

Alert

If your window clerk at the local post office is being methodical and fastidious (what you might call slow) during the transaction, be patient and bear this in mind: If postal clerks do not balance their cash drawers at the end of their shift, they must cover the difference out of their salary.

In the Field

Once the mail has been processed and sorted, letter carriers deliver it all across the country. These men and women travel established routes in big cities, small towns, and out-of-the-way rural routes. Some travel by foot, and others drive mail trucks. They mostly deliver mail, but they also pick it up from individual mailboxes as well as post boxes. They also collect money for postage due and COD (cash on delivery) items and take signatures for certified mail. The duties are more substantial for letter carriers on rural routes than for those who trek through major metropolises. Rural carriers sell stamps and money orders and other things that are usually sold by window clerks at post offices.

Letter carriers are often early risers—some shifts begin as early as 4 A.M. Overtime is often required. On the plus side, they are not confined in the office with a supervisor breathing down their necks. Unfortunately, they have to traverse the sidewalks and roads in all kinds of weather, and hazards come in the form of icy roads and the occasional angry dog. Letter carriers often carry a little can of dog repellent to squirt at an aggressive pooch, but be warned: In most states it is a crime to use the same spray on a human being, no matter how aggressive or hostile.

Requirements

In order to work for the USPS, applicants must be a minimum of eighteen years of age. He or she must be a U.S. citizen or have permanent alien-resident status. Men must be registered with the Selective Service program.

Fact

Originally, letter carriers worked fifty-two weeks a year, typically nine to eleven hours a day from Monday through Saturday, and, if necessary, part of Sunday. In 1884, Congress passed legislation granting them fifteen days of leave per year. In 1888, Congress declared that eight hours was a full day's work and that carriers would be paid for additional hours worked per day.

You must have what is described as a "basic competency" in the English language. This will be determined in a written test that checks your speed and accuracy in dealing with names and numbers, as well as your ability to comprehend mail distribution protocols.

A physical exam is also required, the thrust of which is that you must be able to lift and carry sacks weighing seventy pounds. There is also the ubiquitous drug test. Those applying for letter-carrier positions must have a driver's license and a good record, and the USPS will administer its own road test in one of its vehicles.

Interested applicants should visit their local post office, or the one where they would like to work, to see when and where examinations will be given. Scores will be posted, with names in descending order of the highest grades. You get a bonus of five points if you are an honorably discharged veteran and an extra ten points if you are a veteran wounded in combat. When vacancies open, the appointing officer picks one of the top three applicants. The others remain on the list for future consideration for two years after the test date.

There is much competition for window-clerk and letter-carrier jobs, and there is a waiting period of between one and two years after the test. Do not wait at home to hear from them. The vast majority of hires leave other jobs to go to work for the USPS. If hired, you will be trained by a veteran worker. You may also be obliged to take courses in safe and defensive driving. You will, of course, be trained on any equipment by a seasoned old hand familiar with the machinery.

You will need, if you do not already have them, the virtues of courtesy and tact. You will be dealing with the general public, and that can be trying to one's soul. You should also be able to deal with your colleagues in a professional manner. Some USPS workers begin as part-time employees before being promoted to full-time status. With seniority comes the chance to bid on preferential shifts or routes.

Because of increased automation and competition from private delivery companies like Fed Ex and UPS, opportunities at the USPS are expected to decline over the next several years. Of course, there will always be the need to replace retiring workers, but you can expect the competition to be great. The best opportunities will be in rural areas, but there will not likely be many opportunities in large urban centers.

E ssential

In 1860, postmasters took the following oath: "I, _____, do swear/affirm that I will faithfully perform all the duties required of me, and abstain from everything forbidden by the laws in relation to the establishment of the Post Office and post roads within the United States. I do solemnly swear/affirm that I will support the Constitution of the United States."

The average annual salary of letter carriers ranges from $37,590 to $50,580, depending on length of service. Window clerks earn between $37,880 and $44,030. The average for sorters, processors, and process-machine operators is between $36,240 and $42,620. All have very good benefits, including vacation pay and health coverage similar to other federal government jobs. You will also be represented by one of these unions, depending on your job: the American Postal Workers Union, the National Association of Letter Carriers, the National Postal Mail Handlers Union, or the National Rural Letter Carriers Association.

Visit your local post office and/or state employment service office for details about entrance examinations and specific employment opportunities for USPS workers. You can also visit the USPS on the Web at ✎*www.usps.com.*

Postal Police Force

You were probably not aware that the USPS has its own law-enforcement division. The U.S. Postal Inspection Service is one of the country's oldest federal law enforcement agencies, founded by Benjamin Franklin. These uniformed, armed officers are mandated to assure that the mail flows freely, to fight the mailing of illicit materials, and to thwart frauds and scams sent by mail. The postal police perform investigative and security functions essential to the stability of the postal system.

The U.S. Postal Inspection Service also operates four forensic crime laboratories that are staffed with scientists and other technical specialists. These professionals assist the postal inspectors in analyzing material needed for identifying and tracing criminal suspects and in providing expert testimony for cases brought to trial.

The postal police have been empowered by Congress "to investigate postal offenses and civil matters relating to the Postal Service." Some of the crimes that fall under the jurisdiction of the postal police include:

- **Assaults:** The protection of USPS employees is a very important responsibility. The postal police investigate assaults and threats directed at on-duty postal employees.

- **Bombs:** Keeping deadly mail from reaching its intended target is, of course, a high priority for postal police.
- **Burglary:** Inspectors investigate the more than 300 burglaries that involve the postal service every year.
- **Child exploitation:** The U.S. Postal Inspection Service is the leading federal law enforcement agency combating the production and distribution of child pornography and other crimes that use the mail to exploit children.
- **Controlled substances:** Postal inspectors investigate crimes related to transporting and distributing narcotics through the mail.
- **Counterfeit stamps, money orders, and related crimes:** Postal inspectors pursue people who forge, alter or counterfeit postage stamps, postal money orders, and other products. They also train postal employees to recognize bogus items.
- **Destruction, obstruction, and delay of mail:** Postal police officers uphold federal statutes related to the desertion, obstruction, delay, or destruction of mail. Postal inspectors implement mail security processes to make sure customers receive their mail intact and free from outside interference.
- **Electronic crimes:** Inspectors protect customers from fraud schemes and crimes that may occur online that involve the misuse of the mail. For example, inspectors try to thwart thieves who try to use or sell stolen credit card numbers or who use e-mail in schemes to defraud. Postal police also investigate people who use fake identities when sending e-mails to mislead or deceive recipients, as in spam.
- **Embezzlement:** Postal inspectors investigate employees and contractors suspected of embezzling money and make sure that USPS financial controls are free from internal theft or abuse.
- **Extortion:** Postal inspectors investigate shakedown and blackmail schemes when demands for ransom are sent through the U.S. mail. Inspectors also strictly enforce laws that prohibit people from using the mail to send threats.

- **Forfeiture:** Postal inspectors use criminal and civil forfeiture statutes, when appropriate, to seize assets associated with criminal acts.
- **Identity fraud:** The U.S. Postal Inspection Service is a "leading federal law enforcement agency in the investigation of identity takeovers, a crime that often begins with the theft of mail or use of the mail to defraud individuals or financial institutions."
- **Mail fraud:** The postal inspectors protect postal customers from misuse and abuse of the mail. They sniff out scams related to health care, insurance, investments, and other consumer frauds, especially those that target the elderly or other vulnerable groups.
- **Mail or mailbox destruction:** The U.S. Postal Inspection Service ensures the safety of the mail by securing letterboxes or other depositories of the U.S. mail. The inspectors catch and arrest people who willfully destroy mailboxes.
- **Money laundering:** Postal inspectors investigate criminals who attempt to conceal the profits of their nefarious deeds through monetary transactions. They identify and seize criminals' assets, denying violators their ill-gotten gains.
- **Obscenity and sexually oriented advertising:** Postal inspectors uphold obscenity standards, which prohibit "obscene, lascivious, indecent, filthy or vile" mailings.
- **Robbery:** Postal inspectors respond to robberies of postal employees and postal contractors.
- **Theft of mail:** Postal inspectors bring substantial resources to bear in the investigation of mail theft by criminals, postal contractors, and postal employees.
- **Workers' compensation fraud:** Thinking of faking an injury to get workers' comp benefits? Think again. The U.S. Postal Inspection Service will be on the case.

Postal inspectors have the same police powers enjoyed by just about any other law-enforcement entity. They make arrests and serve search warrants and subpoenas. They work closely with other law-enforcement agencies to investigate cases and prepare them for prosecution in the courts. There are about 1,970 postal inspectors enforcing more than 200 laws. In addition to these plainclothes inspectors, there are some 1,100 uniformed postal police officers assigned to postal facilities across the land. They provide security, ride shotgun with valuable mail shipments, and perform other protection duties.

Chapter 7

Infrastructure

People tend to take things like roads, bridges, tunnels, and mass transit for granted. They expect the garbage to be picked up and the water to flow from their faucets. But in order for all these mundane aspects of life to be serviceable and available to the general public, there must be a dedicated group of people willing and able to work to keep the infrastructure running. This chapter provides a snapshot of some of those jobs.

Engineering

Simply put, engineers use science and math to develop solutions to technical problems. There are many kinds of engineers, each specializing in a particular aspect of building, planning, or problem solving. Engineers can find careers in government in the fields of aerospace, agriculture, biomedicine, chemistry, civil engineering, electricity, and the environment. They can also help protect public health and safety, design ocean-going vessels, or develop mechanical innovations in engines and turbines.

Aerospace

Aerospace engineers design and test aircraft, spaceships, and missiles and oversee their manufacture. They develop new technologies in structural design, guidance, navigation and control, instrumentation and communication, and production methods. Some also specialize in specific types of aerospace products, including commercial aircraft, military fighter jets, helicopters, spacecraft, and missiles and rockets. As changing times call for new innovations, including the possibility of a need to fight new kinds of wars, these kinds of engineers are likely to be in demand. There always has been, and it appears there always will be, a need for engineers who design weapons of war.

Agriculture

Agricultural engineers use their knowledge of technology and science to determine the efficient use of biological resources. They design machinery and equipment. They specialize in areas like power systems, machinery design, structural and environmental engineering, and food engineering. They find ways to conserve soil and often work in areas like research and development, production, sales, or management.

Biomedicine

Biomedical engineers build devices and devise procedures to solve medical and health-related problems by combining biology and medicine with engineering practices. They also create new technologies in medicine, in the form of machinery and medicine. The famous film director John Huston was once asked what steps he took that resulted in such a long and creatively productive life. "Surgery," was his answer. Indeed, there have been great strides in the medical profession in the last few decades. Many people are alive today because of cutting-edge procedures that did not exist until recently, including new surgical techniques, new ways to transplant critical organs, and new ways to fight fatal diseases such as some forms of cancer and even AIDS.

 Fact

The history of the United States is full of notable engineers. The Holland Tunnel, used by scores of Manhattan commuters each day, was named for its chief engineer, Clifford Holland. Twentieth-century Renaissance man Buckminster Fuller engineered the geodesic dome as a sturdy and inexpensive living structure. And the Brooklyn Bridge was designed by engineer John August Roebling.

Chemistry

Chemical engineers apply principles of chemistry, physics, mathematics, and mechanical and electrical engineering. They may specialize in fields like materials science, where they participate in and contribute to the development of specific products such as plastics, medicine, detergents, and fuels.

Civil Engineering

Civil engineers design and supervise the building of roads, buildings, airports, tunnels, dams, bridges, and water-supply and sewage systems. Civil engineering is one of the oldest engineering disciplines and includes many specialties: structural, water resources, construction, environmental, transportation, and geotechnical engineering. Many civil engineers work in supervisory positions, whether that means supervising a construction site or working as a city engineer.

Electricity

Electrical engineers design, develop, and manufacture electrical equipment, such as electric motors, machinery controls, lighting, wiring in buildings, planes, trains, automobiles, and more.

The Environment

Environmental engineers endeavor to create solutions to environmental problems using the sciences of biology and chemistry. They are involved in curbing water and air pollution, encouraging recycling, waste disposal, and solving public health issues. They deal with the proper disposal of hazardous waste. They struggle to reduce the effects of acid rain, global warming, automobile emissions, and ozone depletion. They are involved with the protection of endangered species.

Health and Safety

Health and safety engineers promote worksite and product safety by applying knowledge of industrial processes and how they interact with mechanical, chemical, and human performance. They identify and measure hazards to people and property, including the risk of fires and the dangers involved in working with toxic chemicals. These are the engineers who are helping to reduce harmful toxins in the air, water, and all other aspects of people's lives, in particular their workplaces.

Industrial Engineering

Industrial engineers determine the best way to produce products and services by inspecting the essential factors of production: people, machines, materials, information, and energy. They then strive to integrate these elements to maximize a company's productivity.

ⲉ Alert

There are many well-trained, English-speaking engineers around the world willing to work at much lower salaries than U.S. engineers. The Internet has made it easy for engineering to be done by professionals in other countries. This trend will tend to hinder employment opportunities. However, the need for onsite engineers to interact with other employees and with clients will not change.

Marine Engineering

Marine engineers and naval architects are involved in the design, construction, and maintenance of ships, boats, and related equipment—everything from aircraft carriers to submarines. They bring knowledge from a variety of disciplines to the design and production process of seafaring vessels. The ocean is truly "the undiscovered country." Scientists know more about the surface of the moon and Mars than they do about the deep recesses of the world's oceans. More and more previously unknown species are being discovered every year, and marine engineers are among those leading the way in discovering this new territory.

Mechanics

Mechanical engineers are involved in the research, development, and building of engines, machines, electric generators, internal combustion engines, and steam and gas turbines, and many other kinds of machines.

Requirements and Opportunities

You will need a bachelor's degree even for an entry-level engineering job, and that degree must be in engineering, of course. Occasionally, however, graduates with a degree in math or the physical sciences may qualify for consideration for these positions. Many engineers can cross disciplines. Most two- and four-year colleges have programs in engineering technology. This subcategory allows you to perform engineering-related work in a variety of fields. A degree in engineering technology does not qualify you to register as a professional engineer, however. As in all things, the more advanced the degree you achieve, the more marketable you are. Graduate training is necessary for teaching and research jobs, but it is not a requirement for most government jobs.

Engineering Degree Programs

There are some 360 colleges that are accredited by the Accreditation Board for Engineering and Technology, Inc. (ABET), and approximately 230 colleges offer accredited programs in engineering technology. ABET accreditation is based on a test of the student's abilities. As with any other college degree, always make sure that any school you attend is accredited.

In order to get into an undergraduate engineering school, you need a background in mathematics (algebra, geometry, trigonometry, and calculus) and science (biology, chemistry, and physics), in addition to liberal arts courses. A standard four-year college curriculum consists of two years studying mathematics, basic sciences, introductory engineering, humanities, and social sciences. The second two years includes courses in engineering, with a concentration in one specialty.

Licensure

All fifty states require licensing for engineers who deal directly with the public. This includes most government engineering jobs. Licensed engineers are called professional engineers (PE). In order to earn a PE license, an engineer must have earned a degree from an ABET-accredited engineering program, have four years of on-the-job experience, and have successfully completed a state examination.

E ssential

Recent graduates can start the licensing process by taking the Fundamentals of Engineering (FE) examination upon graduation. If you pass this you are called an engineer in training (EIT) or an engineer intern (EI). After some work experience, EITs can take the Principles and Practice of Engineering exam.

Most states recognize engineering licenses from other states. Most civil, electrical, mechanical, and chemical engineers are licensed PEs. Fledgling engineers work under the supervision of experienced engineers who serve as their mentors. As new engineers gather more experience, they are given more difficult projects and more independence.

Employment Opportunities

There are about 1.4 million engineers working today. Federal, state, and local governments employ some 194,000 engineers. About 91,000 are in the federal government, mostly in the Departments of Defense, Transportation, Agriculture, Interior, and Energy, as well as in the National Aeronautics and Space Administration (NASA). Most engineers in state and local government agencies work in highway and public works departments.

In 2005, salaries for government engineering jobs (for employees who had earned at least a bachelor's degree) averaged between $70,086 and $100,059.

Mass-Transit Operations

Driving for public transit systems can be stressful since the work involves dealing with passengers, timetables, and traffic. Drivers pick up and drop off passengers at prearranged stops in their assigned routes. They collect fares, answer questions about schedules and transfer points, and announce stops. Depending on the size of your city or town, drivers may also clean the bus at the end of the day.

☀ Alert

To protect drivers from hostile passengers, many cities and states have enacted new laws that make assaulting a bus driver the equivalent of assaulting a police officer, which has a greater penalty than an assault against a civilian. Postal employees also have similar protection under the law.

Bus drivers with regular routes and subway operators generally have consistent weekly work schedules. Those who do not have regular schedules may be on call. They must be prepared to report on short notice. In order to accommodate commuters, many operators work split shifts, such as 6 A.M. to 10 A.M. and 3 P.M. to 7 P.M.

Bus drivers have to earn a commercial driver's license (CDL) to operate vehicles that transport sixteen or more passengers. In order to qualify for a commercial driver's license, applicants have to pass a written test on rules and regulations and show that they can safely operate a commercial vehicle.

Subway and streetcar operator applicants with at least a high school education have the best chance of being hired. In some cities, potential subway operators are required to work as bus drivers first. Successful candidates should be in good health, have communication skills, and be able to use good judgment and think quickly on the job.

Public Works

Departments of public works are usually run by the state or city government. They handle solid waste management (including garbage collection and recycling), environmental services (including litter and graffiti removal), and highway maintenance. They may also handle energy and conservation services.

Waste Management

As a waste management worker, you would be responsible for collecting, transporting, and recycling or disposing of waste materials. In general, solid waste (garbage) is collected and then driven to a landfill for disposal. Material for recycling is usually separated by type and collected in dedicated bins alongside general waste.

Departments of waste management need sanitation workers to drive around cities and suburbs to pick up household rubbish and recycling every day. In some locations, sanitation workers are also required to operate street cleaning equipment and do some snow removal during the winter.

Sanitation workers must have a high school diploma, and they must be able to perform physically demanding work for several hours every day. As a driver, you would also need a commercial driver's license. Salaries vary, but they usually start at around $30,000 per year.

Water and Sewer

Municipal water and sewer departments provide drinking water and wastewater services (including collection and treatment) to residential and commercial customers in their cities and towns. In a large municipal area, the water and sewage authority might deliver and process hundreds of gallons of water every day. They need thousands of employees to run the wastewater treatment facilities and keep the tap water flowing.

A wastewater treatment facility laborer must possess a high school diploma and be able to perform physically demanding work (including some heavy lifting). As with other government jobs, you would need to pass a drug test at the time of application. Random drug testing at any time after hiring is also common. Hourly wages for a laborer begin around $20, but a water-services foreman can earn a salary up to $72,000 per year.

Fact

A number of state and local government jobs require weekend or night work. This is especially true in public works jobs. Because cities need sewer systems and clean water continuously throughout each day, weekend and night shifts are the norm for utility workers.

Highway Maintenance

Highway maintenance workers provide upkeep for the highways, municipal and rural roads, airport runways, and other pathways in cities and towns. They repair broken pavement, guardrails, and high-way markers. They plow snow and mow and clear brush from along roads. Highway maintenance workers earn an average of $14 an hour. Maintenance workers earn about $15 an hour. For more information on jobs like these in your area, check the Web site of your city, county, or state government public works department. These sites generally list available positions or provide a link to this information elsewhere on the Web.

Chapter 8

Walk on the Wild Side

Government jobs come in a wide range of environments, from a cubicle to a laboratory. For some jobs, you don't even have to stay inside at all! This chapter describes how it is possible to get paid to do government work in the great outdoors.

National Park Service

The National Park Service is a division of the U.S. Department of the Interior. It was created in 1916 to preserve the environment, designate certain areas as historical landmarks, and create national parks for conservation and recreational purposes. Parks range from Yellowstone National Park where the grizzlies roam free, to Liberty State Park in Jersey City, New Jersey, where you can see Lady Liberty in New York harbor and the skyline of lower Manhattan. There are more than 80 million acres of land in the national parks system.

Becoming a Park Ranger

Park rangers patrol and manage federal and state parks, historical sites, and other recreational facilities. They do a little bit of everything, functioning as law-enforcement officers, conservationists, tour guides, and much more. They will tell you the history of that giant redwood and give you a fine if you leave a messy campsite behind. You may be a park ranger in places as different as Yellowstone National Park and Jersey City, New Jersey, but no matter where you work, you will have to contend with the local wildlife.

There are many skill levels for a park ranger. Entry-level positions with no requirements are available, along with an entry-level salary. You can start at a higher level if you have a high school diploma, and higher still with a college degree. Education or life experience in natural or earth sciences, law enforcement, business or public administration, and other related fields are all helpful when it comes to getting one of these positions.

As a park ranger, your job might require skills that come from any of the previous fields at any time. It is a job that is nothing if not eclectic and crosses many disciplines. Of course, your people skills should be above average. Though you will be in the wide-open spaces, you will not be alone amid the flora and fauna. You will need to help tourists to better enjoy and appreciate the park, and you might even get a chance to be a hero by guiding a lost hiker or two.

These are some general requirements for hiring consideration by federal job candidates. All employees for government outdoor jobs must be the following:

- At least eighteen years old
- U.S. citizens
- In good physical shape and good health (physical examinations may be required)

Training and Advancement

When you are finally in the woods, much of your training will be on the job. The experience you accumulate will help you rise within the ranks if you so desire. You may also be required or inspired to upgrade your skills through career-related courses offered at training centers in Arizona, West Virginia, and Georgia.

As you begin to investigate the possibilities for employment with these agencies, the first place to check out is the Web site ✍*www .usajobs.opm.gov*. This site has a comprehensive listing on available positions in hundreds of fields. Because jobs performed outdoors may fall under a variety of different agencies, this all-in-one resource is the best place to start. Through this Web site, you can receive information about the examination required. Like any civil service position, you will need to take a test.

You will initially start at a certain level based on your examination score and experience. There are several levels, and there is naturally more responsibility the higher you rise within the system. You will need to have good managerial skills if you choose to advance, since your domain will cover a lot of geography and an assortment of personalities who report to you. Starting salaries are low, and even higher-level paychecks will not make any employee a millionaire. You should know this going in, and your decision should be made for the other, less tangible, perks that a park ranger position provides.

Fact

Jobs with the National Park Service, the U.S. Forest Service, the U.S. Fish and Wildlife Service, and the Bureau of Land Management comprise the majority of outdoor government jobs. Smaller federal and state agencies are also looking for paid and volunteer outdoor workers.

State Jobs

People who want to work in outdoors jobs need not only look for positions at the federal level. You might find more opportunities by checking out your state and local governments. The competition to work in Yellowstone National Park or the Grand Canyon is fiercer than a hungry grizzly, and entry-level people may have to work their way up by working at a state-run outdoor park or recreational facility.

State outdoor agencies hire seasonal workers to do things like fight wildfires; build walking, hiking, and biking trails; assist visitors in a customer-service capacity; and run rest and concession areas. There are full-time jobs in agriculture, aquaculture, parks and forests, conservation and geology, research, and maintenance.

Many of these jobs are identical to those with federal agencies. It is an irony that while the federal government has an overabundance of applicants, the states often have trouble filling similar positions. Check with the Web site of your state or local government, and you will very likely find job postings for the above positions as well as many others.

Zoo Workers

If you love animals, you might consider a career in a zoo. You really have to love critters of all kinds if you want to make a living working with them. It can be very hard and sometimes heartbreaking work. Zoo workers cannot expect to earn huge salaries, but the benefits of working with animals can more than make up for a lack of financial rewards.

At one time, you could start at the entry level and work your way up the ranks through on-the-job training and continuing education. These days, although you do not need to be a veterinarian to work with animals, most of the jobs in zoos require some kind of specialized degree. Although practical experience with animals is helpful, most entry-level zookeeper positions require at least a four-year college degree, in addition to animal-handling experience. Specific training in biology, wildlife management, animal science, zoology, marine biology, or animal behavior is preferred. The higher-level positions (such as curator or researcher) typically require advanced academic degrees.

 Fact

The 163-acre National Zoological Park in Washington, D.C., was created by an act of Congress in 1889, and is now part of the Smithsonian Institution. The National Zoo houses more than 2,400 individual animals of 400 different species. Its most famous resident is probably the giant panda Tai Shan, who was born in captivity on July 9, 2005.

A zoo worker's hours are irregular. Zoos are usually open seven days a week. Animals have to be fed at specific times that do not always fall within regular business hours. You will often be called upon to work nights, weekends, and holidays. It is a physical job as well. You can anticipate lots of bending, kneeling, crawling, squatting, and lugging heavy sacks of feed and hay and other supplies.

As with most jobs, salaries for zoo employees vary depending on the location of the institution. Zoos in or near metropolitan areas generally offer higher salaries. On average, an animal keeper's salary ranges from minimum wage to more than $30,000 a year, depending on the keeper's skills and experience.

Fish and Wildlife

The U.S. Fish and Wildlife Service (FWS) has been around for about twenty years in its current form. It is an amalgamation of other related organizations, the first of which, the U.S. Fish Commission, was established in 1871. It has worn many hats since then, sometimes environmental, sometimes aiding the big business that once was the fishing industry. It also got involved in the repopulation of the buffalo, which had been rendered nearly extinct during the "taming" of the Wild West. When the Endangered Species Acts of 1966 and 1973 were passed by Congress, the FWS overtook responsibility for protecting the nation's diminishing wildlife. Now the FWS is perhaps best known as the government agency that places plants and animals on the endangered species list.

E ssential

To find jobs in the FWS (online at ✍*www.fws.gov*), you will use CARES, the Conservation Applicant Referral Evaluation System. With it, you can search for job openings, create and edit your resume, and apply for jobs online. You can also enter information about the type of jobs you are looking for, and the system will notify you by e-mail when that kind of job becomes available.

These days the U.S. Fish and Wildlife Service maintains and administers more than 500 wildlife refuges, encompassing more than 92 million acres across the land, including the Caribbean. Typical work might involve keeping the landscape hospitable for the wildlife by removing alien nonnative plant and animal life, making sure creatures that graze have enough grass and water, and regulating the burning of overgrowth. Most of the lands under the service's jurisdiction are wetlands, though the FWS also controls the lush forests of the Pacific Northwest and Alaska. The FWS also manages fish hatcheries and research facilities.

Life Guarding

There is always a need for lifeguards in bodies of water regulated by the government, from beaches and lakes in national parks to the local city swimming pool. The requirements are pretty much standard across federal, state, and local lines, so the following description draws from the New York City public pools as an example.

Of course, you have to know how to swim—very well. You have to be in good physical condition.

Lifeguard jobs are usually seasonal, unless you work at an indoor pool that is open year-round. The season is usually between Memorial Day and Labor Day, although seasons may vary in other parts of the country. In Florida, for example, the climate is conducive to swimming most of the year.

In the New York City public pools, lifeguards work a forty-eight-hour week, and the pay is $10.71 an hour for the first year, with raises after that. The Parks Department's Lifeguard School administers a test to candidates. The minimum requirements to pass the test are the following:

- You must be able to swim 50 yards in 35 seconds.
- You must have a minimum of 20/30 vision in one eye and 20/40 in the other.
- You must be at least sixteen years old when the position begins.
- You must be able to provide a certificate of good health on doctor's stationery.
- You must successfully complete thirty-five hours of training and a CPR course to become certified as a New York City lifeguard.

You can also take advantage of conditioning classes offered by the city in order to get you in shape to pass the test. These classes are conducted at the city's public pools. If you pass the test and meet the requirements, you will be given free training and are guaranteed a steady job for the summer. New York City lifeguards may work in one of the city's fifty-two outdoor pools or on any of fourteen miles of beach property.

Landscaping

Jobs in landscape architecture are likely to be increasingly in demand. Environmental concerns and regulations are leading businesses and individuals to create landscapes that blend in with the natural world. Builders no longer simply blast and level the landscape before slapping up ugly edifices.

People want attractive grounds enveloping the areas where they work, live, and play. A landscape designer typically plans the location of buildings and paths; determines the location of plants, trees, and shrubbery around the buildings; and undertakes numerous other tasks that will lend beauty to otherwise sterile surroundings. The goal of a landscape architect is to combine functionality and aesthetic appeal to create a pleasing environment that can soothe the senses and calm a troubled mind.

☀ Alert

Government-employed landscape architects usually work regular business hours and are salaried, rather than paid by the hour, meaning that there is no overtime pay even when overtime is necessary to meet a deadline. A bachelor's or master's degree is usually required.

Landscapers work on projects of all kinds. Municipalities at every level of government are always building and renovating. Working closely with surveyors, engineers, and others, landscapers are often involved in the development of a site from day one. At other times they are brought in to add the finishing touches. They also work with environmentalists and others to conserve the natural world around the site, and they often work to restore nature to its pristine form in the process. They conform to any state and federal codes pertaining to building and development in the area. They produce detailed plans of their ideas in advance. In the old days, this was done with sketches and blueprints. These are still used, of course, but today's high-tech landscape architects use computer-generated imagery (CGI) to create a 3D image of their designs for their clients. This is becoming more and more common. In fact, it is virtually a necessity for landscape architects to have strong computer skills. Finally, landscape architects supervise all the work done by contractors and see that it meets their specifications.

Landscape architects who work for government agencies ordinarily design government buildings, courthouses, roadways, recreational parks and other publicly owned property, including national parks and forests. They have to be able to prepare reports on the environmental impact of what they are planning and then design according to the government's guidelines. Landscapers also restore land and property that has laid fallow and/or has deteriorated over the years, such as landfills and mines.

As of 2004, most states required landscape architects to have a license. Interested applicants have to take the Landscape Architect Registration Examination (LARE), sponsored by the Council of Landscape Architectural Registration Boards and administered in two sections: graphic and multiple choice. Standards vary from state to state, but you often have to have a degree or have been working in the field as an apprentice for at least one year, sometimes longer. Fourteen states insist that their own test be taken in addition to the LARE. For federal jobs, the applicant does not need to be licensed, but he or she must have a bachelor's degree or higher in the field. It is a growing field, particularly in the public sector. In fact, some estimates indicate landscape architecture will be one of the most in-demand occupations through 2014.

The Nature Conservancy

Although it is not a government agency, you might consider a job with the Nature Conservancy if you are interested in helping to preserve the great outdoors. Nature Conservancy jobs are in high demand. So many people want to work for this organization that a lot of them start as volunteers in order to get a foot in the door.

Based in Arlington, Virginia, the Nature Conservancy's worldwide office hosts the majority of staff connected to the key institutional support functions of the organization, including external affairs, finance, general counsel, human resources, information systems, and marketing.

Fact

The conservancy has a twenty-four-hour job hotline that lists all job postings across the country. Call (703) 247-3721 to hear a recorded list of jobs ranging from secretarial/administrative assistants and journalists to field biologists and ecologists. They also have positions in locations around the world, from Virginia to Hawaii to Alaska to the Solomon Islands in the South Pacific.

The conservancy collaborates with a number of organizations to achieve its conservation goals. On the nonprofit's Web site, at ✍*www* *.nature.org*, you can search for a job by geographical area or by particular jobs. Many require a college degree. When you find a job that interests you, submit your resume and cover letter to the contact person listed for that job. Be aware that if you simply send your resume to the conservancy, the nonprofit will not consider it, so make sure you are applying for a specific job.

Chapter 9

Government Jobs in Communications

Students in college often major in communications to prepare for careers in journalism, public relations, marketing and advertising, writing, and broadcasting. If you have an interest in both communications and government, you could consider a career as a political speechwriter or publicist. You might even end up one day as the White House press secretary! This chapter describes the tools you need to explore communications jobs in government.

Nonfiction and Copy Writing

Writers produce nonfiction text for books, magazines, trade journals, online publications, company newsletters, radio and television broadcasts, motion pictures, and advertisements. Many writers prepare material directly for the Internet. They may write for electronic newspapers or magazines or produce technical documentation that is available only online. They may write content for Web sites. These writers must be well versed in graphic design, page layout, and multimedia software. They should also be familiar with the interactive nature of the Internet in order to create a cyber-symphony of text, graphics, and sound.

Nonfiction writers either propose the subject matter or are assigned a subject by the editor or publisher. They research and find information about the given topic through various methods: personal knowledge/experience, library and Internet research, and interviews. They then select the material, organize it, and convey the information in a readable and coherent manner.

Copywriters come up with catchy advertising copy for use by publications or the broadcast media to promote the sale of goods and services. Newsletter writers compile information for distribution to various associations, corporate employees, clients, or the general public.

E ssential

Every government entity now has a Web site, and every Web site has to convey information. This is where the copywriters come in. Dazzling Flash and Macromedia presentations are nice to look at, but the written word still reigns supreme because, though the graphics and animations are pretty, people are visiting these sites to get information.

Technical Writing

Technical writers produce technical matter like equipment manuals and operation and maintenance instructions. It is their job to turn technical jargon into easily understandable language. They write operating and maintenance manuals, catalogs, assembly instructions, and sales promotion materials, and depending on the job description they may take on other assignments as well. Science and medical writers compose documents on the physical or medical sciences. They may also work with researchers on technical subjects to help make the information comprehensible to the layman.

Technical writers usually command a higher salary than nontechnical writers. Technical writing often requires a degree in, or at least some knowledge of, a specialized field. Remember, your job as a technical writer is to take obscure, very technical jargon and come up with a simplified version that any average layperson can understand.

Editing

Editors review and rewrite the work of others. The responsibilities vary with the kind of publisher and the type of editorial position. Editorial duties include planning the content of books, technical journals, trade magazines, and other general-interest publications.

Editors offer comments to improve the work. They may also oversee the production of the publications. Editors examine proposals and select material for publication or broadcast. They also review a writer's work for publication.

An executive editor oversees assistant editors, who are responsible for specific subjects. Executive editors have the final say about what stories are published. Managing editors are responsible for the daily operation of the department. Assignment editors decide who will write about what. Copy editors review and edit the writer's text for content, grammar, and style.

Fact

According to the Society for Technical Communication, the average annual salary for entry-level technical writers was $42,500 in 2004. The average for midlevel nonsupervisory technical writers was $51,500, and for senior nonsupervisory technical writers it was $66,000.

In small organizations, such as publications departments of nonprofit or government agencies, one editor may do everything or share responsibility with just a few people. Executive and managing editors hire writers, reporters, and other employees. They also negotiate contracts with freelance writers.

In the publishing world, the entry-level position is that of editorial assistant. Editorial assistants, along with copy editors and production assistants, review text for errors in grammar, punctuation, and spelling, and they check manuscripts for style and conformity with editorial policy. They might suggest revisions to improve clarity. They sometimes conduct research for writers to confirm facts and dates. Production assistants arrange pages in their final form and get the material ready for printing. Publication assistants who work for publishing houses may also read and evaluate manuscripts submitted by freelance writers.

Freelancing

There are about 320,000 writers and editors working today, and more than 33 percent are freelancers. Freelance writers and editors have diverse workplaces. Some are in sedate offices; others work in chaotic environments with a lot of background noise. The quest for information can take writers to various locales, but many more find that the world can come to them through the Internet. Laptop computers and wireless communication allows writers to work from home and on the road. The ability to e-mail, transmit, and download stories, research, or editorial materials using the Internet allows writers and editors greater freedom and flexibility.

Alert

While many freelancers enjoy the advantages of working flexible hours, most face the pressures of either dealing with multiple simultaneous projects or of sitting by a phone that is ominously silent for days at a time. This combination of deadline pressures and erratic assignments can cause stress and burnout. In addition, the daily use of computers can cause back pain, eyestrain, or fatigue.

Freelance writers sell their work to numerous entities: publishers, public relations departments, advertising agencies, and many other venues for the written word. Sometimes, they contract with a publisher to write a book or an article, or they may be hired to complete specific assignments.

Writing and Editing Job Requirements and Opportunities

A position as a writer or editor usually requires a college degree. Some employers accept a broad liberal arts background, but most prefer people with degrees in communications, journalism, or English. Good writers can usually write about anything and can pick up specialized knowledge on the job.

In larger companies and certainly in government agencies, jobs are formally structured, unlike the chaotic maelstrom of the freelancer's life. Beginners do research, fact checking, or copy editing. Advancement to full-scale writing or editing assignments happens more slowly for new writers and editors in larger organizations than for employees in small companies.

E ssential

High school and college newspapers, literary magazines, community newspapers, and local radio and television stations are good things to have on your resume. If you are still young and thinking about getting into the writing game, get involved in one or more of the above right away.

About 50 percent of salaried jobs for writers and editors are in the information sector, including newspapers, book publishers, radio and television broadcasting, software publishers, Internet service providers and search portals, and Internet publishing. The remaining 50 percent work in computer and electronic product manufacturing, government agencies, religious organizations, and many other types of businesses.

Opportunities are best for technical writers and those with a specialty. If you can write well and have a thorough understanding of law, medicine, economics, and/or other areas you will be in demand. The average salary for an American writer is $44,350. Some earn a lot less and others much more. The median for salaried (non-freelance) editors is $43,890.

Advertising and Public Relations

Advertising and public relations people create advertisements for companies and organizations and design campaigns to promote businesses and the public image of their clients. Media representatives sell advertising space to all media. Many government agencies have their own public relations departments. Politicians have press secretaries.

Internal and external public relations departments can influence how governmental bodies make decisions. Public relations strategists work behind the scenes to plan and plot public exposure strategies. This process might be as simple as writing and issuing a press release that is disseminated in various media outlets, or it can be as complex as a mass saturation of an elaborate campaign on everything from billboards to the Internet.

Goals and Objectives

The objective is always to favorably influence public opinion. People in public relations use things like polling and focus groups to get a handle on how Americans are feeling about a particular issue. They write speeches for politicians and high-level bureaucrats, coach them on how to deal with the press, and many other tasks.

 Fact

Sometimes government agencies contract advertising agencies to help polish their image. For instance, the Pentagon recently decided it wanted a new ad campaign for army recruitment. They felt that the "Be all that you can be" was getting stale, so they came up with "An Army of One."

Most employees in advertising and public relations services function in a team environment. The phrase "team player" is not just a cliché—you had better be one if you want to work in this field. You had also better be willing to work long hours, including evenings and weekends. Yes, the work can be fast-paced and exciting, but it can also be quite stressful. The ability to be creative while a deadline looms large on the horizon, even at times when the Muse does not inspire you, can be emotionally draining.

Account managers represent the agency to the client and the client to the agency. They are responsible for the quality of the advertisement or public relations campaign. Account managers monitor the activities of all aspects of the account to make sure that everything runs smoothly. They analyze what the competition is doing and also analyze consumer trends, handle billing issues, and serve as cheerleader to bring the talents of the creative, media, and research areas together.

The creative director supervises the copy chief, art director, and their staffs. Public-relations managers direct the publicity programs to a targeted public. They specialize in a specific area like crisis management or in a specific industry like health care. Public relations specialists deal with media, community, consumer, and governmental relations. They are involved with political campaigns. They also deal with special interest groups, conflict mediation, and other issues. They write press releases and contact people in the media.

Copywriters write the words—the written part of print ads, Web site content, and, if applicable, the scripts of radio and television spots. The art directors develop the visual concepts and designs of the project. They prepare layouts for print ads and television storyboards. These are cartoon-style representations of how an ad will appear. They sometimes oversee filming the television commercials and photo sessions.

Graphic designers use print, electronic, and film media to create designs that meet clients' specifications. They develop the layout and design of print ads for magazines, newspapers, and other publications. They also produce brochures for products and services, design distinctive company logos, and signs that deliver the message in an eye-popping, eye-pleasing fashion.

Research executives compile data and conduct research. They organize and run focus groups, where a cross-section of the general public is brought into a conference room to give their input on the client's product or service.

Media planners gather information on the public's consumer habits, and evaluate editorial content to determine if it is best suited for newspapers, magazines, radio, television, or the Internet. They track the media space and times available for purchase, negotiate and purchase time and space for ads, and make sure ads appear exactly as scheduled.

Question

Job Requirements and Opportunities

Entry-level professional and managerial positions in advertising and public relations require a bachelor's degree, preferably one with broad liberal arts exposure. Entry-level hires usually enter the business in the account management or media department. If you are young enough, getting into some kind of advertising-related internship while in school will give you an advantage. In fact, internships are more and more necessary even to get your foot in the door. Courses in marketing, psychology, accounting, statistics, and creative design are also helpful.

Assistant account executive positions require a bachelor's in marketing or advertising, and some require a master's degree in business administration (M.B.A.).

Assistant art directors usually need at least a two-year degree from an art or design school. Assistant media planner or assistant media buyer positions always require a bachelor's degree with a major in marketing or advertising.

E ssential

For public relations jobs, employers want applicants to have degrees in communications, journalism, English, or business. Some four-year colleges and universities offer a concentration in public relations. The competition for entry-level public relations jobs is ruthless, so you should gather experience through internships and other means. Time served and talent displayed may help you be promoted from an entry-level account management position to account executive, account supervisor, vice president, and maybe even higher. Employment in this industry is expected to grow 22 percent over the next ten years.

Chapter 10

Social Services

People sometimes need a helping hand, and they often turn to the government for that help. It is estimated that 50 percent of the federal budget goes to entitlement programs. The government is heavily invested in the helping business, and that means it has a wide variety of potential job opportunities for prospective helpers.

Social Workers

People who go into social work usually have an interest in the welfare of others, as well as a desire to help people in need. Social workers help their clients become more functional members of society by working to improve their relationships and personal and family problems. They work with clients facing everything from inadequate housing to unemployment to a serious illness, addiction, or disability. Social workers also help people who have domestic problems like child or spousal abuse. Most social workers have a specialty. They might focus on social issues pertaining to the elderly or to families and children, for instance, or they might work with people who suffer from chronic diseases, mental illness, or substance abuse.

Children and Families

Some social workers work with children, families, and schools to provide assistance to improve the social and psychological condition of children and their families. These social workers are called child welfare social workers, family services social workers, child protective services social workers, and/or occupational social workers. Some help single parents, arrange adoptions, or help find foster homes for neglected and abused children. In schools, they deal with teenage pregnancy, misconduct, and truancy issues. They guide the teachers when it comes to dealing with problem students. Social workers who focus on helping this segment of the population typically work for individual and family services agencies, schools, or state and local governments.

Working with the Elderly

Other social workers work with senior citizens. They run support groups for families and the adult children of aging parents. They advise elderly people and their families in areas like housing, transportation, and long-term care. There are instances in which adult children can no longer care for a truly ailing parent, and professionals must be called upon. This is where the social workers come in. The fact that most people are busy with jobs and their own children can make it extremely difficult for them also to give ailing parents the care they need. This keeps social workers busy.

Fact

In 2006, the first wave of baby boomers turned sixty, including President George W. Bush and former President Bill Clinton. The children of the 1960s are the senior citizens of tomorrow. They will need care and assistance. Social workers who deal with the elderly will find no shortage of clients in the years ahead.

Medicine and Public Health

Medical and public-health social workers provide the needy with support to cope with chronic, acute, or terminal illnesses, such as Alzheimer's disease, cancer, and AIDS. They also counsel patients and help them plan at-home services, including things like at-home meal delivery or even hospice care. Medical and public-health social workers work for hospitals, nursing and personal care facilities, individual and family services agencies, and local governments.

Mental Health and Substance Abuse

Mental-health and substance-abuse social workers treat individuals who have been diagnosed with psychological conditions or who have developed a chemical dependency such as alcoholism or addiction to other drugs. The services these social workers provide include individual and group therapy, crisis intervention, rehabilitation, and training in coping skills. They also help plan for supportive services to make it easier for patients to return to the community, such as working with them in a halfway house. Mental-health and substance-abuse social workers work in hospitals, substance abuse treatment centers, individual and family services agencies, and local governments. They are sometimes called clinical social workers.

Planners and Policymakers

Beyond working directly with clients to help them deal with various kinds of life-related issues, social workers also perform the function of planning how such work can best be performed. They also help develop the social and governmental policy that directs and governs such care. These men and women devise programs to address problems like child abuse, homelessness, substance abuse, poverty, and violence. They research and analyze policies, programs, and regulations. They identify social problems and offer solutions. They may help raise funds or write grants to support their programs.

Social Work on the Job

Government social workers usually work a forty-hour week. Some work evenings and weekends to meet with clients, attend community meetings, and deal with emergencies. They spend most of their time in an office or patient facility, and some travel to visit clients or to attend meetings. Others use several offices within a local area to meet with clients. The work can be emotionally draining. If you decide to become a social worker in the employ of the government, you will find yourself dealing with human suffering on a daily basis. It is important to maintain some perspective and to remember that you cannot save the world. Social workers have many successful clients, but they suffer many casualties as well.

Statistically speaking, even successful social workers "lose" more than they "win" when it comes to their clients. This is not the fault of the worker. In the final analysis, clients must take charge of their recovery, and the social worker is there to facilitate and help. For example, it is estimated that only one out of fifty alcoholics ever goes to an Alcoholics Anonymous meeting. Out of that group, only one in five is still sober five years later—and AA is regarded as the most successful treatment for alcoholics. It is staffed by volunteers and it is self-supporting, so it does not employ professional social workers.

Degrees Required

A bachelor's degree in social work is the common minimum requirement for a job as a social worker. Majors in psychology and sociology may qualify for some entry-level jobs. While a bachelor's degree is sufficient for entry into the field, an advanced degree is the new standard for many jobs. A master's in social work is fast becoming a requirement for most jobs in both government and private agencies.

The Council on Social Work Education accredits 442 programs that award bachelor's degrees in social work and 168 programs that award master's degrees in social work. The Group for the Advancement of Doctoral Education lists eighty Ph.D. programs in social work. Bachelor's degree programs prepare graduates for positions such as caseworker, in which the social worker goes out into the field to spend time with clients. These programs include courses in social work values and ethics, dealing with a culturally diverse clientele, recognizing and treating at-risk populations, human behavior, social welfare policy and services, social work practice, social research methods, and field education. Accredited programs require a minimum of 400 hours of supervised field experience.

Master's degree programs prepare graduates for work in their chosen concentration while continuing to develop the skills required to perform tasks like preparing clinical assessments, managing large caseloads, taking on supervisory roles, and handling other aspects of the job. A typical master's degree program lasts two years and includes a minimum of 900 hours of supervised field instruction or internship. You do not have to have a bachelor's degree in social work to go for a master's degree in the field. Nowadays, a second language—especially Spanish—can be helpful.

E ssential

It is a sad fact that many people abuse drugs and alcohol. Those who do not make it into treatment on their own or with family help often end up in jail or government-run rehabilitation programs. As a result, social workers with a specialty in drug and alcohol rehabilitation are generally kept busy.

All fifty states and the District of Columbia have their own licensing, certification, and registration requirements regarding social work practice and the use of professional titles. Most states demand 3,000 hours of supervised clinical experience to get a license as a clinical social worker. The National Association of Social Workers offers voluntary credentials. Based on their work experience, social workers with a master's degree can be eligible for the Academy of Certified Social Workers, the Qualified Clinical Social Worker, or the Diplomate in Clinical Social Work credential.

Salaries and Employment Outlook

Child, family, and school social workers earn an average salary of $40,620 for local government and $35,070 for state government. Medical and public-health social workers average $39,390, while mental-health and substance-abuse social workers average $35,720. Other social worker specialties average $42,570 working for the local government and $40,940 working for state government.

There are about 562,000 social workers in the United Sates. Nine out of ten are in health-care and social-assistance industries or in state and local government agencies. Most social workers are employed in cities or suburbs, but some work in rural areas.

The rapidly growing elderly population and the aging baby boomer generation are going to create a greater demand for health and social services, resulting in rapid job growth among gerontology social workers—those who specialize in service to the elderly. Social workers with backgrounds in gerontology should be in a good position because of the growing numbers of assisted-living and senior-living communities. This expanding senior population will also increase the demand for social workers in nursing homes, long-term-care facilities, and hospices.

E ssential

Competition for social worker jobs is greatest in cities, where the demand for services is highest. Opportunities are better in rural areas, where it is often difficult to attract and retain qualified staff. Job prospects are best for social workers with a background in substance-abuse treatment.

There is also expected to be a high demand for substance-abuse social workers over the next ten years. More and more substance abusers are being placed into treatment programs rather than being sent to prison. Demand is going to increase for treatment programs and social workers to help addicts stay clean and sober one day at a time. Many convicts become clean and sober behind bars, with the help of social workers, chaplains, and twelve-step meetings.

Employment in state and local government agencies is expected to grow along with the rising numbers of people on public welfare and of people who require family services or child protective services. However, the availability of federal, state, and local funding will be a major factor in determining the actual job growth.

Psychologists

Psychologists are students of the human mind and human behavior. Psychologists in the health-service field provide care for patients in hospitals, clinics, schools, or private settings. Psychologists employed in business, industry, government, or nonprofit organizations provide training and conduct research. Psychologists gather information on the human condition through controlled laboratory experiments or by administering a variety of personality, performance, aptitude, and intelligence tests. They also observe people, conduct interviews, and have people fill out questionnaires and surveys. Psychologists ply their trade in many areas, including health and human services, management, education, the law, and more.

Psychology Specialties

Clinical psychologists are most commonly employed in counseling centers, independent or group practices, hospitals, or clinics. They treat mentally and emotionally disturbed clients and counsel them with the goal of returning them to ordinary, productive lives. They interview patients and give diagnostic tests. They provide individual, family, or group therapy. Some administer community mental-health programs.

 **Question**

What are the job opportunities available for research and experimental psychologists?
Experimental or research psychologists work in universities, private research centers, businesses, and governmental organizations. They study the behavior of both human beings and animals like lab rats, monkeys, and pigeons to learn about motivation, thought, attention, learning and memory, the effects of substance abuse, and genetic factors that affect behavior.

The specializations available within the realm of clinical psychology include health psychology, neuropsychology, and geropsychology, which is the study of the effects of aging on the psyche. Health psychologists promote good health through counseling programs designed to help people achieve goals like quitting smoking and losing weight. Neuropsychologists study the relationship between the brain and behavior. They often work in stroke and head injury programs. Geropsychologists deal with the special problems faced by the elderly.

The following specialties are those most commonly found in government social work:

- School psychologists work with students in elementary and secondary schools, collaborating with teachers, parents, and school personnel to create a safe and healthy learning environment.
- Industrial-organizational psychologists apply psychological principles and research methods to the workplace in the interest of improving productivity and the quality of working life. They are also involved in research on management and marketing problems.
- Developmental psychologists study the physiological and social development that takes place over the course of a person's life. Some specialize in behavior during infancy, childhood, and adolescence; others monitor changes that occur during maturity or old age.
- Social psychologists examine people's interactions with others. Prominent areas of study include group behavior, leadership, attitudes, and perception.

Working Conditions

A psychologist's specialty determines his or her working conditions. Psychologists in private practice have their own offices and set their own hours. They offer evening and weekend hours to accommodate clients, since the average citizen is working during weekday business hours.

Psychologists who work for the government do not have that luxury. Psychologists who work in hospitals, nursing homes, and healthcare facilities work shifts that include evenings and weekends, while those who work in schools and clinics generally work regular hours.

Psychologists in government and industry have the most structured schedules.

Qualifications

A doctoral degree is mandatory to be a licensed clinical or counseling psychologist. Psychologists qualify for a wide range of teaching, research, clinical, and counseling positions in the government. A doctoral degree usually takes between five and seven years of study. The doctorate ends with a dissertation based on original research. In clinical or counseling psychology, the requirements for the doctoral degree include at least a one-year internship.

 **Question**

What is the difference between a psychologist and a psychiatrist?
A psychiatrist is a medical doctor—that is, a person who has been through medical school and has chosen psychiatry as his or her medical specialty. While a psychologist can treat patients and offer therapy and counseling, only a psychiatrist can write prescriptions for medications like antidepressants, anti-anxiety drugs, and other medications designed to treat psychiatric conditions.

A specialist degree is required in most states to work as a school psychologist. A specialist degree in school psychology requires a minimum of three years of full-time graduate study and a one-year internship.

People with a master's in psychology can work as industrial-organizational psychologists and psychological assistants under the supervision of doctoral-level psychologists. A master's degree in psychology requires at least two years of full-time graduate study. Requirements usually include practical experience and a master's thesis based on original research. Competition for admission to graduate psychology programs is intense. Some universities require students to have an undergraduate major in psychology.

A bachelor's degree in psychology qualifies a person to be an assistant to a psychologist in community mental health centers, rehabilitation offices, and correctional programs. Those with a bachelor's degree can work as research or administrative assistants for psychologists. Some work as technicians in fields like marketing research.

 Fact

Psychologists hold about 179,000 jobs. Government agencies at the state and local levels employ psychologists in public hospitals, clinics, correctional facilities, and other areas. Increased demand for psychological services in schools, hospitals, social-service agencies, mental-health centers, substance-abuse treatment clinics, and the government will contribute to job growth in the coming decade.

In the federal government, candidates having at least twenty-four semester hours in psychology and one course in statistics qualify for entry-level positions. Be warned that competition for these jobs is especially fierce because the government is one of the few employers that hires psychologists who do not have advanced degrees.

The American Psychological Association accredits doctoral training programs in clinical, counseling, and school psychology. It also works conjunction with institutions that provide internships for doctoral students in school, clinical, and counseling psychology. The National Association of School Psychologists, with the assistance of the National Council for Accreditation of Teacher Education, is also involved in the accreditation of advanced-degree programs in school psychology.

Aspiring psychologists who are interested in working with patients (rather than performing research) should be stable, mature, compassionate, and able to deal well with emotionally disturbed people. Research psychologists should be detailed-oriented and be able to work both independently and as part of a team.

Salaries

Median annual earnings of wage and salary clinical, counseling, and school psychologists are $54,950. Other salaries fall into the following ranges:

- Copractitioners with other health professionals: $64,460
- Elementary and secondary schools: $58,360
- Outpatient care centers: $46,850
- Individual and family services: $42,640

Opportunities and Outlook

School psychologists, particularly those with advanced degrees, will enjoy the best job opportunities. Growing concern about students' mental health and behavioral problems, such as bullying, will keep them busy. Since the awful day of the Columbine High School massacre at Littleton, Colorado, school psychologists have remained on red alert. They no longer simply focus on the underlying problems behind falling grades or attendances issues. They are now on the lookout for malcontents and misfits who might be planning to commit acts of violence or destruction of property.

Clinical and counseling psychologists are always in demand to help people deal with depression, marriage and family problems, job stress, and addiction. An increase in the number of employee assistance programs that help workers deal with personal problems should also create job growth in clinical and counseling specialties.

Master's-degree holders will face keen competition for jobs because most positions that require an advanced degree give preference to those holding a Ph.D. They may find jobs as psychological assistants or counselors, providing mental health services under the direct supervision of a licensed psychologist. Others may find jobs involving research and data collection and analysis in the government.

Government agencies at the state and local levels employ psychologists in public hospitals, clinics, correctional facilities, and other settings. After several years of experience, some psychologists, usually those with doctorates, enter private practice or set up private research or consulting firms. In addition to the previously mentioned jobs, many psychologists hold faculty positions at colleges and universities and as high school psychology teachers.

E Alert

Opportunities will be severely limited for bachelor's-degree holders. Some might find jobs as assistants in rehabilitation centers or in other jobs involving data collection and analysis. Those who meet state certification requirements may become high school psychology teachers.

Child Care

Child-care workers care for children who have yet to enter school as well as older children during the hours before or after school, or at other times when parents are unable to provide supervision. They play an important role in a child's development by caring for the child when parents are at work. Child-care workers are usually classified in three groups:

- Workers who care for children at the child's home, called private household workers
- Workers who care for children in their own home, called family child-care providers
- Workers at child-care centers

Child-care workers spend their day working with children, but they must maintain contact with the parents or guardians through meetings and conferences to discuss their child's progress and needs. Government employees work at the increasing number of day-care centers in offices. Single parents and new mothers want to keep their young ones nearby, and they are being accommodated more and more.

The government is jumping on the family-friendly bandwagon, and more and more onsite day-care centers are popping up in government facilities. This makes good business sense, and it's socially responsible. Having their children on the premises decreases workers' lateness and absenteeism, particularly with the increasing number of single parents, who depend on child-care facilities to help them raise their children.

E ssential

State or local regulations require a certain ratio of workers to children. This ratio varies with the age of the children. Most child-development experts recommend that a single caregiver be responsible for no more than three or four infants (less than one year old), five or six toddlers (one to two years old), or ten preschool-aged children (between two and five years old).

Child-care workers may work a variety of different shifts. Child-care centers are usually open year round, with long hours so parents can drop off and pick up their children before and after work. Some centers have full-time and part-time staff with staggered shifts to cover the entire day. Public preschool programs operate during the typical nine- or ten-month school year, employing both full-time and part-time workers.

The qualifications required of potential child-care workers also vary. Each state has its own licensing requirements that regulate training. These range from a high school diploma to community-college courses to a college degree in child development or early childhood education.

State requirements are generally higher for workers at child-care centers than for family child-care providers. Publicly funded programs have more demanding training and education requirements. Some employers only hire child-care workers who have earned a nationally recognized Child Development Associate credential or the

Certified Childcare Professional designation. More and more employers require an associate's degree in early childhood education.

Opportunities for advancement are limited, but as a child-care worker gains experience, she or he can rise to supervisory or administrative positions in large child-care centers. These positions generally require additional training and education, such as a bachelor's or master's degree.

Employment Outlook

There are about 1.3 million child-care workers, many of whom work part time. Some 62 percent of them work in local government educational services, nursing and residential care facilities, religious organizations, amusement and recreation industries, private educational services, or civic and social organizations. State and local governments operate nonprofit child-care programs.

There are always good job opportunities for qualified child-care workers. Many must be replaced every year as they leave the occupation. Many leave because of dissatisfaction with hours, low pay and benefits, and stressful conditions. Employment is expected to increase over the coming decade. This statistic is based on the number of women of childbearing age in the work force, combined with the fact that the number of children under five years of age is expected to rise over the next ten years. Only a few states provide targeted or universal preschool programs at the moment, but this is likely to change.

Salaries for Child-Care Workers

Salary depends on the education of the worker and kind of child-care center. Sadly, the pay is very low. As always, however, more education usually means higher potential earnings. The median hourly wage of child-care workers is $8.06. Benefits are minimal, if any.

Juvenile Services

Departments of juvenile services usually address issues of school truancy, run education programs such as Drug Abuse Resistance Education (DARE) and manage juvenile corrections services. In the old

days, the government was also responsible for running state reforma-
tories for delinquent youth, but these days the trend is to use different
tactics to control and treat juvenile delinquency.

Juvenile Court

Juvenile services programs are generally administered by the
state or county in which they are located. State departments of juvenile services also administer their own court system, so juvenile
lawbreakers can seek justice separately from the places where adult
criminals are tried and convicted. The juvenile court system needs
lawyers to work as juvenile advocates and protect the rights of under-
age offenders. If you are interested in a career helping youth, this
might be a good fit for you.

Mental-Health Services

Many of the mental-health issues that plague adults manifest
themselves differently in minors, so mental-health services for young
people must be tailored specifically to treat their needs. Young people often suffer from undiagnosed and untreated ADD (attention
deficit disorder) and ADHD (attention-deficit hyperactivity disorder),
learning disabilities such as dyslexia, and substance abuse. Juvenile
mental-health services try to reduce criminal activity and alleviate
recidivism in minors by coping with the underlying illnesses that
often contribute to antisocial behavior.

In addition to mental illness, many juvenile offenders have also
suffered from stressful living environments, often including physical or sexual abuse, and parents or guardians who abuse drugs and
alcohol.

For the health and safety of youth suffering from mental illness,
the National Mental Health Association (@*www.nmha.org*) strongly
recommends that young people convicted of minor or nonviolent
offenses be offered treatment, services, and supervision, rather than
incarceration. NMHA suggests that the juvenile-justice system and
the mental-health system work together to develop programs and
services within juvenile systems for these children. The most effective services would focus on treatment, rather than punishment, and

would take into account the child's age, gender, culture, and family circumstances.

Fact

The rate of mental illness is often found to be higher among youths in the juvenile justice system than among youths in the general population. Federal studies indicate that possibly 60 to 75 percent of incarcerated minors suffer from mental-health disorders, and as many as 20 percent may suffer from severe disorders.

Requirements and Outlook

Positions in most Departments of Juvenile Services include the investigation, control, or supervision of juvenile offenders who have been detained, are awaiting placement, or are otherwise in the custody of the department. Candidates for these positions must generally pass a physical examination to ensure that they are physically capable of performing the duties of the job, along with a mental exam to determine whether they are emotionally and mentally prepared for their new position.

Many lawyers and even juvenile advocates do not know how to help juvenile offenders navigate the mental-health system to get the care they need. Juvenile court personnel will be increasingly relied upon to advise youth and their families on their rights to access mental-health services.

Social and Human Services

"Social and human service assistant" is the generic term applied to people who hold many different job titles, including human-service worker, case-management aide, social-work assistant, community-support worker, mental-health aide, community-outreach worker, life-skills counselor, and gerontology aide. Each works under the direction of supervisors in many fields, including nursing, psychiatry, psychology, rehabilitative or physical therapy, and social work.

Social and human service assistants deal directly with clients to help them reach their maximum level of independence. They determine the clients' needs and establish their eligibility for benefits like food stamps, Medicaid, or welfare. They keep case records on clients and report progress to supervisors and case managers.

Social and human service assistants wear many hats. They organize and lead group activities, help clients in need of counseling or crisis intervention, and administer food banks or emergency fuel programs. In halfway houses, group homes, and government-supported housing programs, they help adults who need supervision and support. They review clients' records and try to ensure that they take correct doses of medication. They talk with family members and confer with medical personnel and other caregivers to get firm insight into their clients' needs.

Question

Do social and human service assistants get to work with other professionals?
In rehabilitation programs and outpatient clinics, social and human service assistants work with professional psychiatrists, psychologists, and social workers, to help clients master everyday living skills and get along better with others.

Working Conditions

Working conditions vary. Some social and human service assistants work in offices, clinics, and hospitals, while others work in group homes, shelters, sheltered workshops, and day programs. Many work under close supervision, while others work on their own. Many social and human service assistants spend most of their working days in the field visiting clients, with one day designated as an office day to catch up on paperwork. Sometimes clients live in bad neighborhoods. This can be dangerous, and sometimes a security officer accompanies the worker. Government employees work a forty-hour week and usually have a light caseload.

If you go into this field, you should have a genuine desire to help people, or at the very least, be willing to do your job without an argument or an attitude.

Requirements

A bachelor's degree usually is not required for an entry-level position; however, some relevant work experience and education beyond high school is becoming more and more of a prerequisite. Certificates or associate degrees in subjects like social work, human services, gerontology, or one of the social or behavioral sciences are helpful. Human-services degree programs have curricula that train students to observe patients and record information, conduct interviews, implement treatment plans, handle crisis-intervention matters, and use proper case-management and referral procedures. Most programs offer the opportunity to specialize in addictions, gerontology, child protection, and other areas. Many degree programs require participation in a supervised internship.

Regardless of the academic or work background of employees, government agencies provide some form of on-the-job training. There may also be additional hiring requirements for group home employees. A valid driver's license may be required, and you may have to submit to a criminal background investigation.

Formal education is always necessary for advancement. A bachelor's or master's degree in human services, counseling, rehabilitation, social work, or a related field is required if you want to advance to supervision and administration duties.

One in three social and human service assistants is employed by state and local governments, primarily in public welfare agencies and facilities for mentally disabled and developmentally challenged individuals.

A Bright Future

Opportunities for social and human service assistants are expected to be excellent, especially for applicants with more advanced degrees. The number of positions is projected to grow much faster than the average for the next ten years. There is going to be more competition for jobs in urban areas than in rural areas, but qualified applicants should find it relatively easy to find a job.

Unfortunately, the salary is not all that high in this field. The median salary for state government workers is $29,270, and the average annual salary for local government employees is $28,230.

E ssential

The number of jobs for social and human service assistants in local governments will grow, but the public sector may fluctuate with the level of funding provided by state and local governments. In addition, some state and local governments are contracting out some social services to private agencies in order to save money.

The demand will expand with the growing elderly population, and more social and human service assistants are going to be needed to provide services to pregnant teenagers, the homeless, the mentally disabled and developmentally challenged, and substance abusers. Job training programs are expected to rise because, as welfare rules change and the system makes people work for their benefits, there will be a demand for people with the training to teach job skills to those who are new or returning to the work force. Since substance abusers are increasingly being sent to treatment programs instead of prison, employment of social and human service assistants in substance-abuse treatment programs also is going to grow.

Social Security Administration (SSA)

The Social Security Administration (SSA) headquarters are located in Baltimore, Maryland. In addition, the SSA has ten regional offices and 1,300 local offices nationwide. The administration pays retirement, disability, and survivor benefits to workers and their families and administers the Supplemental Security Income (SSI) program. It also issues Social Security numbers.

Public Contact Workers

Public contact workers deal with the general public. They are "the voice of Social Security." Opportunities exist throughout the country in field offices, program service centers, teleservice centers, and the headquarters in Baltimore, Maryland.

A public contact representative's daily duties include the following:

- Speaking with beneficiaries about their rights under Social Security laws
- Gathering facts and evidence to establish eligibility for benefits
- Making critical decisions to determine the amount of benefits paid to individuals
- Using state-of-the-art computer technology to access and update information about claims

Opportunities also exist for claims representative, claims authorizer, benefit authorizer, service representative, and teleservice representative positions. Public contact representatives receive thorough training in Social Security programs and state laws. Bilingual individuals have an advantage in the hiring process. Many of Social Security's executives and managers began as public contact representatives and moved on to technical, analytical, and supervisory positions.

Information Technology (IT) Jobs

Social Security has one of the world's largest computer installations in its Baltimore headquarters. Its database management and telecommunications systems are among the best in the world. The operation of the administration's computer systems affects nearly all Americans. Information technology (IT) professionals who work for the SSA keep the systems up to date with the constantly changing

Social Security programs. Career opportunities in the IT field exist in the following areas:

- Software development
- Network services
- Systems analysis
- Web development
- Data management

SSA computer specialists have experience in fields such as client/server development, mainframe development, and telecommunications/networking technologies. Training is available for entry-level positions.

E Alert

Special salary rates are available for most IT positions. Translation: the job market in this field is competitive, and the government has to compete with the private sector. Many of the government's computer specialists move on up to become managers.

Office of Hearings and Appeals

Social Security pays benefits to more than 40 million people each year. Those who disagree with the agency's decisions regarding their claims for benefits may appeal through the Office of Hearings and Appeals. Staff attorneys and administrative law judges work nationwide to provide the public with a fair appeal process for Social Security benefits. In their headquarters, attorney-advisers and attorney-examiners review and act upon the decisions of their administrative law judges.

Opportunities exist for staff attorneys, attorney-advisers, administrative law judges, and attorney-examiners. All attorneys must be in good standing with their state bar association. Entry-level attorneys begin with admittance to the bar, and administrative law judges should be practicing attorneys for at least seven years, of which two have been spent preparing and trying cases.

Criminal Investigators

Criminal investigators work nationwide fighting fraud and abuse. Social Security's law enforcement professionals work with the Office of the Inspector General to investigate abuses of Social Security's operations and programs.

A criminal investigator's day might include the following tasks:

- Planning and conducting surveillance of a suspect
- Serving search warrants and subpoenas
- Interviewing suspects, witnesses, and informants
- Testifying before grand juries or courts
- Researching to determine whether violations of law have occurred

Experience as a criminal investigator may lead to higher-level positions in the Office of the Inspector General.

Administrative Positions

More career opportunities for administrators include management analysts, budget analysts, human resource specialists, and staff assistants. If your talents are more specialized and technical, the SSA has the following positions as well: actuaries, auditors, economists, social science research analysts, and statisticians. Visit *www.ssa .gov* to learn about the many additional opportunities within the Social Security Administration.

Department of Veterans Affairs

The Department of Veterans Affairs (VA) was created on March 15, 1989. It replaced the former Veterans Administration. This department is responsible for providing federal benefits to veterans and their families. It is headed by the Secretary of Veterans Affairs and is the second-largest of the fifteen Cabinet-level federal departments. It operates nationwide programs for health care, financial assistance, and burial benefits.

Ⓔ Fact

A famous case of disability fraud occurred in New York City when a former firefighter, out of work on permanent disability due to physical injuries sustained on the job, won a contest. The contest was a race up to the top on the Empire State Building—via the stairs! The media attention surrounding his victory got him in trouble with the disability police.

The VA has experienced unprecedented growth in the medical system workload over the past few years. The number of patients treated increased from 4 million in 2001 to more than 5 million in 2004. There are about 24.8 million veterans currently alive, and nearly three-quarters of these served during a war or an official period of conflict. Some 63 million people are eligible for VA benefits and services because they are veterans, family members, or survivors of veterans.

The VA is most often associated with benefits and health care. The VA's health-care system includes 157 medical centers, with at least one in each state, Puerto Rico, and the District of Columbia. The VA operates more than 1,300 "sites of care," including 862 ambulatory care outpatient clinics, 134 nursing homes, forty-two residential rehabilitation treatment programs, 207 veterans centers, and eighty-eight comprehensive home-care programs. All these facilities need to be staffed by trained professionals.

The VA runs the largest medical-education and health-professions training program in the United States. VA facilities are affiliated with 107 medical schools, fifty-five dental colleges, and more than 1,200 other schools across the country. About 83,000 health professionals are trained in VA medical centers. More than half of the physicians practicing in the United States received some of their professional education in the VA health-care system.

Counseling Services

For returning veterans who often face challenges readjusting to civilian life, the VA's Readjustment Counseling Service operates veterans centers that provide psychological counseling for war-related trauma such as post-traumatic stress disorder, community outreach to homeless and addicted veterans, and supportive social services to veterans and family members. There are 207 veterans centers, and approximately 2 million veterans have been helped since 1979. The veterans centers serve more than 130,000 veterans and make house calls to 1 million veterans and their families.

Fact

More than 5 million people received care in VA facilities in 2004. About 78 percent of disabled and low-income veterans enrolled with the VA for health care. In 2004, VA inpatient facilities treated 587,000 patients, and the VA's outpatient clinics received 54 million clients.

The veterans centers are open to any veteran who served in combat during wartime or anywhere during a period of armed hostilities. Veterans centers also provide trauma counseling to veterans who were sexually assaulted or harassed while on active duty. The staffs of these centers help more than 100,000 homeless veterans each year. Medical staff, medical assistants, therapists, social workers, receptionists, and many more types of workers are employed in these centers.

Science Jobs with the VA

The VA also employs scientists and researchers. There are approximately 3,000 researchers at 115 VA medical centers, and the department's career development program provides young scientists an opportunity to develop skills as clinician-researchers. The VA has become a leader in research areas such as aging, women's health, AIDS, post-traumatic stress disorder, and other mental health issues.

VA researchers played an important role in developing the cardiac pacemaker, the CAT scan, and improvements in prosthetic limbs. The first liver transplant in the world was performed by a VA surgeon/ researcher. VA clinical tests also established the effectiveness of new treatments for tuberculosis, schizophrenia, and high blood pressure.

E ssential

The VA wants you. If you are interested in joining this department in its mission, visit ✍*www.va.gov/jobs*. The VA's goal, in the department's own words, is "to provide excellence in patient care, veterans' benefits and customer satisfaction. We can provide you with challenging, interesting, meaningful work to care for the veterans who have risked their lives to protect our freedom."

The "Seattle Foot" developed by VA scientists allows people with amputations to run and jump. Contributions to medical knowledge have won VA scientists many awards, including the Nobel Prize. Functional electrical stimulation, a technology that uses controlled electrical currents to activate paralyzed muscles, is being developed at VA facilities and laboratories throughout the country. Through this technology, paraplegic patients have been able to grasp objects, stand, and even walk short distances.

National Cemeteries

The VA also maintains 120 national cemeteries in thirty-nine states and Puerto Rico. In 2004, VA national cemeteries conducted 93,033 interments. That number is expected to increase to 109,000 by 2008. The VA has provided more than 8.7 million headstones and markers since 1973. The department opened five new national cemeteries between 1999 and 2002, and plans to open five more in the next five years.

The nation's most famous cemetery, Arlington National Cemetery in Virginia, is ironically on property that once belonged to the Civil

War Confederate General Robert E. Lee. Lee was offered command of the Union Army by President Abraham Lincoln. He declined and opted to fight on the opposing side. His land, which was very close to Washington, D.C., was seized very early in the war. He was never able to return to his home, but his land is now the final resting place for thousands of Americans who have given their lives over the years since the Civil War.

Fact

The VA operates one of the largest life insurance programs in the world, comprising six different life insurance options. These programs provide $746 billion in insurance coverage that covers 4.3 million veterans, active-duty members, reservists and National Guardsmen, plus 3 million spouses and children. This means there are jobs for accountants, actuaries, and other office workers in the VA.

Employment Outlook and Benefits

The VA has about 236,000 employees on its rolls. In the federal government, only the U.S. Department of Defense has a larger work force. Of the total number of VA employees, 215,000 are in the Veterans Health Administration; 13,000 work in the Veterans Benefits Administration; 1,600 work in the National Cemetery System; 3,200 are employed in the Veterans Canteen Service; and 400 in the Revolving Supply Fund. The remaining 3,700 employees work in various staff and facilities offices.

The VA is also a leader in hiring veterans. In addition to receiving its many benefits, you can go work for them. About 57 percent of all male employees are veterans, and some 16,000 women employees served in the armed forces.

At the U.S. Department of Veterans Affairs, you can break away from the traditional nine to five, forty-hour workweek without sacrificing the opportunities and benefits that come with job security. The VA lets you choose a schedule that accommodates your needs and lifestyle. You can vary your arrival and departure times, working longer but fewer days during your pay period. You may even be eligible to work from home on a regular or part-time basis. Working remotely gives you flexibility and helps you balance work and family responsibilities. You can also take your child to work every day. This is an option for some VA employees because of onsite child-care centers. Child-care programs are offered for children of different ages. Parents can enjoy lunch with their children in a learning environment that is safe and convenient to working parents.

The Application Process

At the U.S. Department of Veteran's Affairs recruitment Web site (online at *www.va.gov/JOBS/index*.asp), you can learn the following:

- The position title provides the official position title for the job being advertised. Sometimes similar positions can have different position titles, so it is important that you read the duty statements and qualification requirements in vacancy announcements.
- The series and grade provides information on the occupational series used in the federal government for positions and the grade level that has been assigned to the position. All positions in the federal government have a position title and a four-digit occupational series number. The complete list of grades and salaries appears elsewhere in this book and in Appendix B.
- The salary range provides the range of salaries for the grades of the position being advertised. For example, if the position is announced as GS-11/12, you will see the salary range for both the GS-11 and GS-12 grade level.
- The promotion potential indicates the highest grade level for the position being advertised.
- The type of appointment indicates whether the position is permanent or temporary and whether it is full-time or part-time.

- The location of the position provides the name of the location, the city, and state where the position is located.
- The announcement number provides the announcement number for the position being advertised. Each position has a different announcement number.
- The opening and closing dates provide the opening and closing dates for the announcement. The vacancy announcement will indicate whether the application must be submitted to the contact person by the closing date or if postmarked or other received date applications will be accepted. You should pay close attention to the closing date. If your application is late, you will probably be excluded from consideration.
- The area of consideration indicates the area from which applications will be accepted. For example, if the area of consideration is "All U.S. citizens," then all U.S. citizens are eligible to apply. "All U.S. citizens in the local commuting area" means that only those U.S. citizens within the particular commuting area would be considered. "Status applicants only" means that only current federal employees may apply. "VA employees only" means that only current VA employees may apply.
- Duties describes the main duties and responsibilities for the position being advertised.
- The qualifications section describes the main qualification requirements for the position being advertised. In this section, you'll find information about education and experience requirements. You will see knowledge, skills, and abilities described in this section in terms of "Specialized Experience" and in some instances as "Selective Factors."
- The application information section lists what must be included in your application package for you to be eligible for consideration. Failure to submit required information may result in your not being considered for a position.
- The "other important information" section provides other information related to the application process and federal hiring rules and regulations.

- Contact information provides information on where and how your application can be submitted.

To apply for VA positions and all other federal positions, you can submit a completed resume, curriculum vitae, or an Application for Federal Employment Optional Form 612, along with other documents requested in each vacancy announcement. You can download the form, as well as other employment forms, on the VA site. You might also want to check out these forms, available online:

- OF-510—Applying for a Federal Job (Instructions for applying)
- OF-612—Optional Application for Federal Employment
- OF-306—Declaration for Federal Employment
- SF-15—Application for 10-point Veteran's Preference

Once you have completed your application, you will need to submit it to the contact person listed in the vacancy announcement. Before you seal the envelope, send the fax, or send your e-mail, take a few moments to be sure that your application is complete. Read it over one last time, checking for spelling and grammatical errors. Make sure that you have included all requested information and documents.

For most jobs, you can submit your application package by postal mail, fax, or through e-mail. If you are using e-mail, you will need to submit any requested documents so that they can be matched up with your application. If you need to send a transcript and you do not have a copy that can be attached to your e-mail, you will have to either fax it or send it via postal mail so it can be attached to your application. If you are sending documents via postal mail that are separate from your application, make sure to indicate on the documents the vacancy announcement number, the position title, and the location of the position.

When positions are announced, they will include both an opening date and a closing date. Some job announcements are opened for one or two weeks, while others may be open for longer periods of time. Once the closing date passes, federal agencies must wait a period of time—typically seven to ten days—for receipt of postmarked applications. During this time period, the assigned human-resources specialist will begin reviewing the applications received to determine if the applicants meet the qualification requirements outlined.

E ssential

The vacancy announcement will specify whether your application must be in by the closing date, must be postmarked by a certain date, or will be tallied according to its received-by date. Because federal jobs are filled using a competitive process, understanding the timing of the process will better prepare you for the wait after you submit your application.

Those candidates who do meet the minimum qualifications will then be reviewed to determine if they are among the "qualified" or "best-qualified" candidates. Sometimes this can take a few days, but it can also take as long as a few weeks, depending on the number of applications received. Once the best-qualified candidates are identified, a "certificate of eligibles" is prepared and sent to the supervisor (or selecting official) for the position. The supervisor will then review the applications and determine who among the best qualified will be interviewed.

Interviews are scheduled and conducted, references are checked, and final candidate selections are made. The recruitment and selection process may take several weeks from the time a position is advertised to when a selection is made. In most cases, you will be sent a notice acknowledging the receipt of your application. You will also be notified once a final selection has been made.

Chapter 11

Office Support Staff

Office staffs are needed in all kinds of businesses, and the government is no exception. In this chapter, you will learn about administrative and secretarial job opportunities, and you can see if you have "the write stuff" to leave a paper trail throughout the hallowed halls of government. Some of these positions are available without college degrees, which means competition for them can be fierce.

Administrative

Administrative assistants are the unsung heroes of any organization. They are the women and men who take care of quotidian details so the big bosses can do whatever it is they do behind closed doors in cushy corner offices. While the head guys plot the fate of different factions of the civilized world, someone has to be the foot soldier, transforming those plans into reams of paperwork.

Administrators supervise secretaries and the temp staff. They engage in office management. They schedule the boss's appointments, change the paper in the printer, and liaison with other departments within the entity. In so many words, the administrator is the jack-of-all-trades who ensures that the office runs like a well-oiled machine.

Administrators must be aware of the strengths and weaknesses of their staffs in order to delegate responsibilities. Diplomacy and people skills are a prerequisite. They must oversee the work of others but strive to resist the temptation to micromanage. Most people do not function well with a supervisor breathing down their necks. Administrators may also participate in performance reviews of people who report to them, play an active role in the hiring of new employees, and take on the occasional uncomfortable and unfortunate duty of firing someone.

Most administrators in government jobs work a typical forty-hour workweek. The forty-hour week has gone the way of the dinosaur in the private sector, but the government is still a place where clock-punching remains. You must be flexible, however, in the event of an office crisis, when you may be asked to go the extra mile.

 Fact

Administrative assistants are employed in every area of the working world, including the government. President Lincoln, for example, had a secretary named Kennedy. President Kennedy had a secretary named Lincoln. Some folks believe this created a "cosmic connection" between the assassinations of these two presidents.

Many administrators rise up from within the ranks; others are recruited from outside the organization. Those eager to climb the ladder had better be willing to demonstrate their ability to go above and beyond the call of duty. Some cynics may believe this trait is not a mainstay of government employees, but it is in your best interest to be a team player and to display problem-solving and leadership abilities. Those brought in from the outside usually start in entry-level positions and work their way up.

There are about 1.5 million administrative workers currently employed in the United States, and the government employs many of them. There is stiff competition to fill these government jobs, as there is for almost every kind of job these days. The number of applicants exceeds the number of job openings. The employment outlook for these jobs is optimistic, but expect the number of opportunities to grow slowly.

The average salary for an office administrator is $41,000. The lowest-paid 10 percent earn less than $25,000, and the highest-paid 10 percent earn more than $67,000.

Secretarial

The stereotypical role of the coffee-fetching, dictation-taking secretary is a thing of the past. The role of the secretary—nowadays referred to as "office support staff"—includes more responsibilities than ever, particularly since the advent of personal computers. Secretaries have more tasks, many of which were once handled by managerial staff.

E ssential

Administrative staff members do not fetch coffee or perform other menial tasks these days. Office employees throughout the ranks are keenly aware of inappropriate behavior in the workplace. Guidelines are distributed and posted for all to see. Administrators may also train new employees and act as the liaison between their superiors and the general public, contractors and vendors, and other department heads.

Secretaries do more than type and take dictation. They must be well versed in the latest word-processing and other relevant software programs. They must be Internet savvy. They must be ready to adapt to new technologies. But the basics of the job remain the same: coordinating the administrative duties of the workplace and supporting the managers and other bosses by being effective "go to" guys and gals.

This involves performing clerical duties, scheduling meetings and appointments, answering the phones and taking messages, keeping a filing system both electronically and in hard copy, handling travel arrangements for bosses and clients, and troubleshooting myriad problems and crises that arise during the day-to-day operations of any organization.

Secretaries should be able to use and maintain standard office equipment such as printers, fax machines, scanners, and videoconferencing technology. The Internet has made meetings easier and less expensive. Executives need not travel to see their counterparts across the country and around the world. They can have real-time conferences through the miracle of modern technology.

Types of Secretaries

There are different kinds of secretaries with different areas of expertise. Some secretaries even have secretaries. For example, executive secretaries work for the big shots. They do not do as much of the clerical work or change the paper in the printer. They handle the boss's more complex needs, such as supervising other secretaries, training employees, preparing reports, and performing other duties.

Alert

Secretarial jobs invariably involve sitting for long periods of time. Too much time at the keyboard spent staring into a computer screen can cause problems like eyestrain, stress, and repetitive motion ailments such as carpal tunnel syndrome. It is important to take regular breaks during the day and use ergonomic equipment to help decrease the possibility of developing these ailments.

Legal secretaries perform specialized work, including preparing legal reports and correspondence. Knowledge of the law is required since the work involves dealing with summonses, subpoenas, and other legal documents. Of course, the final responsibility for these higher-level tasks will be under the supervision of a lawyer or paralegal, but a legal secretary should still have a grasp of the material. Hence, legal secretaries will make more money than generic support people. The same applies to medical secretaries. They must know about insurance regulations, medical records, prescription information, laboratory procedures, and other things related to doctors, patients, and health care.

Telecommuting

More and more companies and government entities allow for flexible work schedules. It's not quite as common in the government, but it is happening. Nowadays, anyone with a decent home computer and a broadband Internet connection can work from home. Approximately 19 percent of secretaries work part of the time from their homes. The majority of secretaries in the government still work in an office during the traditional forty-hour week.

The future will see more and more workers telecommuting. There will be an increasing number of duties that need not be performed at the office. There is still a need for a brick-and-mortar locale for people to conduct meetings and other face-to-face functions, but even this may go the way of the dinosaur eventually.

Training Required

A high school graduate can qualify for an entry-level secretarial position. Some computer knowledge is necessary before you even send out a resume, though most companies will give you additional on-the-job training. Word processing, spreadsheet, and database management skills are essential. You must have a command of good grammar, spelling and punctuation skills, and be a reasonably fast typist. And people skills are mandatory, of course. You have to work well with others, be able to take direction and constructive criticism, and be able to work independently.

You may have the opportunity or be required to take courses to become up to date on the latest programs and technologies to increase your skills. Your employer should pay for this or provide reimbursement. Take advantage of everything that will enhance your skills and aid in your career development.

Associations

Some professional organizations that offer training and support are the International Association of Administrative Professionals, the National Association of Legal Secretaries, Inc., and Legal Secretaries International, Inc. Through these organizations, you can earn certifications such as the following:

- Certified professional secretary
- Certified administrative professional
- Accredited legal secretary
- Professional legal secretary
- Certified legal secretary specialist

Job Outlook

There are about 4.1 million secretaries currently employed in the United States. It is one of the largest occupations in the economy. Nine out of ten work in services industries, including the government. Growth is anticipated to be higher in the private sector, but overall growth is expected to be slow between 2006 and 2014. In order to be competitive, you need to learn as many software programs and other office technologies as you can.

Salaries

The average salary for a secretary is $34,970. The lowest 10 percent earn less than $23,810, and the highest 10 percent earn more than $53,460. Secretaries in the government earn, on the average, between $30,750 and $36,940.

Customer Service

Customer service is one facet of the economy that is growing steadily, and job prospects are very good. Customer-service jobs are plentiful in the private sector, but the government has lots of opportunities as well. Many of these jobs are at the state and local level. You might, for example, find yourself fielding complaints about tickets in a traffic-control office. Or you might be a person's first point of contact at one of the agencies in a state's department of human services.

You may be involved in fielding routine requests and general problems and complaints, or you may specialize in solving specific issues. You will have a headset and be sitting in front of a computer screen, and most questions and issues can be resolved by looking up the customer's information in the database. In other instances, further research and a return call may be necessary. If you cannot resolve the issue, or if the customer is unreasonable, you may have to bump the issue to a supervisor, who can deal with the issue and is authorized to make changes or issue refunds or do any number of things an entry-level customer-service person cannot.

Working in Call Centers

Most customer-service representatives work in what are called customer contact centers or call centers. Their environment is a cubicle, and the tools of their trade are a telephone, headset, and a computer. Some call centers are open around the clock, seven days a week, or at least beyond regular business hours. That means there are many shifts available, including weekends. About 20 percent of customer-service representatives work part-time, and many work from home, the calls being forwarded to their home telephone numbers.

E ssential

Most jobs require a minimum of a high school diploma, but more rigorous educational requirements are becoming common. As a customer-service representative, you are responsible for answering customers' questions and solving their problems. You will be communicating primarily over the phone, though you will also sometimes use faxes and e-mail. You will even occasionally communicate in person.

Call centers are a hectic environment. They are often crowded and noisy. Combine this with the monotony and repetition of the work, and the occasional disagreeable customer, and you can see that customer-service representatives are in a stressful environment. If that's not enough to heighten your heart rate, keep in mind that most of your calls will be recorded. Many a customer service representative has found himself or herself called into the supervisor's office after a call to review his or her performance.

There are also quotas that are supposed to be achieved during the course of a business day. Representatives are coached on how to get the caller off the line as quickly as possible while still ensuring customer satisfaction. It is a delicate balancing act that does not always work.

When you are confronted with an irate caller, you will be taught to keep your cool at all costs. Do your best to accommodate his needs. If all else fails, call your supervisor to deal with the person.

Qualifications and Advancement

Most customer-service jobs require at least a high school diploma, though more and more are requiring an associate or a bachelor's degree. A working knowledge of computers and software systems is required. Training is usually provided for the company's particular system. The ability to speak English well is important, and if you are bilingual, your chances of getting a good job definitely increase.

Job Outlook

Customer service is one industry with more jobs than job seekers. It is one of the easier jobs to get, if you are willing to comply with and endure the above description of what it takes. Employment in this job will increase steadily over the next decade. There is a downside to this—a controversial and unpopular trend known as "outsourcing" or "off-shoring." Many American companies are shutting down their call centers in the United States and opening them overseas, primarily in India.

☀ Ạlert

Customer-service jobs do not pay that well. Again, it's a job with plenty of openings and not enough willing workers. The average salary is $27,020. The lowest 10 percent earn less than $17,680, and the highest 10 percent earn more than $44,160. Perhaps, if the number of applicants remains low, better pay will be offered as an incentive.

With current technology, an American business can have people halfway around the world fielding its calls, and pay them pennies on the dollar of what American workers earn. From a corporation's perspective, this is good business sense. For the American job seeker, it is an unfortunate practice. So far, however, the government has chosen not to outsource its customer-service jobs.

Labor Relations

Human-resources, training, and labor-relations managers and specialists find the most qualified employees and match them to jobs for which they are a good fit. In addition to hiring the best people, they are also involved in keeping up morale and thus increasing productivity, limiting job turnover, and helping their companies improve performance.

These managers and specialists also help their firms provide training and development opportunities to improve skills and increase employees' satisfaction with their jobs and their working conditions. The ability to deal with people is the most important part of the job.

E ssential

The responsibility of human-resources people varies widely. In large corporations and government entities, human-resources executives develop and manage human-resources programs and policies. These policies are then implemented by a director or manager of human resources.

The director of human resources supervises several departments, each headed by a manager who is likely to specialize in one aspect of human resources, such as employment, compensation, benefits, training and development, or employee relations.

Recruiters maintain contacts within the community, often traveling to job fairs and college campuses to find qualified job applicants. Recruiters screen, interview, and test applicants. They also check references and are often the ones to extend the official job offer. They must be familiar with their company and its human-resources policies in order to discuss wages, working conditions, and promotional opportunities with prospective employees. They also must keep informed about Equal Employment Opportunity (EEO) and affirmative action guidelines and laws, such as the Americans with Disabilities Act (ADA).

Compensation/Benefits Management

Compensation, benefits, and job-analysis specialists conduct programs for employers in specific areas such as pensions and other employee benefits. Job analysts, occasionally called position classifiers, collect and examine detailed information about job duties in order to prepare job descriptions.

Establishing and maintaining a company's pay system is the job of a compensation manager. Compensation managers design ways to ensure fair salaries. They conduct surveys to see how their firm's salaries compare with those of other firms, and they determine whether pay scales comply with changing laws and regulations. Compensation managers also manage their firm's performance evaluation system, and they may design reward systems such as pay-for-performance plans.

Employee-benefits managers and specialists oversee their companies' employee benefits programs, including health-insurance and pension plans. They need expertise in designing and administering benefits programs. Businesses today confront an ever-changing landscape, in which employer benefits account for a growing proportion of overall compensation costs, and benefit plans are becoming increasingly complex. An employee-benefits manager is the gardener for this landscape. Familiarity with health benefits is critical, since nearly all firms are dealing with the rising cost of health care for employees. In addition to health insurance and pension coverage, some firms offer their employees life and accidental death and dismemberment insurance, disability insurance, and new benefits designed for a changing workforce, like parental leave, child care, and employee assistance and wellness programs. Benefits managers must be well versed in the changing federal and state regulations that affect employee benefits.

Employee-assistance plan managers are responsible for many programs covering occupational safety and health standards and practices, health promotion, physical fitness, medical examinations, and minor health treatment, such as first aid. They are also involved with office security, food service, recreation activities, car pooling and transportation programs, such as transit subsidies. Child care and elder care are growing more common because of the growing number of two-income households and the increasing elderly population. Managers and specialists are involved in securing counseling to help employees deal with emotional disorders, alcoholism, or marital, family, legal, and financial problems.

 Fact

Equal Employment Opportunity (EEO) officers, representatives, and affirmative action coordinators handle EEO matters in large organizations and government entities. They investigate and resolve EEO grievances, examine employer practices for possible violations, and submit EEO statistical reports.

Training Positions

Training and development managers and specialists, as their titles suggest, supervise training and development programs for employees. Companies have come to understand that training develops skills and enhances productivity and the quality of work. It also builds worker loyalty.

Training managers provide training either in the classroom or onsite. This includes setting up teaching materials prior to the class, teaching the class, and issuing completion certificates at the end of class. Training managers are responsible for the entire process. They plan, organize, and direct a variety of training activities. Training managers help employees improve their job skills. At the same time, they help supervisors improve their interpersonal skills in order to deal effectively with employees.

Training can take many forms. Almost all companies offer new employees a course on what constituted sexual harassment and how to recognize and report it in the workplace. More experienced employees may get training on how to use their benefits most effectively, how to start an on-the-job savings plan, and how to find out about the latest technology that can make their lives easier.

Employer-relations representatives often work in government agencies. They maintain relationships with local employers and promote the use of public employment programs and services. Interviewers, whose numerous job titles include human-resources consultants, human-resources development specialists, and human-resources coordinators, help to match employers with qualified candidates.

Occupational Analysis and Industrial Relations

Occupational analysts conduct research in large companies and government agencies. They are concerned with occupational classification systems and study the effects of industry and occupational trends on worker relationships. They may serve as the liaison between a firm and other firms, the government, and/or labor unions.

The director of industrial relations establishes the labor policy, oversees labor relations, negotiates collective bargaining agreements, and coordinates grievance procedures to handle complaints resulting from management disputes with unionized employees.

Labor-Relations Specialists

Labor-relations specialists prepare information for management to use during the collective-bargaining process. Collective bargaining is the name for the specialized kind of negotiation that takes place between an employer and one or more unions. This is a process that requires the specialist to be familiar with economic and salary data and to have a thorough knowledge of labor law and collective bargaining trends. The labor-relations staff administers the contract with respect to grievances, wages and salaries, employee welfare, health care, pensions, and union and management practices. As union membership continues to decline in most industries, industrial-relations personnel are working more often with employees who are not members of a labor union.

Mediators

Dispute resolution has become increasingly important as parties attempt to avoid costly litigation, strikes, and other disruptions of business. Dispute resolution is complicated. It involves employees, management, unions, and government agencies. Specialists involved in dispute resolution must be knowledgeable and experienced. Mediators advise labor and management to prevent and resolve disputes over labor agreements. Arbitrators decide disputes that bind both labor and management to specific terms and conditions of a contract. Labor relations specialists who work for unions perform the same functions on behalf of the union and its members.

Work Week

Most human-resources, training, and labor-relations managers and specialists work forty-hour weeks, but longer hours are sometimes necessary. Labor-relations managers, arbitrators, and mediators work round the clock when contracts are being negotiated. Most work in their offices, but some traveling is necessary. Recruiters attend professional meetings and visit college campuses to interview prospective employees. Arbitrators and mediators have to go to the site of negotiations. These are usually held in a neutral location, rather than in the corporate headquarters or the union hall.

Employment Requirements

Educational backgrounds vary because of diverse duties and responsibilities. Entry-level positions require a college degree, preferably with a major in human resources, human-resources administration, or industrial and labor relations. For some employers, a bachelor's degree with a business concentration or even a liberal arts focus will suffice.

Most colleges have programs leading to a degree in personnel, human resources, or labor relations. An interdisciplinary background is best in this field, so a combination of courses in social sciences, business, and behavioral sciences is ideal. Some jobs may require a specialized background in engineering, science, finance, or law. It is advisable that you take courses in compensation, recruitment, training and development, and performance appraisal, plus courses in management, organizational structure, and industrial psychology. Other worthwhile courses to consider are business administration, public administration, psychology, sociology, political science, economics, and statistics. Additionally, courses in labor law, collective bargaining, labor economics, labor history, and industrial psychology would be useful.

E ssential

The International Foundation of Employee Benefit Plans confers a designation to people who complete a series of college-level courses and pass exams covering employee benefit plans. The American Society for Training and Development Certification Institute also offers certification, and the Society for Human Resource Management has two levels of certification. Both require experience and a passing grade on their exam.

Many jobs in labor relations demand graduate study in industrial or labor relations. A background in industrial relations and law is desirable for contract negotiators, mediators, and arbitrators. Often, people in these jobs are lawyers. Previous experience is certainly an asset, but for advanced positions it is essential. Many employers will go for an entry-level worker who has some experience in an internship or work-study program while in school.

Human-resources, training, and labor-relations managers and specialists have to be able to speak and write well. They have to work with or supervise people from various cultural backgrounds. They have to keep a cool head under pressure. This is not your grandfather's workforce. All sorts of issues that Grandpa could not even conceive of come into play these days: onsite day care for the little ones, benefits packages that apply to married couples as well as same-sex life partners, sexual harassment policies, and many other issues that went unaddressed until recent times.

Entry-level employees learn the trade by working as administrative assistants. They enter data into computer systems, compile employee handbooks, and answer the phone and handle routine questions. They often enter formal or on-the-job training programs in which they learn how to classify jobs, interview applicants, or administer employee benefits. They may ultimately advance to managerial positions.

Government Human-Resources Job Outlook

Federal, state, and local governments employ 17 percent of human-resources managers and specialists working today. They handle the recruitment, interviewing, job classification, training, salary administration, benefits, and employee relations for public employees.

Competition for these jobs is intense. Changing legislation and rules and regulations in occupational safety and health, equal employment opportunity, salaries, health care, pensions, and family leave will increase demand for human-resources training and labor-relations experts. That's the good news for you, prospective job seeker. The bad news is that you will have to do your homework before you arrive for an interview. And once on the job, you will wish for more hours in the day to keep up with all of the constantly changing legislation related to working life in these United States.

The rising cost of health care will increase the need for specialists to develop compensation and benefits packages. Demand is expected to be strong for certain specialists. Employers are expected to devote more of their resources training programs due to the growing complexity of many jobs, the aging of the workforce, and other changes in the working world that will increase the demand for training and development specialists.

Salaries

The average salary for compensation and benefits managers is $66,530. It is $67,460 for training and development managers. The median for all other human resources managers is $81,810. Employment, recruitment, and placement specialists make an average of $41,190. Local government salaries average $40,540 for all of the above specialties, and state governments average $35,390. The average annual salary of compensation, benefits, and job-analysis specialists is $47,490. Local governments average a little higher, at $51,430, and state governments average a bit less, at $39,150. The median annual salary for training and development specialists is $44,570. Local governments average $45,320, state governments $41,770, and the federal government $38,930.

The average salary for human-resources managers employed by the federal government is $71,232. Employee-relations specialists make $84,847. Labor-relations specialists earn $93,895, and employee-development specialists make $80,958.

Personnel Assistants

Personnel assistants are responsible for maintaining and updating human-resource records and databases. This includes keeping up with employee names, addresses, job titles, salaries, and benefits including health and life insurance and tax withholding. When an employee receives a promotion or switches health insurance plans, human-resources assistants update the records. They also prepare reports for managers within the organization. It goes without saying that these are positions for the meticulous.

Types of Jobs

Personnel assistants often have specific job titles. Assignment clerks notify existing employees of upcoming job openings, identify applicants who qualify for the vacancies, and reassign those who are qualified for new positions. They track new openings within the company or agency, and they complete the paperwork that advertises the vacancies. When a selection for the position is made, assignment clerks notify all of the applicants of their acceptance or rejection.

Identification clerks are responsible for security matters at defense installations. They compile and record personal data about vendors, contractors, and civilian and military personnel. Their job duties include interviewing applicants, writing correspondence with law enforcement officials, and preparing badges, passes, and other forms of identification.

Assistants typically work a forty-hour week, and most employers look for applicants with a high school diploma or equivalent. Training beyond high school is not usually required, but once on the job, training in computers, filing systems, organization, and human-resources practices will happen. Proficiency in Microsoft Office and other computer programs is desirable. Many of these skills are learned in vocational high school programs, and what you have not learned in the classroom you can pick up on the job.

E ssential

Personnel assistants may perform some clerical duties, including answering inquiries and sending out announcements of job openings or job examinations. Assistants also interact with payroll departments and insurance companies to verify changes to records. Some personnel assistants are involved in the hiring process. They may also screen job applicants, administer tests, explain employment policies, and request references from present or past employers.

Required Skills

Personnel assistants must also be able to communicate with colleagues at every level of the organization. They must have good interpersonal skills and have discretion in dealing with sensitive and confidential information like salaries and Social Security numbers. Confidentiality is paramount in this field. An employee entrusted with personal data must be the very model of discretion.

Compensation

The average annual salary of personnel assistants is $31,750. The federal government average is $35,490, and the state and local government average is $32,460. The federal government pays entry-level human-resources assistants with a high school diploma or six months of experience an average annual salary of $20,984. The average salary for all human-resources assistants employed by the federal government is $36,576.

The Judicial System

The federal judiciary system includes the U.S. Supreme Court, twelve regional courts of appeals, and district courts, all operating in ninety-four federal judicial districts. In addition to the federal courts, there are numerous state and county courthouses across the country. If you've ever wanted to experience what it's like to work inside a courthouse, you might consider a job as a court officer, clerk, court reporter, or corrections officer.

Court Officer

Court officers, also known as bailiffs or marshals, are the law-enforcement officers who maintain safety and order in courtrooms. Their duties vary by location but include enforcing courtroom rules, assisting judges, guarding juries from outside contact, delivering court documents, and providing security for courthouses.

When you see court officers depicted on television (in shows such as *Night Court* and *Judge Judy*), you might note that their workload seems light; it consists mostly of bringing documents from the litigants to the judge. Do not be misled. For one thing, the bailiff is the messenger who brings the important verdict from the jury to the judge. More importantly, bailiffs are also law-enforcement officers who are sometimes called to action, and some have lost their lives in the line of duty.

Each state and local judicial system has its own guidelines, so check with your local courthouse to find its hiring practices and policies. Most judicial systems do not have an upper age limit, however. Typically, if you are in your late thirties and want to be a law-enforcement officer, you might as well give up any notions of starting as a rookie at the federal, state, or local level. But that is not always the case for court officers. In the New York City court systems, for example, there is no age requirement. A cantankerous forty-something can still apply for the position and take the civil service test. If he scores high enough, he can be hired.

Court Clerk

Court and municipal clerks perform a variety of state and local government administrative tasks. They prepare case dockets, get information for judges as per their requests, and contact witnesses, lawyers, and attorneys to find out information asked for by the court. They draft agendas for town or city councils, record minutes of meetings, answer correspondence, keep financial records and accounts, and prepare reports. State and local governments also employ many secretaries, administrative assistants, and general office clerks. For most professional jobs, a college degree is required.

E ssential

The average starting salary for court officers is $30,410 in local government. The high end is $54,770, and the low end is $17,930. This does not include benefits packages or overtime pay. These vary state-by-state, county-by-county, so drop by your courthouse or visit your county's Web site to learn the particulars for your area.

Salaries in state and local government are projected to increase about 10 percent by 2012. Job growth will come from an increased demand for services at the state and local levels. The winds of change affect government jobs. When economic times are good, the government increases spending on programs and employment. When times are tough, the government enacts hiring and salary freezes. Salaries vary by size of the state and region of the country. As in most industries, professionals and managers earn more than other workers.

Employer-provided benefits include health and life insurance. Retirement benefits are more common and often better for state and local government employees than in the private sector.

Court Reporter

Court reporters create a word-for-word transcript of speeches, conversations, meetings, and other events during legal proceedings. They play a critical role in judicial proceedings and every meeting in which the spoken words must be recorded verbatim. They are responsible for seeing that the transcript is complete and accurate. Court reporters also help judges and trial attorneys in several ways, including searching for information in the official record and advising judges and attorneys regarding courtroom procedures. An increasing number of court reporters provide closed-captioning and live translation services to the deaf and hard-of-hearing.

There are several styles of court reporting. The most widely used method is called stenographic. These court reporters use a stenotype machine. It is not a traditional typewriter or keyboard. Stenotypists record every statement made in judicial proceedings. This machine lets them press multiple keys at a time to record combinations of letters representing sounds, words, or phrases. The symbols are electronically recorded and then translated as text in a process called computer-aided transcription. "Real-time court reporting" is another kind of court reporting. Stenotype machines used for real-time captioning are linked directly to a computer. As the reporter keys in the symbols, they instantly appear as text on the screen. This process is called communications access real-time translation (CART). It is used in courts, classrooms, official meetings, and for closed captioning televised proceedings for the hearing-impaired.

Electronic reporting involves using audio equipment to record court proceedings. The court reporter monitors the process, takes notes, identifies speakers, and listens to the recording to ensure clarity and quality. The equipment used ranges from analog tape recorders to digital equipment. Electronic reporters and transcribers are also used to produce a written transcript of the proceeding.

Another method is called "voice writing." The voice-writing method has the court reporter speak directly into a voice silencer, which is a hand-held mask containing a microphone. As the reporter repeats the testimony into the recorder, the mask prevents the reporter from being heard during the court proceedings. Voice writers record everything that is said by judges, witnesses, attorneys, and all other parties. They even record the gestures and emotional reactions of trial participants.

Some voice writers produce a transcript in real time, using computer speech-recognition technology. Other voice writers translate their voice files after the proceeding is over, or they transcribe the files manually. Speech-recognition–enabled voice writers can not only find careers in court reporting, but they can also be employed as closed-captioners, CART reporters for hearing-impaired individuals, and Internet streaming text providers.

Court reporters who use the stenographic or voice-writing method are responsible for a number of duties before and after transcribing events. They have to create and regularly update the computer dictionary they use to translate stenographic strokes or voice files into written text. They can customize the dictionary with parts of words, entire words, or terminology specific to the proceeding. They must also edit their translation for correct grammar and for accuracy of names and places. They prepare written transcripts, make copies, and provide a transcript to the judge, all parties in the proceedings, and the public, if requested.

Most court reporters record official proceedings in the courtroom, but others work outside the courtroom. They take depositions for attorneys in offices and document the proceedings of meetings, conventions, and other activities. Some record the proceedings that take place in government agencies, ranging from the U.S. Congress to state and local governments.

Working Conditions

Court reporters work in offices of attorneys, courtrooms, legislatures, and conventions. Many work from home as independent contractors or freelancers. While not a dangerous job, court reporting does have its physical perils. Sitting in the same position for long periods can be tiring, and you can be afflicted with wrist, back, neck, eyestrain, and repetitive stress injuries such as carpal tunnel syndrome. The pressure to maintain consistent speed and accuracy can be stressful.

Court reporters usually work a forty-hour week. The court system moves slowly. There are nearly always delays, recesses, and jury deliberations. Courts are closed on all federal and state holidays.

Job Requirements

The training necessary to become a court reporter varies with the type of reporting. It usually takes less than a year to become a voice writer, but electronic reporters and transcribers often learn their skills on the job. The average length of time to become a stenotypist is thirty-three months. Training is offered by 160 vocational and technical schools and colleges. The National Court Reporters Association (NCRA) has approved about seventy programs, all of which offer courses in stenotype computer-aided transcription and real-time reporting. National Court Reporters Association-approved programs require students to capture a minimum of 225 words per minute, a requirement for federal government employment as well.

Some states make it mandatory for court reporters to be notary publics. Some also require that candidates get the certified court reporter designation. A reporter must pass a state test administered by a board of examiners. The National Court Reporters Association gives an entry-level designation called registered professional reporter to those who pass a four-part examination and participate in mandatory continuing-education programs. This is a voluntary certification, but it is highly recommended that you go for one. A reporter can also obtain additional certifications that demonstrate higher levels of proficiency, including the registered merit reporter or registered diplomate reporter. The registered diplomate reporter is the highest level of certification available to court reporters. To earn it, a court reporter must either have five consecutive years of experience as a registered merit reporter or be a registered merit reporter and have a bachelor's degree.

The NCRA also offers these designations: certified real-time reporter, certified broadcast captioner, and certified CART provider. These promote and recognize competence in converting the spoken word into the written word.

E ssential

Court reporters working in government have a median salary of $41,070. Salaries for court reporters vary by the type of reporting job, experience and level of certification achieved, and the region of the country. Official court reporters earn a salary and a per-page fee for transcripts. Many salaried court reporters supplement their income by doing freelance work.

Some states require voice writers to pass a test and to earn a state license. As a substitute for state licensure, the National Verbatim Reporters Association offers three national certifications to voice writers: certified verbatim reporter, the certificate of merit, and real-time verbatim reporter. If you earn these certifications, it is comparable to being licensed in states where the voice method of court reporting is permitted. To get the certificate of merit or real-time verbatim reporter license, you must first earn the certified verbatim reporter license. Candidates for that license must pass a written test covering spelling, punctuation, vocabulary, legal and medical terminology, and must also pass three five-minute dictation and transcription tests for speed, accuracy, and silence.

The American Association of Electronic Reporters and Transcribers certifies electronic court reporters. This is a voluntary certification that includes a written and a practical examination. To be eligible to take the exams, you must have at least two years of court reporting or transcribing experience, and you must be eligible for notary public commissions in your state. The association offers three types of certificates: certified electronic court reporter, certified electronic court transcriber, and certified electronic court reporter and transcriber. Some employers require electronic court reporters and transcribers to obtain certificates as soon as they are eligible.

In addition to possessing speed and accuracy, court reporters must have excellent listening skills, as well as good grammar, vocabulary, and punctuation skills. Voice writers must learn to listen and speak simultaneously while also identifying speakers and describing activities in the courtroom. Those who work in courtrooms must have an expert knowledge of legal terminology and criminal and civil case procedures. Because recording the proceedings requires the use of computerized stenography or speech-recognition equipment, court reporters must be knowledgeable about computer hardware and software applications.

Employment

About 18,000 people are employed as court reporters in the United States. Sixty percent work for state and local governments. Job opportunities for court reporters are expected to be excellent. Job openings outnumber job seekers. Court reporters with certification will have the best job opportunities. Fewer people appear to be entering this profession.

Federal legislation has mandated that all new television programming must be captioned for the deaf and hard-of-hearing. The Americans with Disabilities Act gives deaf and hard-of-hearing students in colleges and universities the right to request access to real-time translation in their classes. Both of these factors are expected to increase demand for court reporters to provide real-time captioning and CART services.

Corrections Officer

Correctional officers supervise individuals who have been arrested and who are awaiting trial or who have been convicted of a crime and sentenced to serve time in a jail or penitentiary. They maintain security, enforce the rules, and prevent disturbances and escapes. They have no law-enforcement responsibilities outside the institution where they work. Police and sheriffs' departments in county and municipal jails or precinct station houses employ correctional officers who are sometimes called detention officers. The majority of the approximately 3,400 jails in the United States are operated by county governments, and about three-quarters of all jails fall under the jurisdiction of an elected sheriff. The average jail population is in flux. New offenders arrive and other prisoners are released on an almost daily basis. Correctional officers in local jails process about 12 million people a year, and about 700,000 offenders are in jail at any given time.

 Fact

Most correctional officers are employed in state and federal prisons, and they supervise about 1.4 million incarcerated offenders. Other correctional officers oversee individuals held by the U.S. Immigration and Naturalization Service, pending release or deportation, or work for correctional institutions run by private for-profit organizations.

Correctional officers maintain order within the institution and enforce rules and regulations. To ensure that inmates are orderly and obey rules, correctional officers monitor prisoner activities and supervise work assignments. Officers must search inmates and their living quarters for contraband like weapons or drugs, settle disputes between inmates, and enforce discipline. On paper, this sounds pretty simple. But it's a tough job for tough people.

Correctional officers inspect locks, window bars, doors, and gates for signs of tampering, and they inspect mail and visitors for prohibited items. The cliché from old movies and television shows is the file inserted into a cake. In reality, most prisons do not allow inmates to receive food from friends and family. The rules for what inmates can receive are quite strict. They can only receive paperback books because a hardcover might be able to be used as a weapon, as could a spiral-bound manual. More and more prisons only allow inmates to purchase items from their internal commissary—including playing cards and other items.

Correctional officers report both orally and in writing on inmate conduct and on the quality and quantity of work done by inmates. They keep a record of convicts' daily activities. In jails and prison facilities with direct supervision cellblocks, officers are unarmed. They carry communications devices to call for help if necessary. These officers often work in a cellblock, alone or with another officer, among the fifty to 100 inmates. Officers enforce regulations primarily through their communications skills and the use of progressive sanctions, such as the removal of some privileges.

In maximum-security facilities, where the most dangerous inmates are housed, correctional officers often monitor the activities of prisoners from a control center with closed-circuit television cameras and a computerized tracking system. In this environment, inmates may not see anyone but correctional officers for days or weeks at a time. Correctional officers escort inmates to leave their cells only for showers, solitary exercise time, or the occasional visitor. Correctional officers may have to restrain the more dangerous inmates in handcuffs and leg irons to escort them safely to and from cells and other areas and to see authorized visitors.

A Dangerous Job

Working in a correctional institution can be stressful and sometimes dangerous. Correctional officers occasionally are injured in confrontations with inmates. Correctional officers work both indoors or outdoors, and they usually work an eight-hour day, five days a week, on rotating shifts. Because prison and jail security must be provided all day, every day of the year, officers work all hours of the day and night, weekends, and holidays. Officers may also be required to work paid overtime.

Job Requirements

The Federal Bureau of Prisons requires entry-level correctional officers to have either a bachelor's degree or three years of full-time experience in a field providing counseling, assistance, or supervision to individuals. Candidates may also have a combination of relevant work experience and education.

Candidates are required to meet standards of physical fitness, eyesight, and hearing. Many jurisdictions use various tests to determine the applicant's suitability to work in a correctional environment. Applicants are screened for drug abuse. They are subject to background checks and are required to pass a written examination.

Federal, state, and some local departments of corrections provide training for correctional officers based on guidelines established by the American Correctional Association and the American Jail Association. Some states have regional training academies. State and local correctional agencies often provide on-the-job training, including training on legal restrictions and interpersonal relations. Many systems require firearms proficiency and self-defense skills. Officer trainees typically receive several weeks or months of training in an actual job setting under the supervision of an experienced officer.

Question

What are the requirements for a position as a correctional officer?
Most institutions require correctional officers to be at least eighteen to twenty-one years of age and a U.S. citizen. Officers must have a high school education or equivalent and usually two years of work experience. And it goes without saying that they cannot have any felony convictions.

Federal corrections officers undergo 200 hours of formal training within their first year of employment. They also complete 120 hours of specialized training at the Federal Bureau of Prisons residential training center at Glynco, Georgia, within sixty days of their appointment. Some correctional officers are members of the prison tactical response teams. They are trained to respond to disturbances, riots, hostage situations, and other dangerous confrontations. They practice disarming prisoners, protecting themselves and inmates against the effects of chemical agents, and other SWAT-team–style tactics.

With education, experience, and training, qualified officers can advance to the position of correctional sergeant. Sergeants supervise the correctional officers, and they are usually responsible for maintaining security and directing the activities of other officers during an assigned shift.

There Is Always a Need

Bailiffs, correctional officers, and jailers hold about 484,000 jobs. Three of every five jobs are in state correctional institutions, including prisons, prison camps, and youth correctional facilities. There are about 16,000 correctional officers in federal correctional institutions, and another 15,000 in privately owned and managed prisons. The remaining jobs are in city and county jails or in other institutions run by local governments.

Job opportunities are and will continue to be plentiful. The increasing demand for jobs stems from the current trend of longer sentences and reduced parole for inmates as well as the new construction of corrections facilities. Layoffs of correctional officers are rare because prisons are filling up. Median annual earnings are $44,700 in the federal government, $33,750 in state governments, and $33,080 in local governments. According to the Federal Bureau of Prisons, the starting salary for federal correctional officers was $26,747 a year in 2005. The average salary of the supervisors/managers of correctional officers is $41,080 in state government and $49,470 in local government.

Correctional officers employed in the public sector are usually provided with uniforms or a clothing allowance to purchase their own uniforms. Civil service systems or merit boards cover officers employed by the federal government and most state governments. Their retirement coverage entitles correctional officers to retire at age fifty after twenty years of service or at any age with twenty years of service.

Chapter 13

Technological Wizards

The men and women who keep computers running are an indispensable component of any organization, especially those in the government. More and more reliance on computers and increasing threats of "cyber-terrorism" make these folks soldiers in the preservation of civil liberties and democracy.

Information Technology (IT) Specialists

Computer and information technology (IT) specialists coordinate all the computer-related activities of a business. They work with management to implement the goals of the organization. They supervise the work of systems analysts, programmers, and other computer support people. They upgrade hardware and software so that the organization stays on the cutting edge of the latest technology, and they see that the network runs smoothly and is free from attack by hackers and viruses. These are the folks who will save you when your computer suddenly crashes.

Chief technology officers report to the organization's chief information officer. The technology officer's job is to be aware of the latest technology and evaluate whether it is valuable, usable, and cost-effective for the company. These men and women must be ahead of the curve when it comes to technology.

Directors of management information systems also report to the chief information officer. They do things like oversee the organization's help desk. They supervise the tech staff that comes to your cubicle or office when you call about a problem with your office desktop or laptop computer. They also make recommendations about upgrading the network and the individual computers in the workplace.

Project managers oversee budgets and schedules for their companies. They coordinate technology projects. This entails working with clients and consultants, vendors, and staff.

IT people spend their days in an office environment. Any traveling is to another office. They are subject to being "on call" since computer crises can arise any time of the day or night. On the positive side, these men and women are well paid for their efforts.

E ssential

According to the National Association of Colleges and Employers, salaries for graduates with a bachelor's degree in computer science start at an average of $50,820. The low end is $36,470, and the high end is in excess of $99,610. In other words, if you are computer savvy, you can practically write your own ticket.

Prerequisites

You need to learn all about computers, with a solid educational background, and have some hands-on experience before anyone will hire you. You also need to develop the ability to "dumb down" advice for computer fixes. Laymen will not understand you unless you convey what needs to be done in the simplest possible terms.

Many colleges offer degrees that combine business and technology classes. It is rare though not unheard of to be hired with only an associate's degree, but such candidates must have extensive job experience to offset their lack of an advanced degree. In general, a bachelor's degree in computer science is the bare minimum requirement, and some organizations require a graduate degree. Some people go for an MBA with an emphasis on technology.

The Job Market

The government is one of the largest employers of IT specialists, if only because the government is large and getting larger. IT people work in every realm of the public and private sectors. Everyone has computers and computer networks large and small, and everyone needs them maintained, upgraded, and serviced. Employment is anticipated to grow faster than other areas of the economy. The never-ending advances in technology will assure the need for qualified individuals to work in the field.

 Fact

LAN/WAN (local area network/wide area network) managers do any number of things, including design and administration of an organization's computer network. They deal with every level of an organization, from the CEO to the building maintenance staff. After all, computers must be in climate-controlled environments. If they get too hot or too cold, the network can suffer.

The security of the government's computerized infrastructure is now a subject of great importance. Terrorism can take many forms, and a blow to the right computer systems could do serious damage to government and military operations. Cyber security is a growing field, and these men and women will be on the front lines in a war against hackers, virus-spreaders, and other evildoers intent on destroying government networks and computer systems. The growth of e-commerce and Internet stores also will create a high demand for computer whiz kids.

The money is not bad, either. Computer and information systems managers vary by specialty and level of responsibility, but even those on the low end of the spectrum can make in the high five figures, while the top tier takes in a nice six-figure salary. The government will have to stay competitive with the private sector in order to attract the best and the brightest.

Computer Scientists and Database Administrators

Computer scientists, database administrators, and network systems and data communication analysts have duties and job titles that change as frequently as computer technology evolves.

Database administrators use database management systems software to organize and store data. They set up and modify computer databases. A database administrator makes sure the system runs smoothly and designs and implements system security.

Communications analysts design and test systems including local area networks (LANs) and wide area networks (WANs), the Internet, intranets, and other communications systems. This can be as simple as connecting two offices in a multinational corporation to a global network.

The focus of telecommunications specialists is the connection between computers and communications equipment. They devise, install, and maintain voice- and data-communication systems. They also service users of the systems after they are installed. The booming, continually growing Internet has created numerous new occupations involving Web site maintenance, service, and design.

Computer scientists and database administrators work forty-hour weeks in offices or laboratories. Evenings and weekends may sometimes be required in order to meet deadlines. Telecommuting is increasingly common. More and more work can be done from remote locations via modems, laptops, e-mail, and the Internet.

Continually evolving technology necessitates a continuing education on the part of those wishing to stay on the cutting edge of the latest bells and whistles. Computers become outdated faster than any other machine designed by man, so successful candidates must keep abreast of the trade journals and be aware of the next new thing coming down the pike lest some up-and-coming graduate aces them out of a promotion or even a job. It is that tough out there.

Most community colleges offer computer courses. Many employers want people with a computer science degree and some business courses. Prospective employees have to navigate more than circuits and fiber optic cables. They must also maneuver the treacherous waters of office politics. You need not go for a full degree. Many college and computer training centers offer certifications in various aspects of information technology. Everything you can do to add to your resume will help make you a more marketable commodity.

The government is one of the largest employers of computer scientists and database administrators. Other entities where the demand is high are financial institutions, colleges, insurance companies, Internet service providers, Web site hosting companies, and related companies. Job prospects are very good in the Information Age.

Ⓔ Fact

Companies, including the government, want people with state-of-the-art skills. A bachelor's degree is the minimum educational requirement for most jobs. An associate's degree may be acceptable when partnered with considerable work experience. The more complex the job, the more advanced the degree required.

The average salary for government IT workers is $52,300, which is in the middle range for this kind of job. The government will have to be competitive in order to attract above-average workers.

Computer Programmers

Computer programmers write, test, and maintain complex instructions, called programs, that computers follow in order to function. Computer programs essentially tell the computer what to do to achieve a desired result, such as perform word-processing operations. There are myriad programs based on the kind of data that needs to be accessed or generated.

Simple programs can be written in a few hours, while complex programs that employ mathematical formulas can take more than a year of work. In these instances, several programmers work together under a senior programmer's supervision.

There are different kinds of computer languages commonly used on most computer systems:

- COBOL is commonly used for business applications.
- Fortran, which is short for "formula translation," is used in science and engineering.
- C++ is widely used for both scientific and business applications.
- Extensible markup language is a popular programming tool for Web programmers.
- J2EE (Java 2 Platform) is another tool for Web programmers.

Programmers usually learn more than one language because it makes them more marketable. They are known by the language for which they are experts—for example, Java programmers—or by the systems they service: database programmers, Web programmers, and so on.

In addition to writing programs, programmers also update and modify existing programs. There are software programs to help them do this. They are called computer-assisted software programming tools.

 **Question**

What are the different types of computer programmers?
These are the two main types of programmers. Applications programmers write programs for a specific job the system needs to perform. Systems programmers write programs to maintain and control computer operating systems, networks, and databases.

The government is one of the largest employers of programmers. Programmers often work long hours, including evenings and weekends. Deadlines and crises arise at any moment, and these men and women must be on call. Telecommuting is increasingly common; more and more work can be done from great distances. Programmers can fix more problems remotely in this global village.

Like the other jobs described in this chapter, your odds of getting a plum job are greatly improved if you have an advanced degree and work experience. If the branch of government that piques your interest is involved with science or engineering, prospective employers will probably be most interested in you if you can show off a degree in either information science or math and the physical sciences. Some positions may require graduate degrees. If the government entity is involved in business, it will look for people who have taken courses in management information systems who also possess programming acumen.

In addition to the older computer languages, many employers are looking for people with proficiency in C++ and Java. The bottom line is that it's a good idea to get as much training as you can. If you are a student or in a position to work for the experience alone, seek out internships with companies in your area.

You must also have a familiarity with the database systems DB2, Oracle, and Sybase. In addition, you should obtain as many certifications as you can. This can be done by taking individual courses at your local college or business school. Product manufacturers also offer certifications in their products. Check that out, too.

Data Entry

Data processors are the foot soldiers of the Information Age. Data entry is an umbrella phrase that covers jobs such as word processors, typists, data-entry keyers, electronic data processors, keypunch technicians, and transcribers. Data-entry keyers input lists, numbers, and other information. They manipulate and edit existing material and proofread databases for accuracy. In addition to computers, keyers use a machine that converts information into magnetic impulses on tapes and disks.

Data entry is not just for computers anymore. Many data-entry workers work with scanners to scan and save whole documents without having to retype them. Keyers sometimes also serve as the archivists of this data, functioning as librarians who catalog and oversee the wealth of information generated by companies and bureaucracies.

Cautions for Data-Entry Workers

Like the other jobs discussed in this chapter, data-entry work is sedentary, meaning you spend most of the day sitting down. The environment is often noisy due to the machines operating around you. You will have to deal with the usual computer-related problems like carpal tunnel syndrome, back pain, eyestrain, and other injuries caused by repetitive motion. The work also can be quite monotonous, but you must remain sharp and focused. One false keystroke can create pandemonium.

E ssential

Word processors use word-processing programs like Microsoft Word to type correspondence, prepare reports, mailing labels and envelopes, and create or maintain any other textual material. More experienced word processors work with complex statistical documents.

Speed is of the essence for data-entry workers. More and more employers expect candidates to have some keystroke experience before being hired. In today's world, private-sector employers are less likely to provide on-the-job training. There are Internet tutorials to help bring you up to speed, and courses are taught in high schools and colleges. You can also buy software programs to practice on your home computer. Of course, speed is only half of the equation. The other half is accuracy. An ideal data-entry worker can type rapidly without making mistakes. The key is practice.

On the Job and Employment Outlook

Data entry is often an entry-level position that serves as an entrée into a company or bureaucracy. People often start in data entry and work their way up through secretarial to administrative to management to—who knows—maybe even president of the United States. Government agencies usually have training programs to help workers increase their skills and advance up the ladder. Others are journeymen data-entry professionals, who work hard for the money while pursuing their dreams after hours.

E Fact

There are about 525,000 data-entry workers in the United States. Most work in offices, but some telecommute from home. One out of five data-entry workers is employed by federal, state, and local government. Data-entry workers employed by the government earn between $27,000 and $29,000.

Data-entry jobs likely will decline over the next few years. Those in the field, or who want to get into the game, are advised to keep their skills honed and to stay up to date on the latest technology. The specter of outsourcing looms over data entry, as it does over many other fields. Many companies are farming out their information processing to workers in foreign lands because they can pay them a fraction of what American workers would expect.

Chapter 14

Hands-On Jobs

If you like to work with your hands, you can find a job with the government. The government needs carpenters, electricians, mechanics, painters, and other workers whose hands-on skills make them essential to keep government buildings and other structures up and running. This chapter describes jobs that allow you to get physical as you earn a living.

Carpenter

Carpenters build, install, and repair structures and fixtures made from wood and other materials. This is a great career for the handy because your work leaves a lasting monument to your craftsmanship.

Sometimes carpenters specialize in one technique, or they might be knowledgeable in many. For example, a carpenter might specialize in cabinetmaking, metalwork, drywall installing, or fence building. The smaller the business, the more a carpenter must know. Employees in large construction companies usually have a specialty.

Most carpenters work from blueprints or instructions from supervisors. They measure and arrange materials in accordance with local building codes. They cut and shape wood, plastic, fiberglass, or drywall using hand tools and power tools. They join the materials with nails, screws, staples, and other adhesives.

Carpentry work is often strenuous. It involves a lot of standing, climbing, bending, and kneeling. The risk of injury exists when one works with sharp or rough materials and uses sharp tools and power equipment. Carpenters also work in areas where slip-and-fall hazards are more common. The numerous home-improvement shows on television will give you an idea of what the work entails. Take some adult education courses at your community college.

Carpenters learn their trade through both formal and informal training programs. It takes about three or four years to become a skilled carpenter by following a regimen of classroom and on-the-job training. Training can begin as early as high school, where, if the curriculum exists, you can study English, algebra, geometry, physics, mechanical drawing, blueprint reading, and general shop. You can continue your training after high school either through additional schooling or by seeking out a mentor. The tradition of mentor and apprentice is an ancient one.

E ssential

You can find information on registered apprenticeships through links to state apprenticeship programs on the U.S. Department of Labor's Employment and Training Administration Web site, online at *www.doleta.gov.*

You can look for a job with a contractor who will provide on-the-job training. Entry-level workers start as helpers. You may be required to join a union in order to work in the trade. Apprentices must be at least eighteen years old and meet local requirements. Some union locals will make you take an aptitude test. Apprentices learn elementary structural design and become familiar with layout, form building, rough framing, and outside and inside finishing. They learn to use the machines, equipment, and other tools of the trade. They are instructed in safety, first aid, blueprint reading, freehand sketching, basic mathematics, and other carpentry techniques, both in the classroom and on the job.

If you do not seek out or successfully find a mentor right away, there are public and private vocational-technical schools and training academies affiliated with carpentry unions.

The Job Market

Carpenters make up the largest of the building trades occupations. There are about 1.3 million carpenters working in the United States today. Approximately 400,000 of those work in building construction, and 260,000 work for special trade contractors. The rest work in a variety of other industries, including government agencies.

⚡ Alert

Many carpenters become members of the United Brotherhood of Carpenters and Joiners of America. The organization has more than 500,000 members who specialize in fields like carpentry, cabinet-making, and roofing. To learn more about this union, visit its Web site, online at *www.carpenters.org*.

Job opportunities are expected to be excellent. The more skills you have and the more skilled you are, the better your chances are to find a decent job in the field. The demand for new government buildings, along with continual maintenance of existing ones, will make for plenty of work. The average hourly rate for carpenters is $16.78. The lowest 10 percent in this field makes about $10.36 an hour, and the highest 10 percent earns about $28.65.

Electrician

Electricians install, connect, and maintain electrical systems for many purposes, including climate control, security, and communications. They also install and maintain the electronic controls for machines in business and industry. Think about the last time you had a power outage, and you will see the important role electricity plays in our lives.

Electricians must be able to understand blueprints. Blueprints indicate the locations of circuits, outlets, load centers, panel boards, and other equipment. Electricians must follow the national electrical code and comply with state and local building codes when they install systems.

Electricians work both indoors and outside. They work at construction sites, in homes, in businesses, and in factories. Work can be strenuous and involves bending and lifting heavy objects, standing, stooping, and kneeling for long periods. They may be subject to unpleasant weather conditions when working outdoors. They also risk injury from electrical shock and must follow strict safety procedures. A small number of electricians die on the job each year, either through carelessness on their part or circumstances beyond their control. Dealing with this potent force of nature on a daily basis is not without risk. You had best learn all the safety precautions you need to know before you ever begin work on a site.

E ssential

Most electricians work a standard forty-hour week, though overtime, nights or weekends, and being on call are often part of the job. Companies that are open twenty-four hours a day may employ three shifts of electricians. And of course, private contractors have the luxury of setting their own hours.

Like carpenters, most electricians learn their trade through an apprenticeship program. These programs combine on-the-job training with classroom instruction. Apprenticeship programs are often sponsored by local unions of the International Brotherhood of Electrical Workers, local chapters of the National Electrical Contractors Association, or local chapters of the Associated Builders and Contractors and the Independent Electrical Contractors Association.

Applicants for apprenticeships must be at least eighteen years old and have a high school diploma or a GED. You should have good math and English skills, since the instruction manuals are in English. You may have to pass a test and meet other requirements. Apprenticeship programs usually last four years and include about

144 hours of classroom instruction and 2,000 hours of on-the-job training.

Classroom studies include electrical theory, installing and maintaining electrical systems, blueprint reading, mathematics, electrical code requirements, safety and first aid practices, communications, fire alarm systems, and many other topics. When on the job, apprentices work under the supervision of an experienced electrician.

Training is offered by many public and private vocational-technical schools and through training academies affiliated with local unions. Employers who hire graduates of these programs start them at a more advanced level than those without the training.

Electricians need to be licensed. Licensing requirements vary from state to state. Electricians must pass an examination that tests their knowledge of electrical theory, the national electrical code, and the local electric and building codes.

Experienced electricians can advance to supervisory positions. In construction, they can become project managers and construction superintendents. Many become electrical inspectors. It is increasingly important to be able to communicate in both English and Spanish. Spanish-speaking workers are making up a larger part of the construction workforce. To understand instruction presented in classes and on the work site, Spanish-speaking workers who want to get ahead need very good English.

E Fact

Many electricians are members of the International Brotherhood of Electrical Workers. Other unions representing maintenance electricians are the International Brotherhood of Electrical Workers; the International Union of Electronic, Electrical, Salaried, Machine, and Furniture Workers; the International Association of Machinists and Aerospace Workers; the International Union, United Automobile, Aircraft and Agricultural Implement Workers of America; and the United Steelworkers of America.

Jobs for electricians are expected to increase over the next decade. More electricians will be needed to install and maintain electrical devices and wiring in homes, factories, offices, and other buildings. New technologies will create the demand for workers. Older structures being rehabilitated require being brought up to meet existing electrical codes.

The median hourly rate of electricians is $20.33. The low end is $12.18, and the high end is $33.63. The average for government-employed electricians is $22.24. Apprentices start at between 40 and 50 percent of the fully trained electrician rate. They receive periodic pay increases throughout the course of their training and job experience.

For details about apprenticeships or other work opportunities in this trade, contact the offices of your state employment service, your state's apprenticeship agency, local electrical contractors or firms that employ maintenance electricians, or local union-management electrician apprenticeship committees. Information is also available from local chapters of the Independent Electrical Contractors, Inc.; the National Electrical Contractors Association; the Home Builders Institute; the Associated Builders and Contractors; and the International Brotherhood of Electrical Workers.

Mechanic

Mechanic is a very general term than covers a wide variety of jobs. Most mechanics specialize in the service and repair of one kind of equipment. For example, motorcycle mechanics repair and overhaul motorcycles and other all-terrain vehicles. They repair engines, work on transmissions, brakes, and ignition systems. Motorboat mechanics, or marine equipment mechanics, repair and adjust the electrical and mechanical equipment of boat engines. Outdoor power equipment and other small engine mechanics service and repair lawnmowers, garden tractors, edge trimmers, and chain saws. Routine maintenance is also part of the mechanic's work.

Due to the increasing complexity of mechanical devices, employers nowadays prefer to hire mechanics who have graduated from formal training programs. Some still learn their skills on the job, and some are prodigies who have an affinity for all things mechanical. Many got their basic skills through working on automobiles, motorcycles, and other equipment as a hobby.

The average hourly earnings of motorcycle mechanics are $13.70. Motorboat mechanics earn $14.74 per hour, and those who service outdoor power equipment and small engines make $11.98 per hour.

Many government jobs for mechanics can be found locally. Cities and states have fleets of vehicles that must be serviced. Your local parks and recreation department contains legions of lawnmowers that occasionally will go kaput. The pay for these jobs can be quite good. The city of Phoenix, Arizona recently advertised for a heavy-duty maintenance mechanic. The pay range was $46,000 to $55,000 per year, but it required four years of skilled experience.

For more details about work opportunities, you can contact your local motorcycle, motorboat, and lawn and garden equipment dealers, boatyards, and marinas. Your state employment service also may have information about employment and training opportunities.

Painter

Everybody needs some painting done at one time or another, so there is always work to be had for painters. Painters apply paint, varnish, and other finishes to buildings and other structures. They prepare the surfaces to be covered, so that the paint will adhere properly. This often requires the removal of the old coat of paint by stripping, sanding, wire brushing, burning, or water and abrasive blasting. Painters also wash walls to remove dirt and grease, fill nail holes and cracks, sandpaper rough spots, and brush off dust.

Painters must stand for long periods and often work on scaffolding and ladders. The job entails lots of climbing and bending. This requires physical fitness because much of the work is done with one's arms raised overhead. Painters sometimes work with hazardous or toxic materials. This often mandates a sealed self-contained suit to prevent inhalation of or contact with hazardous materials.

Painting is learned mostly through on-the-job training and by working as a helper to an experienced painter. Besides these apprenticeships, some novice painters attend technical schools that offer training. These schools take about a year to complete. Some receive training through local vocational schools. Applicants should have good manual dexterity and color sense. A colorblind painter is not a good thing.

Apprenticeships for painters usually involve two to four years of on-the-job training, and 144 hours of related classroom instruction each year. Apprentices must be at least eighteen years old and in good physical shape. A high school education or equivalent is necessary to enter an apprenticeship program. Instruction includes study in color harmony, use and care of tools and equipment, surface preparation, application techniques, paint mixing and matching, characteristics of different finishes, blueprint reading, and safety.

Painters can advance to supervisory jobs with painting and decorating contractors. A lot of them establish their own painting businesses. As is true of all the jobs described in this chapter, bilingualism is a plus. The average hourly salary for painters is $14.55. The government pays a little more, averaging $18.36. Some painters join the International Brotherhood of Painters and Allied Trades.

Printer/Reproduction

The printing industry produces materials ranging from newspapers, magazines, and books to brochures, labels, newsletters, postcards, memo pads, business order forms, checks, maps, T-shirts, and packaging. Printing methods include lithography, flexography, gravure, screen-printing, and letterpress.

Lithography uses the basic principle that water repels oil. It is the most widely used printing process in the industry. Flexography produces vibrant colors with little rub-off. This is used in the printing of newspapers, directories, and books. Gravure's high-quality reproduction, flexible pagination and formats, and consistent print quality are used in packaging and product printing. Screen-printing prints designs on clothes and other fabric items, like caps. Letterpresses print images from raised surfaces on which ink sits. The raised surfaces are generated by means of casting, acid etching, or photo emulsion.

The printing industry is undergoing technological changes as computers and technology change the way work is performed. Many of the things once done by hand are now automated. The influence of technology is seen in the three stages of printing:

1. Prepress is the preparation of materials for printing.
2. Output is the actual printing process.
3. Post press, or finishing, is the folding, binding, and trimming of printed sheets into their final form.

The most significant change is in the prepress stage. Rather than cutting and pasting articles by hand, printers now produce entire publications on a computer, complete with artwork and graphics. Columns can be displayed and arranged on the computer screen exactly as they will appear in print. Almost all prepress work is now computerized, and prepress workers need a good deal of training in computers and graphic design software.

Workers enter the printing industry with diverse educational backgrounds. Helpers usually have a high school or vocational school background, while management trainees usually have a college background. Job applicants must be high school graduates with mathematical, computer, and verbal and written communication skills. Training and experience in desktop publishing is becoming extremely important.

Workers are generally trained informally on the job. The length of this training varies. New hires learn their trade under the close supervision of a more seasoned employee. Through experience and training, workers can advance to more responsible positions.

Employment in the printing industry is expected to decline over the next decade, both in the public and private sector. This is because of the growing computerization of the printing process as well as the increasing use of the Internet, which reduces the need for printed materials.

The average weekly earnings for production workers in the printing industry is $604. The main union for this industry is the Graphic Communications Conference of the International Brotherhood of Teamsters.

Other Jobs in the Construction Trade

Construction laborers are found on all construction sites, and they perform a variety of tasks from the very easy to the dangerous. They work in buildings, on highways, construction sites, bridges and tunnels, and many other sites. Their jobs require physical strength plus training and experience. Others require little skill and can be learned quickly. Most laborers specialize in one kind of construction, but there are many generalists who perform different tasks during all stages of construction. The more you know, the more marketable you are.

Ⓔ Fact

Information on apprenticeships and other training opportunities may be obtained from local employers such as printing shops, local offices of the Graphic Communications International Union, local affiliates of Printing Industries of America/Graphics Arts Technical Foundation, or local offices of the state employment service.

Construction laborers clean and prepare construction sites, and this sometimes requires the removal of asbestos or lead-based paint from buildings. They erect and disassemble scaffolding and other temporary structures. They load, unload, identify, and distribute building materials to the appropriate location according to project plans. They mix concrete using a portable mixer, or they might tend a machine that pumps concrete, grout, cement, sand, plaster, or stucco through a spray gun for application to ceilings and walls. They assist other workers, including carpenters, plasterers, operating engineers, and masons.

At highway construction sites, construction laborers clear highway work zones and rights of way; install barricades, cones, and markers; and control traffic in and around work zones. Construction laborers operate a variety of equipment including pavement breakers, jackhammers, concrete mixers, electric and hydraulic machines, and other equipment. Government construction projects mean that jobs for laborers are available at the local, state, and federal level. If the government hires laborers directly—that is, if you become an employee of a government agency, such as the Department of Transportation—you will receive excellent government benefits. Sometimes, the government contracts with private companies. In that case, you will be an employee of the contracting company, and your benefits will vary.

☀ Alert

Physical laborers have demanding jobs. They lift and carry heavy objects. Their jobs require them to stoop, kneel, crouch, and crawl. They work at great heights and outdoors in all kinds of weather. Construction laborers are sometimes exposed to harmful materials or chemicals, fumes, odors, loud noise, and dangerous machinery. On the plus side, they develop muscles of steel.

Construction laborers generally work eight-hour shifts, although longer shifts and overnights are common. Many of these jobs require little skill other than strength and the ability to follow instructions, but others require specialized training and experience. Many employees learn from on-the-job training. Entry-level workers start as helpers, assisting more experienced workers. Beginners perform routine tasks like cleaning the worksite and unloading materials. They can learn from experienced construction workers how to do more difficult tasks like operating tools and equipment.

The most skilled laborers usually have more formal training. Some employers offer their employees formal apprenticeships. These programs include between two and four years of classroom and on-the-job training. The curriculum consists of basic construction skills like blueprint reading, the proper use of tools and equipment, and knowledge of safety and health procedures. Advanced studies include specialized skills training in three of the largest segments of the construction industry: building construction; highway construction; and environmental cleaning, including lead, asbestos, mold, and hazardous-waste removal. Workers who use dangerous equipment or handle toxic chemicals receive specialized training in safety awareness and procedures. Apprenticeship applicants usually must be at least eighteen years old and meet local requirements.

Fact

The average hourly wage for construction laborers is $12.10. Highway, street, and bridge construction, often employed by local governments, make an average hourly wage of $13.55. Pay levels increase as apprentices learn new skills.

Construction labor accounts for about 1 million jobs in the U.S. economy. They work throughout the country but are concentrated in metropolitan areas. Opportunities are always best for those with experience and specialized skills and for those willing to relocate to areas with new construction projects. Opportunities are also anticipated to be good for workers specializing in the removal of lead, asbestos, and other hazardous materials.

For information about a job as a construction laborer, contact local building or construction contractors, local joint labor-management apprenticeship committees, apprenticeship agencies, or the local office of your state employment service.

Chapter 15

Science and Medicine

The government needs doctors, food scientists, nutritionists, pharmacologists, and other scientists to help establish safety regulations for the food and medicines Americans consume and use every day. This chapter explains who does what and why, and how you can be a part of this important work.

U.S. Food and Drug Administration

The U.S. Food and Drug Administration (FDA) is one of the nation's oldest consumer protection agencies. Its mission is "to promote and protect the public health by helping safe and effective products reach the market in a timely way, to monitor products for continued safety after they are in use, and to help the public get the accurate, science-based information needed to improve health."

The FDA is typically the agency that alerts Americans about the potential health risks of certain foods.

E Fact

In September of 2006, people in numerous states began to get very ill. The FDA determined that their illness was caused by loose, bagged spinach. Some spinach had been infected with deadly E. coli bacteria. At first, the FDA did not know which company had processed the tainted spinach, so all bagged spinach was removed from supermarket shelves.

The FDA also changed how we take over-the-counter medication, due to a series of murders that took place in Chicago in 1982. Seven people in the Chicago area died suddenly and unexpectedly. Author-ities traced the deaths to Tylenol capsules, which had been laced with cyanide. The perpetrator of the act was never caught. Soon after the incident, the FDA toughened product-tampering laws. In time, all over-the-counter capsules were replaced with today's familiar caplets.

Here are some of the main functions of the FDA:

- It makes sure all ingredients used in foods are safe and that food is free of contaminants, including disease-causing organisms, chemicals, or other harmful substances.
- It approves new food additives before they can be used.
- It monitors the safety of dietary supplements and the content of infant formulas and medical foods.
- It monitors medical products, making sure they are safe and effective before they can be used in the treatment of patients. These products include vaccines, gene therapy, as well as blood and biotechnology products.
- The FDA regulates all medical devices, from very simple tongue depressors and thermometers to complex technolo-gies such as heart pacemakers, kidney dialysis machines, microwave ovens, cell phones, X-ray equipment, lasers, medical ultrasound and MRI machines, and many other con-sumer, industrial, and medical products.
- It monitors mammography facilities to make sure that their equipment is safe and they are properly run.
- It regulates drugs and devices used on animals, both pets and livestock.
- The FDA monitors cosmetic products to make sure that they are safe.

Most of FDA's budget goes toward paying its highly skilled work force. Its employees are drawn from science and public health pro-fessions, including biologists, chemists, physicians, biomedical engi-neers, pharmacologists, veterinarians, toxicologists, and specialists in public-health education and communication.

In order to carry out its mission, the FDA employs about 9,000 people who work in locations around the country. This network of field offices is generally the first point of contact for the public and regulated manufacturers. The employees in these offices focus on inspection and surveillance, laboratory work, and public and industry education.

The FDA staff that works in the Washington, D.C., office focuses on product review and regulatory policy.

E ssential

To learn more about what the FDA does and why, check out its Web site, online at ✐www.fda.gov. You can find information for consumers, health professionals, industry, and the latest news on FDA-regulated products. The FDA Web site also provides a link to job opportunities available within the agency.

New Product Review

The FDA reviews results of laboratory and animal and human clinical testing done by companies to determine if their products are safe and do what their makers claim.

The FDA does this for new human drugs, complex medical devices, food and color additives, and animal drugs. The FDA then tracks the product to make sure the manufacturers continue to maintain their standards of production and monitors cases of adverse side effects. FDA employees make more than 16,000 visits a year to facilities that make FDA-regulated products.

Research

The FDA's research provides the scientific basis for its regulatory decisions and the tools needed to identify risks. The agency uses its research results to guide standard setting, evaluate new products, develop test methods and other support for product monitoring, and to study emerging risks.

Enforcement

When problems arise, the FDA takes numerous actions to protect the public health. It works with manufacturers to correct the problem voluntarily. Failing this, legal remedies may be necessary, including impelling the manufacturer to recall a product, having federal marshals seize products if a voluntary recall is not implemented, and confiscating imported products at the port of entry.

FDA Career Opportunities

Employees are usually hired into the federal government under a career-conditional appointment. This means that the employee must complete three years of substantially continuous service before becoming a full-career employee. This three-year period is used to determine whether the government is willing and able to offer the employee a lifetime career, which is called tenure. Once you have tenure, it is next to impossible to lose your job.

The first year of service is considered a probationary period. The probationary period is really the final and most important step in the testing process that begins when an employee first fills out an application. This year gives the supervisor an opportunity to evaluate the employee's performance on the job. Previous federal civilian service counts toward completion of probation if it is in the same agency, the same line of work, and without a break in service.

At the FDA, three years of continuous service must not include any breaks of more than thirty calendar days. If an employee does not complete the three-year period or has a single break in service of more than thirty calendar days, he or she will be required to serve a new three-year period. Career-conditional employees automatically become full-career employees upon completion of these requirements.

Biologists

An FDA biologist reviews and evaluates scientific and clinical data to determine the safety and effectiveness of medical products; screens out products that may pose a public health hazard; conducts research on the preparation, preservation, and safety of blood and blood products; and studies the biological effects of various additives found in foods.

Grade (Salary) Levels

The federal General Schedule (GS) grade levels at which biologist positions are commonly filled are GS-9 ($38,175) through 13 ($65,832) at the headquarters level and GS-5 ($25,195) through 11 ($46,189) at the field level. Higher grade levels in both headquarters and field offices are available based on peer review of individual accomplishments or responsibilities.

Qualifications

The basic qualifications required for all grades in this position include a degree in biological sciences, agriculture, natural resource management, chemistry, or related disciplines, or a combination of education and experience. In order to qualify for higher-graded positions, candidates must have additional amounts of specialized experience or related education. The amount of additional experience or education needed depends on the grade of the position. FDA biologists are located in the administration's headquarters in suburban Washington, D.C., and in FDA facilities throughout the country.

Chemists

An FDA chemist's job entails reviewing and evaluating new drug applications; evaluating the methods, facilities, and controls used to manufacture drugs; reviewing proposed labels; summarizing findings; and recommending approval or disapproval of applications. The administration also conducts research projects that study the effects of food components and dietary supplements. Studies are also designed to investigate the effects of drugs, antibiotics, and agricultural chemicals on cattle, small laboratory animals, and other domestic livestock.

Qualifications

The necessary requirements for all chemist grades include a degree in physical sciences, life sciences, or engineering; thirty semester hours in chemistry supplemented by coursework in mathematics, including differential and integral calculus, and at least six semester hours of physics; or a combination of education and experience.

Fact

The federal General Schedule (GS) grade levels at which chemist positions are most commonly filled are GS-9 ($38,175) through 13 ($65,832) at the headquarters level and GS-5 ($25,195) through 12 ($55,360) at the field level. Higher-grade levels in both headquarters and field offices are available based on experience.

To qualify for higher-graded positions, applicants must have additional amounts of either specialized experience or education. The more you know, the further you will go. FDA chemists also are located in Washington, D.C., and facilities across the country.

Pharmacologists

Pharmacologists who work for the FDA review and evaluate the pharmacological and toxicological data contained in new drug applications (NDAs) and investigational new drug applications (INDAs). FDA pharmacologists review the results of preclinical pharmacological and toxicological studies submitted in support of NDAs and INDAs. In addition, they assess the safety of drugs based on toxicity experiments conducted by the investigator. FDA pharmacologists then prepare a summary of data reviewed and submit recommendations and conclusions for approval.

The grade levels at which these positions are most commonly filled are GS-9 ($38,175) through 15 ($91,507) at the headquarters level. Prerequisites for all grades in this position include a degree with a major in pharmacology or in a biological, medical, veterinary, or physical science, including a minimum of thirty semester hours in chemistry and physiology and twelve semester hours in pharmacology. Pharmacologists are located only in the headquarters, not in field offices.

 Question

What sort of lab work does a pharmacologist do?
In the laboratory, a pharmacologist is likely to conduct research on the absorption of chemicals in skin; investigate the effect of antibiotics in normal and diseased animals; investigate the effects of drugs and toxins from the molecular level to the total body response; and develop new methods to evaluate chemicals, drugs, and toxins.

Microbiologists

FDA microbiologists who work in the field perform duties that include the evaluation of the chemical, microbiological, and manufacturing data submitted in new drug applications and preclearance actions for antibiotic drug products. Those who work in the laboratory might conduct research on the development of procedures for isolating and identifying pathogens in foods and studying foodborne bacteria to determine how it grows and survives, in order to destroy it.

Microbiologists conduct research and prepare reports in the areas of bacteriology, virology, parasitology, mycology, serology, tissue culture, hematology, and immunology. They oversee programs related to coordination of the regulation of cytokines that are used in the treatment of AIDS. Grade levels for microbiologists range from GS-9 ($38,175) through 15 ($91,507) at the headquarters level and GS-5 ($25,195) through 11 ($46,189) at the field level.

FDA microbiologists are required to have a degree in microbiology or biology, chemistry, or basic medical science, which must include a minimum of twenty semester hours in microbiology and related subjects geared toward the study of micro-organisms. Applicants must also have twenty semester hours in physical and mathematical sciences, combining coursework in organic chemistry or biochemistry, physics, and college algebra, or their equivalent.

A combination of education and relevant experience may also be accepted. The amount of additional experience or education required will determine your GS level. FDA microbiologists work in the Washington, D.C., headquarters and throughout the field. Job opportunities for microbiologists are likely to be consistently available in the coming years.

Medical Officers

Medical officers at the FDA make sure that all human drugs manufactured for interstate sale are safe and effective, with truthful and informative product labeling. They ensure the safety and effectiveness of vaccines, blood products, certain diagnostic products, and other biological human products. Medical officers also ensure the safety of medical devices and eliminate unnecessary human exposure to manmade radiation from medical and consumer products. The GS grade levels for these positions are GS-14 ($77,793) and 15 ($91,507). Nonsupervisory positions are subject to a peer review of individual accomplishments.

☰ⱻ☰Alert

In order to be hired as a medical officer with the FDA, you must have earned an MD or doctor of osteopathy degree and have graduated from an accredited school in the United States or Canada. Graduates of medical schools in other countries must demonstrate that they hold a degree equivalent to the MD awarded by accredited schools in the United States.

In order to earn the GS-14 salary, the applicant must have four years of residency training in the specialty of the position to be filled or equivalent experience and training. GS-15 candidates must have five years of residency training in the specialty. A residency program involves training in a specialized field of medicine in an institution accredited for training in the specialty by a recognized body of the American Medical Association. Medical officers work in FDA offices located in suburban Washington, D.C., headquarters and in the field.

Chapter 16

The Money Managers

A large proportion of government agencies have responsibility for collecting, printing, and managing money. If you are looking for a job in government and are interested in crunching numbers for a living, this might be the place for you. Perhaps you majored in accounting or finance, or maybe you worked in a bank for a few years. You can put that knowledge and experience to work in a career in government. In this chapter, you will learn about the possible government jobs for a person of your talent and interests.

Internal Revenue Service (IRS)

David Letterman is not the only guy with a top-ten list. The Internal Revenue Service (IRS), the government entity that taxes your hard-earned dollars, also has a top-ten list of reasons why, if you are so inclined, you should work for the agency:

- Enjoy great benefits and job security.
- Have time to spend with your family and friends.
- Work in a diverse and culturally rich environment.
- Be trained by experts in their field.
- Have continuous opportunities to improve your skills.
- Develop the kinds of talents that other top U.S. employers demand.
- Work with the nation's top tax professionals.
- Become independent and accountable.
- Have frequent opportunities to advance your career.
- Be responsible for important work from day one!

Accounting Professionals

IRS accounting professionals have responsibilities that include the design, development, operation, or inspection of accounting systems; keeping up with accounting standards, policies, and requirements; the examination, analysis, and interpretation of accounting data, records or reports; and the provision of accounting or financial-management advice and assistance to management. IRS accountants develop new accounting and financial information systems and maintain and improve established systems.

Business and Finance Professionals

Your business and finance skills can be used in virtually all of the IRS's professional fields. You will receive training from the IRS, and the agency will keep you up to date throughout your career. You can take advantage of training delivered by what the IRS Web site calls "some of the best instructors in and outside of the government." There is also tuition reimbursement should you wish to further your education. You will have the opportunity to advance within the government's largest agencies, which is also one of the largest financial institutions in the world. The IRS is one of the largest employers of professional accountants.

Internal Revenue Agent

You can enter the IRS as an internal revenue agent. From this position, a wealth of training and skills development is available. Many members of the IRS leadership and executive teams began their careers as internal revenue agents. You are eligible for an entry-level position if you are a recent college graduate with at least thirty hours of accounting courses. If you already have professional accounting experience, you can apply for advanced opportunities.

Agents work with customers, businesses, corporate executives, and members of the legal and financial communities. As an entry-level agent, you will learn the latest in computers, telecommunications and data management systems, and gain expertise in tax laws and accounting practices.

Senior Internal Revenue Agent, Large- and Mid-Size Business (LMSB) Division

The large- and mid-size business (LMSB) revenue agent is a professional accountant who examines and audits individual, business, and corporate tax returns to determine correct federal tax liabilities. These specialized agents also conduct examinations relating to compliance with technical requirements imposed by the Internal Revenue Code.

E ssential

You may receive e-mail notification of internal revenue agent openings and all other positions by becoming a registered user at Career-Connector, the agency's online applicant management system (online at ✐*http://jobs.irs.gov/careerconnector.html*). When you register, you will be able to apply online. U.S. citizenship is required for all positions.

At this level, agents are responsible for administering the tax examinations of the largest corporations in America. They work on teams and individually, coordinating examinations of multinational and national corporations and other complex entities. Economists, international examiners, financial products specialists, and engineers assist the LMSB agent in determining the appropriate amount of tax owed. These agents frequently deal with corporations on complex concerns such as tax shelters, mergers and acquisitions, global operations, transfer pricing, and other issues. They deal with the senior levels of corporate tax departments and their representatives.

The LMSB division has a number of important specialists within the tax examination programs, including those described in the following sections.

Financial Products and Transactions Examiners

These agents work with other parts of the IRS to provide examination support. They are responsible for examining, researching, and assessing corporate tax returns in order to determine an appropriate amount of tax as it relates to financial transactions and activities. They interact with corporate taxpayers, their representatives, and other agents regarding many of the most complex financial activities and the resulting tax issues.

Question

What does an international examiner do?

International examiners provide international tax expertise to the corporate tax program. They also work with other parts of the IRS to provide support. They are responsible for examining, researching, and assessing corporate tax returns in order to determine the appropriate amount of tax as it relates to international transactions and activities.

Employment-Tax Specialists

These agents conduct examinations of employment tax returns filed by large and multiconglomerate business firms. The businesses generally have extensive operations and contain several operating subdivisions. The examinations require the agent to have a special ability in accounting and auditing, as well as a highly advanced knowledge of tax law and industry practices. An employment-tax specialist conducts independent examinations and serves as the employment-tax expert on an audit team in the examination of a large case.

Computer-Audit Specialists

These agents provide analyses of complex computerized accounting systems, determining and recommending the most effective method for providing audit data, providing computer analyses of large volumes of data, independently designing applications, and continually searching for creative and innovative ways to use computer-assisted audit techniques.

Internal Revenue Officer

Internal revenue officers are responsible for protecting the interests of the federal government. This entails responsibilities involving the collection of delinquent tax accounts and securing delinquent tax returns. Officers conduct research, interviews, and investigations. IRS training includes classes in tax law, business law, investigative techniques, and enforcement procedures. Internal revenue officers work in IRS field offices across the country. Requirements include excellent communications skills and a bachelor's degree.

Tax-Resolution Representative

Tax-resolution representatives are the IRS's goodwill ambassadors, putting a friendly face on an agency many folks find scary. Representatives provide face-to-face assistance to taxpayers. This assistance includes resolving examination, collection, and account issues related to pre-filing, filing, and post-filing processes. This is a technical position wherein agents provide procedural assistance, tax guidance, and tax-related accounting assistance to taxpayers. Tax-resolution representatives are also involved in compliance-outreach activities, education, and volunteer programs. The skills required include customer-service ability, good communication skills, and knowledge of accounting principles and practices.

Tax Specialist

Tax specialists have a number of key responsibilities. They provide technical tax guidance, tax-related accounting consultation, and other services related to filing processes. They conduct surveys, studies, and focus groups to determine the effectiveness of agency products, services, and communications. They work to influence voluntary compliance. They serve as liaisons at IRS functions involving compliance-outreach activities, education, and volunteer programs. They also provide support to walk-in taxpayers during the filing season.

Tax Examiner

Tax examiners review filed returns for accuracy, and to make sure the filer is taking no more than the allowable deductions. They verify that the Social Security numbers on each tax return are legitimate, and that they belong to the filer. They also make sure the filer has filled out the tax return properly. In general, tax examiners handle the simple returns with few deductions that are filed by most individuals and small businesses. Once they've reviewed the documents, the examiner will then call the filer to discuss any discrepancies. They may also perform some general administrative tasks, such as entering the information from the tax returns into a computer system for processing.

⚡ Alert

The tax specialist position is less "accounting heavy" than some of the other positions you've read about in this chapter. Therefore, it's well suited for business majors who have taken a minimum number of accounting courses. Successful candidates must have six semester hours of accounting and be able to pass an accounting proficiency test.

Administrative/Clerical

These ground-level positions are crucial to the operation of the IRS. Employment opportunities range from file and mail clerks to administrative assistants. These men and women are integral to the smooth functioning of the IRS. There are also openings in IRS Service Centers in field offices across the country and at the agency's headquarters in Washington, D.C. The IRS guarantees "unrivaled growth potential," adding that you can further your education and take on new responsibilities. In addition, if you demonstrate a "willingness to be mobile, you can rise to any level you desire. Additional training is always available. You can also take advantage of our HR Investment Fund that provides monetary support for applicable educational courses."

Qualifications for administrative and clerical openings include a high school diploma or the equivalent, proof of U.S. citizenship, and the ability to pass a work/skills test.

Information Technology (IT)

Most computer-savvy folks already have a head for numbers, and you can put that talent to use for the IRS. The agency has an information technology (IT) environment dealing with some of the most sensitive data in the country. Tracking, organizing, and ensuring the security and confidentiality of that data is paramount. Opportunities exist for telecom specialists, programmers, computer specialists, network administrators, web designers and more. In these positions, IT people can advance while learning valuable skills.

Law Enforcement

Criminal investigation is the law-enforcement branch of the IRS. Its mission is to investigate potential criminal violations of the Internal Revenue Code and related financial crimes. An IRS criminal-investigation special agent combines accounting skills with law-enforcement techniques to investigate financial crimes. Special agents are duly sworn law-enforcement officers. Because of the expertise necessary to conduct these complex financial investigations, IRS special agents are considered the finest financial investigators in the federal government. These gun-toting tax collectors are busier than ever. The government has always been on the lookout for bogus businesses that are merely fronts for money laundering by organized and disorganized crime. Now more than ever they are checking out organizations that may be secretly funding terrorist organizations.

Treasury Department

The U.S. economy is more connected than ever before to the economies of other nations. The secretary of the treasury is the chief financial officer of the federal government. He is the manager of a team of more than 100,000 employees, including those in the U.S. Department of the Treasury. According to the treasury department Web site, online at ✐*www.ustreas.gov,* a career with the treasury means helping people every day and ensuring "the legacy of the world's most open trade regime." Treasury employees help to preserve and maintain the economy and to thwart illegal activities.

Treasury employees receive benefits such as flexible work schedules, health- and fitness-club memberships, emergency child care, and tuition assistance. The mission statement of the treasury is "to promote the conditions for prosperity and stability in the United States and encourage prosperity and stability in the rest of the world."

The U.S. Department of the Treasury is the federal agency that is responsible for the economic and financial prosperity and security of the United States. Its activities include advising the president on economic and financial issues and promoting the president's agenda. In the international realm, the treasury department works with other federal agencies, the governments of other nations, and international financial institutions to promote economic growth, raise the standards of living, and predict and hopefully prevent economic crises.

E Fact

The treasury department was created in 1789 by an act of Congress. The department's first secretary was Alexander Hamilton. In 1814, during the War of 1812, the British burned the treasury building. It was rebuilt by White House architect James Hoban. Twenty years later, American arsonists burned the treasury building again. Portions of the current treasury building date back to 1842.

The treasury department is organized into two major divisions: departmental offices and operating bureaus. The departmental offices are responsible for policy-making and management, while the operating bureaus carry out the specific operations assigned to the department. The operating bureaus comprise 98 percent of the treasury workforce. The basic functions of the treasury include the following:

- Managing federal finances
- Collecting taxes and other money paid to and due to the United States and paying all bills of the United States
- Printing postage stamps and currency
- Managing government accounts
- Supervising national banks
- Advising on domestic and international financial, monetary, economic, trade, and tax policy
- Enforcing federal finance and tax laws
- Investigating and prosecuting tax evaders, counterfeiters, and forgers

The treasury department states that it provides a work environment "that relies on open communication and respect of every individual contribution. By promoting a workplace that is fair and values-based, we hold our employees to the highest standards of trust and accountability so that we can give the American people our best."

Government Accountability Office (GAO)

The Government Accountability Office (GAO) is at the center of government decision-making. The GAO helps Congress make the right decisions by providing legislators with information on policy issues and offers recommendations to improve government operations. The office claims to be "one of the most respected organizations in both the private and public sectors because our program reviews, policy analyses, audits, and investigations are professional, objective, fact-based, non-partisan, and non-ideological."

The GAO's work covers whatever the U.S. government has done, is doing, or is considering doing. Employees investigate issues including national defense, international affairs, education, the environment, health care, transportation, financial management, and information technology. They work with local and state governments, federal agencies, and foreign governments.

Accountability office employees are at the vanguard of congressional oversight, and their work depends on knowledge, analysis, and specialized skills. The entire staff has a voice in all operations and management. The GAO helps its employees balance work and personal lives through flexible work schedules and onsite services. It invests in employees' continuing education through training and mentoring programs, and rewards high-performing individuals through a pay-for-performance system and incentive awards.

E ssential

GAO employees testify before the Congress several hundred times a year. They are cited regularly in the news media and are the second most-referenced organization in the world. The office's recommendations result in hundreds of actions, including landmark legislation, that lead to improvements in government operations.

More than half of the GAO staff has a doctoral or master's degree in areas like public administration, public policy, law, business, computer science, accounting, economics, and the social sciences. The GAO employs more than 3,000 employees from coast to coast, two thirds of whom work at the Washington, D.C., headquarters.

Career opportunities at the GAO include positions for analysts, financial auditors, and various specialists in information technology, economics, and communications analysis. The office also has a student intern program. The GAO also wants you to know that it "is an Equal Employment Opportunity employer, promoting and supporting diversity through recruitment, employee associations and councils, diversity training and events, and outreach programs."

Chapter 17

Other Agencies

You've read about a lot of different options for getting into a career in government, but perhaps you still haven't found what you're looking for. Believe it or not, there are even more government departments and agencies that this book has not yet explored. In this chapter, you will learn about a few of the other agencies in the government that you might find to be interesting places to work.

U.S. Department of Housing and Urban Development

The U.S. Department of Housing and Urban Development (HUD) was established in 1965. It was one component of President Lyndon Johnson's "Great Society" programs, the largest expansion of the federal government since Franklin Roosevelt's New Deal in the 1930s. Three years later, Johnson helped push the Civil Rights Act of 1968 through Congress. As a follow-up to Johnson's Civil Rights Act of 1964, the legislation passed in 1968 focused principally on fair housing for minorities. The Civil Rights Act of 1968 forbids housing discrimination on the basis of race, religion, national origin, sex, disability, or family status. HUD is responsible for enforcing its edicts.

HUD describes its mission as follows: "To increase homeownership, support community development and increase access to affordable housing free from discrimination. To fulfill this mission, HUD will embrace high standards of ethics, management and accountability and forge new partnerships—particularly with faith-based and community organizations—that leverage resources and improve HUD's ability to be effective on the community level."

HUD is involved with the following:

- Community planning and development
- Demonstrations and university programs
- Fair housing
- Health-care facility loans
- Indian programs
- Lead hazard control
- Public housing
- Single-family housing programs

Students, recent graduates, and others who are willing to work for free in exchange for experience can apply for the HUD Intern Program. It was created to find talented people who have the skills that match HUD's employment needs. Through its numerous and varied intern positions, the HUD Intern Program hopes to attract exceptional individuals to myriad occupations within HUD. Interns benefit from professional experience and formal training. There are several kinds of internship programs.

E ssential

HUD jobs can be found at the USAJOBS Web site, online at *www.usa jobs.com*. You can search the site by state, program, or keyword. USA Jobs is a valuable resource for HUD and other federal government jobs. You can also create and post a resume on the site and opt to make your resume searchable by any other agency representatives looking for new employees with your skills.

U.S. Department of the Interior

Talk of creating an interior department for the United States began in 1789, but the department was not actually formed until 1849. When the department was first created, it had a broad range of concerns. It oversaw the construction of the national capital's water system, the colonization of freed slaves in Haiti, exploration of the West, running the District of Columbia jail, regulation of territorial governments, management of hospitals and universities, management of public parks, and the basic responsibilities for Indians, public lands, patents, and pensions. Nowadays, the U.S. Department of the Interior is the nation's main conservation agency.

Fact

The mission statement of the U.S. Department of the Interior is "to protect America's treasures for future generations, provide access to our nation's natural and cultural heritage, offer recreation opportunities, honor our trust responsibilities to American Indians and Alaska Natives and our responsibilities to island communities, conduct scientific research, provide wise stewardship of energy and mineral resources, foster sound use of land and water resources, and conserve and protect fish and wildlife."

The agency has more than 70,600 employees and 200,000 volunteers located at approximately 2,400 operating locations across the United States, Puerto Rico, and U.S. territories.

Land

The interior department manages 504 million acres of surface land. This comprises about one-fifth of the land in the United States, with a breakdown as follows:

- 261.9 million acres which are managed by the Bureau of Land Management
- 96 million acres managed by the Fish and Wildlife Service
- 84.4 million acres managed by the National Park Service
- 8.7 million acres managed by the Bureau of Reclamation
- 55.7 million acres managed by the Bureau of Indian Affairs

More than 190,000 acres of abandoned coal-mining sites have been reclaimed through the Office of Surface Mining's Abandoned Mine Land Program.

Water

The U.S. Department of the Interior also has responsibility for managing numerous water and underwater resources, including 471 dams and 348 reservoirs that provide irrigation water to one out of five farmers and water for more than 31 million people. The Minerals Management Service has jurisdiction over approximately 1.76 billion acres of the Outer Continental Shelf, on which are more than 7,300 active oil and gas leases on 42 million acres.

The U.S. Geological Survey conducts groundwater and surface water studies with offices in all fifty states.

Recreation and Cultural Opportunities

There are more than 68 million visitors to 3,300 recreational sites provided by the Bureau of Land Management, with a departmental breakdown as follows:

- 276 million visits to 388 places, including parks, monuments, seashore sites, battlefields, and other cultural and recreational sites provided by National Park Service
- 39 million visits to 545 wildlife refuges provided by the Fish and Wildlife Service
- 90 million visits to 308 recreation sites provided by the Bureau of Reclamation

Native American Lands and Needs

The U.S. Department of the Interior oversees 55.7 million acres of land belonging to 562 Indian tribes. The Bureau of Indian Affairs (BIA) provides educational services to 47,588 Indian children in 184 schools and dormitories. The BIA serves as a liaison with all of the country's 562 Indian tribes.

U.S. Energy Needs

The U.S. Department of the Interior is in charge of energy projects on the federally managed lands and offshore areas that supply about 30 percent of the nation's energy production, as follows:

- 34.5 percent of the nation's natural gas
- 34.7 percent of the nation's oil
- 43 percent of the nation's coal
- 17 percent of the nation's hydroelectric power supply
- 50 percent of the nation's geothermal energy sources

Scientific Research

U.S. Geological Survey scientists monitor, analyze, interpret, and report findings on earthquakes, volcanoes, and other information pertaining to the geology of the United States. They also assess water quality, stream flows, and ground water at thousands of sites across the nation. They produce more than 55,000 different maps and conduct research on biology, geology, and water.

Benefits

The U.S. Department of the Interior has many benefits that you may or may not find in the private sector. As you have been learning throughout this book, government jobs often make up in benefits and security what they lack in salary. You will get ten paid holidays a year, two-and-a-half weeks of both vacation and sick days, family and medical leave as needed, paid jury duty, bereavement leave, and military duty. You can find out all the details about the interior department at the department's Web site, online at *www.doi.gov*.

You will get the standard health-care benefits for you and your dependents, including medical, dental, and vision insurance. Some sites even have health-care units on the premises. You can choose from several life insurance policies. The department's retirement program is better than the ever-diminishing benefits on the private sector. There are also telecommuting opportunities, child-care facilities at some locations, relocation assistance (in some cases), an employee assistance program (should you or a family member need counseling), tuition assistance, and even a gym at some locations. And how does free parking and a full-service low-cost cafeteria at most locations sound? Not bad.

U.S. Department of Education

The U.S. Department of Education was created in 1980 when several other federal agencies were combined. Its creation was not without controversy. Unlike many nations, the United States does not have a centralized public education system. The maintenance of public schools is left up to states and to individual school systems.

E ssential

You can find jobs with the education department's EdHIRES system, online at *www.ed.gov*. With it you can search for jobs, input your qualifications, or submit your resume. You can also search for education department jobs by visiting *www.usajobs.com* and performing a search by location or keyword.

Many Republicans believed that a U.S. Department of Education was irrelevant. Democrats, on the other hand, believed that a centralized federal education department was necessary to provide assistance to underperforming schools and to be a clearinghouse for scholarships.

The U.S. Department of Education has about 4,500 employees, and its mission is to do the following:

- Establish policies on federal financial aid for education, and distribute as well as monitor those funds.
- Collect data on America's schools and disseminate research.
- Focus national attention on key educational issues.
- Prohibit discrimination and ensure equal access to education.

- Strengthen the federal commitment to assuring access to equal educational opportunities for every individual.
- Supplement and complement the efforts of states, local school systems, and other instrumentalities of the states, the private sector, public and private nonprofit educational research institutions, community-based organizations, parents, and students to improve the quality of education.
- Encourage the increased involvement of the public, parents, and students in federal education programs.
- Promote improvements in the quality and usefulness of education through federally supported research, evaluation, and sharing of information.
- Improve the coordination of federal education programs.
- Improve the management of federal education activities.
- Increase the accountability of federal education programs to the president, the Congress, and the public.

Salaries and Other Benefits

U.S. Department of Education salaries are based on position, level, and geographic location. Entry-level professional salaries range from $22,000 to $27,000 annually. Locality pay is provided to offset the cost of living in many areas. For example, it is more expensive to live in Jersey City, New Jersey, than Des Moines, Iowa.

There are flexible work options available to some employees, such as telecommuting from home. More than 20 percent of education department employees telecommute. Depending on time served, you will be eligible for between thirteen and twenty-six vacation days per year, as well as thirteen days of sick leave. Good health coverage, life insurance, and retirement benefits are available. You can earn extra days off by taking part in volunteer activities such as community, education, and youth programs. You will get time off to attend teaching-related conferences, and you will get a mass transit subsidy of up to $100 a month if you take mass transit to work. There is also a child-care subsidy and tuition reimbursement.

U.S. Environmental Protection Agency

The U.S. Environmental Protection Agency (EPA) was created on December 2, 1970, during the presidency of Richard Nixon. The EPA was created in response to increased concern over environmental pollution. Its mission is "to protect human health and to safeguard the natural environment—air, water, and land—upon which life depends. For more than thirty years, the EPA has been working for a cleaner, healthier environment for the American people."

 **Question**

Besides providing environmental protection, what does the EPA do?
The EPA is involved in everything from regulating auto emissions to cleaning up toxic waste, banning the use of potentially dangerous pesticides, protecting the ozone layer, and increasing recycling efforts. The EPA leads the nation's environmental science, research, education, and assessment efforts.

Federal employment benefits in the EPA are among the best available. The EPA is committed to paying people well and providing progressive incentives and excellent benefits. They are more or less the same as others mentioned in this chapter. For instance, you may carry forward 240 hours (six weeks) of annual leave to the next year. The EPA's method of accumulating vacation and sick leave is a little different. It works as follows:

- Four hours of annual leave (vacation time) per pay period for the first three years of service
- Six hours of annual leave per pay period for three to fifteen years of service
- Eight hours of annual leave per pay period for more than fifteen years of service
- You will earn sick leave at a constant rate regardless of the length of service

- Four hours of sick leave per pay period (regardless of length of service), with all hours carrying forward

There are more than 18,000 employees of the EPA. These men and women protect the nation's natural environment in order to protect people's health and conserve our country's natural wonders for future generations to enjoy. The EPA protects America's resources through regulations, research, and education.

The EPA works with private-sector industries, nonprofit organizations, and state, local, and tribal governments to fulfill its mandate. More than 50 percent of its employees are engineers, scientists, and policy analysts. Others specialize in legal and public affairs or finance and information technology.

There are ten regional offices, each with responsibility for several states and territories. These regional EPA labs focus on research and testing involving environmental impacts, enforcement, and more.

Department of Motor Vehicles

The Department of Motor Vehicles (DMV) is a state-run bureaucracy, so there are fifty of them—one for each state. To find your state's DMV, go online to ✐ *www.dmv.org*. Each state has its own DMV, but the processes and procedures are similar. This section uses the Commonwealth of Virginia to provide an example of a typical DMV. You will find that it is more or less the same as your state's DMV.

As a DMV employee, you will receive the standard perks and benefits that most federal and state jobs offer, including these:

- Flex-time
- Alternative hours
- Competitive pay
- Twelve paid holidays per year
- Health care—medical and dental
- Life insurance
- Short-term and long-term disability
- Vacation and sick leave
- Retirement plan

- Low-cost (or no-cost) parking
- Employee recognition programs
- Work-site wellness opportunities
- Paid training opportunities

The Commonwealth of Virginia's DMV has a customer base of more than 5 million people. Your state will have more or less, but it probably, like Virginia's, offers more face-to-face interaction with the public than any other state agency.

The Commonwealth of Virginia's DMV's mission statement, typical of the other forty-nine, is to "Administer motor vehicle-related laws, advance transportation safety and collect/distribute transportation revenues in a manner that is ethical, security-sensitive and focused on customers and employees."

Chapter 18

Applying for a Government Job

The path to any new job can be strewn with obstacles and hoops that every applicant must jump through. When your path takes you toward a government job, you may find even more hoops and bumps than usual. In this chapter you will learn in more detail what these various tests, screenings, and clearances entail.

USAJOBS

One of the first steps to finding a government job is to log on to USA-JOBS, the automated Web-based recruitment system that allows government job seekers to apply for positions online (*www.usajobs.opm.gov*). You have to apply for a USAJOBS vacancy and wait to be contacted via e-mail, as there are so many applicants vying for a finite number of jobs.

Before you register, you should familiarize yourself with the USAJOBS service and review the FAQ and "How to Apply" sections. When you register, make sure you save your registration information in a safe location. You will be using this information to re-enter the system. If you cannot remember or have lost your registration (user ID, e-mail address or password), do not re-register. Just follow the instructions under the "forgotten password" section.

You will set up your e-mail notification preferences during the registration process, and USAJOBS will notify you of available vacancies based on your preferences.

You should prepare your resume in advance using word-processing software such as Microsoft Word, then copy and paste your resume in the appropriate space during the registration process. You can edit or update your resume at any time. To edit your resume, log in using your ID and password and select the "Edit My Registration Profile" option.

USAJOBS forwards your resume to the appropriate human resources office immediately upon the closing date of the vacancy announcement for which you applied.

You can use the resume check-length button to make sure that you do not exceed the maximum space requirement of 16,000 characters, including spaces. This corresponds to about eight single-spaced pages of text.

During the application process, make sure that you prepare your responses to questions that require long answers using word-processing software in advance. Then copy and paste responses in the appropriate place in the job application. Use the "check length" button to avoid error messages.

Fact

All government jobs open to the public are announced on the Office of Personnel Management's USAJOBS Web site. You can register for e-mail notifications at ✑www.usajobs.com.

It is advisable that you set aside a minimum of forty-five minutes to an hour of uninterrupted time to apply for jobs. Do not wait until the last minute to begin the process. All vacancies close at 11:59 P.M. EST on the closing date of the announcement. If you cannot finish the session, get interrupted, or want to save work you have completed, go to the end of the job application questions and click on "Finish" to save the information you have provided so far. Any questions marked with a red asterisk are required in order to finish. You can return any time and edit your responses as long as the vacancy announcement has not closed. Always select the option to have your application e-mailed back to you when you have finished. Save this copy for confirmation purposes.

The Application

Most government agencies require to you to fill out their official application form, and this is the primary document that is used to determine your qualifications. The application will essentially repeat the information that is on your resume. Some might consider this an example of needless bureaucracy. Nevertheless, the agencies do want both.

E ssential

When applying for a job with the federal government, check to see if you can use a resume or if you can use the Optional Application for Federal Employment—OF 612. If you need the form, you can download it from the Office of Personnel Management Web site at *www. opm.gov/forms.*

You must fill out the application to exact specifications. Of course, the information you supply must be accurate and must stand the test of reference checks and other scrutiny. If the space provided is not sufficient, you will have to add an attachment. In the space allotted, be sure to alert your reader that more material is being provided with a note that reads "See Attached" or "Attachment." Neatness counts, as does legibility. This is the document that will be circulated among the various officials who make the hiring decisions, hence everything must be perfect.

If you're downloading the application from a Web site, print multiple copies. After you've completed your application, print it so you can see how it will look to potential employers. Most likely, you'll feel a need to change some of your answers for clarity. Make changes in pen or pencil on your printed application. Then, go ahead and type up the changes. Print out the new and improved application. Once again, take a look at it. Once you're happy with the final result, you're ready to send it to Uncle Sam.

Background Checks

Certain government jobs will require a thorough background check of prospective candidates. This is not confined to those entering law enforcement or homeland security positions. Do not be surprised if you are asked for a list of references, and fully expect that your references will be contacted for a lengthy interview.

The Field Interview

For the field interview, the interviewer will appear at your reference's home, so choose references who can be relied upon to say the right things about you. When the government interviewer shows up at the door of your reference, he will ask detailed questions about your integrity and trustworthiness. The government official should offer to show proper identification, and your reference would be within her rights to request to see it. Pick people who know you well, especially those who know your skills and abilities. The bottom line is that you need to let your references know they are likely to be contacted. Give them notice, and even let them know what you might like them to say, if you feel comfortable doing so. Most of all, it is important to make sure that your reference is not caught by surprise.

Subject Interviews

You will also be subjected to a comprehensive onsite interview when seeking certain kinds of government jobs. Your interviewer will most likely not be the same person who interviews your references. The questions will be similar. For instance, you're likely to be asked about your family, health, alcohol and drug use, financial affairs, time spent in foreign countries, and other matters that may be applicable. Naturally, you should be honest in all your answers. Rest assured they will be verified, and a lie, large or small, will disqualify you from that and probably any other government job.

The interviewer will be doing more than listening to your answers. He or she will be reading your nonverbal cues, including body language and facial expressions. If you are seeking a job that will involve sensitive and secret matters, you must convey that you are reliable and not a potential security risk. Be honest and forthright at all times, but do not try to be overly familiar. Be friendly but not flippant, relaxed but not sloppy. Show that you view the interview process and the job for which you are applying with the utmost seriousness.

Drug Tests

Drug testing is more and more common in both the private sector, and it is definitely the norm in government jobs, courtesy of Ronald Reagan. In 1986, Reagan made it mandatory for all federal employees to "Just say no." The Drug Free Workplace Act followed in 1988. This made drug tests a requirement for any company that contracted more than $25,000 worth of business with the federal government. Insurance companies got into the act by providing discounts to companies that have a drug-testing policy. The main drug test is called a "five screen" because it tests for these five drugs:

- Cannabinoids (includes marijuana and hashish)
- Cocaine (test detects the metabolite benzoylecognine)
- Opiates (such as heroin, opium, codeine, and morphine)
- Amphetamines (includes amphetamines, methamphetamines, commonly known as speed)
- Phencyclidine (commonly known as PCP or angel dust)

Many drug-testing companies are now offering a "ten screen" that includes these five additional drugs:

- Barbiturates (including phenobarbital, secobarbitol, pentobarbital, butalbital, amobarbital)
- Methaqualone (contained in Quaaludes)
- Benzodiazepines (contained in the tranquilizers Diazepam, Valium, Librium, Ativan, Xanax, Clonopin, Serax, Halcion, Rohypnol)
- Methadone
- Propoxyphene (found in Darvon compounds)

Some legal drugs such as codeine (a prescribed painkiller) will show up in a standard drug test. Other opiate-based painkillers may also show up in your results. You should be candid in advance about any medication you are taking so neither you nor your prospective employer are surprised by a possible positive result.

Included in this list are prescribed painkillers and anti-anxiety drugs. If you are being treated for severe pain or a panic disorder, you will test positive, so you will have to be up front about your medical history.

☰E☰Alert

Be careful what you have for breakfast in the days before your scheduled drug test. A poppy-seed bagel can cause a false positive for heroin! Opium and heroin are derived from the poppy flower. Have bacon and eggs instead. It might not be healthy, but at least it won't affect your drug test.

Even if you are clean and sober you can still fail a drug test, and get what is called a false-positive result. The following over-the-counter drugs can cause this result:

- Ibuprofen (Advil, Motrin)
- Midol
- Nuprin
- Sudafed
- Vicks Nasal Spray
- Neosynephren
- Ephedra and ephedrine-based products (often used in diet products)
- Detromethorphan
- Vicks 44

If you do receive a false positive, you may be asked to take a second test. Some employers do not offer a second test because they are expensive. If you have the money, you can offer to pay for it yourself. Be sure to ask if you can use a different testing company. If the employer refuses to give you another test, even if you have disclosed your prescription and have not used illegal drugs, legal recourse may be your only option.

Security Clearances

The military and intelligence communities deal with information that is highly sensitive. Keeping the secrets is critical to national security, and the ability to have access to this information is reserved for those who are willing to undergo the process of getting what is called a security clearance.

A security clearance investigation is like a background check, only more extensive. It delves deeply into a person's honesty, trustworthiness, reliability, financial responsibility, criminal activity, emotional stability, and other similar and pertinent areas. It also consists of checks of national records and credit checks.

In the military, all classified information is divided into one of three categories:

- **Confidential:** This refers to information or material that, if disclosed, would cause some damage to national security.
- **Secret:** This refers to information or material that, if disclosed, would cause serious damage to national security.
- **Top secret:** This refers to information or material that, if disclosed, would cause severe damage to national security.

There are even levels classified as "above top secret." Anyone who works with and has access to a minimum of confidential information requires a security clearance. Some military positions require clearance even if you never get to sneak a peek at classified material.

If it is determined that you need a security clearance, you have to complete a Security Clearance Background Investigation Questionnaire. Since May 2001, the U.S. Department of Defense has required that this form be completed via a software program called EPSQ (Electronic Personnel Security Questionnaire). When completing the questionnaire for confidential and secret clearances, you have to provide information for the previous five years. For top-secret clearances, you must provide information for the previous ten years. It is important to make sure that you tell the truth because if it is proved that you gave false information, you could go to prison for five years. If you are in the military, false testimony can result in not only five years in the brig (military prison) but also a dishonorable discharge and forfeit of all benefits.

Fact

If you work for the U.S. Department of Defense, the Defense Security Service is the office that is most likely to conduct your security clearance investigation. The Office of Personnel Management conducts security clearance investigations for most other branches of the federal government.

Credit Checks

More and more companies conduct credit checks before employment. If you are informed in advance that it is going to happen, you can refuse to submit to it, but the employer can also decline to hire you. It is unfair, but it is an inescapable reality. The best you can do is try to avoid credit card and student loan debt and monitor and try to improve your credit score. The credit reporting bureaus are each required to provide you with one free credit report every year; go to *www.annualcreditreport.com* to access your free report. There are also other online credit monitoring services that will send you free copy of your credit report, and various services can help you repair and rehabilitate your credit history.

Fair Credit Reporting Act

Under the Fair Credit Reporting Act, an employer must obtain your written authorization before it commences with a background credit check. The authorization must be on a document separate from all other documents such as an employment application. Under federal law, if the employer uses information from the consumer report for an "adverse action—that is, denying the applicant a job, terminating the employee, rescinding a job offer, or denying a promotion"—it must take certain steps. To learn more about employer obligations when it comes to credit reports, visit the Federal Trade Commission's Web site, online at *www.ftc.gov*.

Before the adverse action is taken, the employer must give the applicant a "pre-adverse action disclosure." This includes a copy of the report and an explanation of the consumer's rights under the Fair Credit Reporting Act. After the adverse action is taken, the individual must be given an "adverse action notice." This document must contain the name, address, and phone number of the employment screening company, a statement that the employer made the adverse decision (rather than the screening company), and a notice that the individual has the right to dispute the accuracy or completeness of any of the information in the report.

Background Checks and Your Credit Report

The three major credit-reporting agencies—Experian, Trans-Union, and Equifax—provide a modified version of a credit report called an "employment report." This includes information about your credit-payment history and other credit habits from which current or potential employers might draw conclusions about your character. An employment report provides everything a standard credit report would provide, except your credit score and date of birth.

E ssential

Employers often use your credit history to gauge your level of responsibility. The logic goes that if you are not reliable in handling your credit, you will not be a reliable employee. If you have no credit history, this can also be held against you. The employer is looking for someone who has an established history of responsible money management and bill paying.

The Fair Credit Reporting Act says only that certain things like negative information more than seven years old cannot be considered. The absence of a credit history can also be considered. But if this bit of information means you don't get the job, the employer has to give you an adverse notice decision.

Steps You Can Take

You can take the following steps to reduce the chances that you and/or the potential employer will be surprised by information found in the background credit-check process:

- Order a copy of your credit report ahead of time. If there is something you do not recognize or that you disagree with, dispute the information with the creditor and/or credit bureau before you have to explain it to the interviewer.
- Do your own background check. If you want to see what an employer's background check might uncover, hire a company that specializes in such reports to conduct one for you. That way, you can discover if the databases of information vendors contain erroneous or misleading information. Or, you can use one of the many online search services to find out what an employer would learn if conducting a background check in this way.
- Ask to see a copy of your personnel file from your old job. Even if you do not work there any more, state law might enable you to see your file. You may also want to ask if your former employer has a policy about the release of personnel records.

Always read the fine print carefully. When you sign a job application, you will be asked to sign a consent form if a background check is conducted. Read this statement carefully, and ask questions if the authorization statement is not clear. Unfortunately, job seekers are in an awkward position, since refusing to authorize a background check may jeopardize their chances of getting the job. The only other information this form can include is your authorization and information that identifies you.

Chapter 19

Your Resume and Cover Letter

These days, your resume has to be more outstanding than ever before, but it is the cover letter that makes your first impression. It inspires your reader to examine your resume thoroughly. Because it is your goal to make your cover letter eye-catching and unique, it is inadvisable to simply reiterate the information that appears on your resume. Your cover letter is your chance to shine before you even meet a prospective employer. This chapter examines the relationship between your resume and the letter that covers it.

Preparing Your Resume

These days, most employers prefer that you send your resume via e-mail. That way, employers can use a software program that scans for format and key words. The resume is no longer a list of your work history and education. You now have to be concerned more than ever about formatting, both for ordinary mail and e-mail. You have to be clued in on the current buzzwords, key words, and catch phrases that fit the bill for the jobs you want.

Always customize your resume for each job application. In other words, if you're applying for a position that requires substantial knowledge of certain kinds of computer software, emphasize the software experienced you've had at previous jobs. These days, it's easy to customize your resume. Just make the changes in your document and save it under another name. Save all your various resumes so you can use them as needed in the future.

With your resume, you are selling yourself to an employer. It is the vehicle to get your foot in the door. The door in this case leads to an interview. Your resume is supposed to show that you are a good fit with the company or organization. It should show how you, and you alone, are the perfect candidate for that position.

The average employer—and this is true for government employers as well—will probably only take thirty seconds to scan your resume before making a decision. If your resume does not stand out, it will likely go into the recycling bin. Hence, you need to catch the prospective employer's attention by using key words and phrases. A good resume should have the following qualities:

- An eye-catching and easy-to-read format
- No typos or other errors
- Perfect grammar
- Emphasis on relevant information
- Your resume should fit on one page. If it's longer than two pages, that alone might send it to the recycling bin.

E ssential

Think of your resume as an organic entity. Unlike the old days, when you could just keep a standard resume on file, this document now needs to be tailored for each particular job you're seeking. It should also convey the maximum impact with a minimum number of words. With few exceptions, resumes should not exceed a single page.

Chronological Resume

This type of resume is exactly what it sounds like, a chronological description of your work history. It is organized as a timeline, with your most recent job first and the rest following in descending order. Companies and job titles are emphasized. A chronological resume is best used when you have stayed in the same line of work during your career and when it demonstrates that you have advanced along the way. It is the preferred format to send out when seeking government jobs.

Functional Resume

In this form, your skills and accomplishments take precedence over job titles, names, and dates. This form is often used by people who have time gaps in their work history, have changed jobs often, and/or have had a variety of different careers. People who fear age discrimination also use the functional resume. It is best to use this format if you fall into the following categories:

- You want to stress abilities not used in your most recent job.
- You want to emphasize personal characteristics.
- You are changing careers or re-entering the work force.
- You want to de-emphasize time gaps in your working life.
- You have eclectic and diverse work experience.
- You have been a freelancer or consultant, or you worked at many temp jobs.

Combination Resume

There is also a style called the combination resume. It combines elements of the chronological and functional resumes. It presents accomplishments and skills in a section called "Areas of Effectiveness" or "Qualifications Summary," but it also includes a work history and education summary.

Key Words

Many companies these days do not want to receive a hard copy of your resume initially. You are more likely to be e-mailing than snail mailing your resume these days. You should be aware that a computer software program will be used to scan your resume for keywords and phrases before it is forwarded to a human being.

In writing both your resume and your cover letter, it is important to use active language and as many verbs as possible. Use the job description as your guide. If it lists data analysis as a core job skill, for instance, you should use the verb "analyzed" whenever applicable.

If you need help, here is a list of words and phrases that will catch the attention of either the machine or the human that is perusing your resume:

- Interaction with
- Acted as liaison
- Edited
- Established
- Formulated
- Handled
- Initiated
- Implemented
- Maintained
- Managed
- Promoted to
- Instrumental in
- Recipient of
- Administered
- Assisted with
- Adept at
- Analyzed
- Assessed
- Arranged
- Coordinated
- Conducted
- Counseled
- Delegated
- Directed
- Demonstrated
- Developed
- Advised
- Budgeted
- Consulted
- Delivered
- Drafted
- Evaluated
- Gathered
- Improved
- Installed
- Instructed
- Investigated
- Negotiated
- Organized
- Performed
- Planned
- Presented
- Recommended
- Successful at
- Expertise and demonstrated skills
- Experienced in all facets
- Knowledge of
- Extensive involvement
- Proficient at
- Specialize in
- In charge of
- Familiar with
- Assigned to
- Worked closely with

In the Proper Order

The order in which you place the sections of your resume should vary based on your age and experience. A recent grad should put her education section first, since she has limited experience. A seasoned veteran of the working world will put her education information at the bottom of the page.

The first thing on your resume should be contact information. This is true regardless of what type of resume you submit. After all, you can't be hired if you can't be found. Make sure your contact information is up to date. Your contact information should contain the following: name, address, city, state, zip code, telephone numbers, and—if applicable—fax number.

⚡ Alert

> At one time, it was commonplace and even expected that you would include an objective statement in your resume, such as "My objective is to attain a position that will allow me to use my excellent interpersonal skills." This is no longer standard practice, and it might even send your resume to the bottom of the pile.

If you are a recent graduate, you should put the education section next. Did you graduate with honors? Make sure you note that. Does your degree focus on a particular skill area? Make sure that's clear too. If you have been out of school for a while, then your experience and work history should be very high on your resume. Provide a brief outline of your qualifications that gives the most amount of information in the fewest words. Focus on any special skills you have, awards you have won, or specialized training you have received.

List your current and past positions in reverse chronological order as follows: employer, job title, dates you worked there, and a description of your responsibilities. You should be more thorough in describing the most recent position; less detail is required as you go back in time. This is also the place where you may customize the descriptions to fit the job for which you are applying.

If you have a great deal of experience, you can save the educational information for a space after your work history. First, list your most recent degree, if you have one, or note where you are studying, if you're still in school. This section should be more extensive the less experience you have. If you're a recent grad, list your GPA and any honors, awards, or extracurricular activities that may be relevant to your job search.

Fact

Unfortunately for many job seekers, most companies no longer give out references out of fear of being sued for giving a bad one. However, most companies still ask for references, even though they are unwilling to give them. This is an unfortunate paradox for the applicant. One solution is to ask supervisors or coworkers to give you written references, which you can then supply to prospective employers directly.

The final section of your resume should contain your references. If you have good ones, go ahead and list them. If you don't, just put, "References available upon request." Most likely, Uncle Sam will only want to check your references if you a strong candidate for a particular job. At that point, a good reference can be the final push that gets you in the door.

Cover Your Resume

The cover letter is just as important as your resume. Regardless of how you submit your resume, and regardless of who the intended recipient is, never send your resume without a cover letter. Your cover letter represents you. It tells your readers what you most want them to know about you and your goals. Just like your resume, your cover letter mirrors your knowledge of self and your knowledge of qualification criteria associated with specific positions or functional areas.

Ideally, every cover letter you send will be addressed to a particular person. "To whom it may concern" and "Dear Sir or Madam" are never appropriate salutations. If you don't know the recipient's name, start the letter immediately following address information, or use a memo format. Correspondence style or memo-formatted documents can be faxed, e-mailed, or actually mailed. Know your target readers and write accordingly.

The best cover letters and resumes can stand alone, soliciting and supporting consideration. Readers can look at either independently and have enough information to judge the candidate's worthiness for an interview. But when they're combined, the impact of the two is much greater. Cover letters have a number of potential target readers (some at first electronic, yet all ultimately human), and they can be titled and defined by a few common terms.

The cover letter is almost as important as the resume. It has gained greater importance in recent years as the job market has become more competitive. The letter introduces a prospective employer to who you are as a person. Your letter will let your employer know if you are a people person, a good communicator, and a competent manager, and it will provide visible evidence that you are detail oriented.

 **Question**

Must I always include a cover letter with my resume?
Even if you are told to "just send a resume," what you should hear is "Send a resume and a supplemental document focusing the reader's attention on your desired goals." Thus, you should always send some form of letter. Resumes should, in good taste, never be naked.

In your cover letter, you should state why you are interested in the job you are applying for and how your previous experience relates to the job. Since the resume and cover letter come as a package, you want to make sure your cover letter says something new about you, beside the straightforward education and experience information that's in your resume. The cover letter is your place to highlight the particular achievements and successes that make you the ideal candidate for the job.

Other Types of Correspondence

There are many other kinds of letters you will be called upon to write as you progress through your job-search campaign. When you're looking for a job in the government, you might need to do some networking with existing contacts, or even make some new ones. You might need to write letters of introduction, letters of application, or letters of inquiry to help you along in your job search. The following sections describe some of these types of job-search correspondence.

E ssential

Remember that spelling, grammar, and punctuation are very important, so make sure to have a friend or family member look over your cover letter before you send it out to prospective employers. Even if you think you have caught all errors, a second pair of eyes can be invaluable when it comes to proofreading your job-search materials.

Letters of Introduction

A letter of introduction does just what it says: It introduces you and describes your circumstances to readers. You also clearly identify what you would like the reader to do next and what you will do next. You can seek assistance, specific information, or referrals. Readers are, most often, prospective network members and advocates, or people who can offer answers to specific questions. They are, less often, potential employers from whom you solicit consideration.

Letters of introduction are most effectively used as research and information-gathering tools. They ask readers to conduct information conversations or for referrals to persons, organizations, or Web sites that might be of assistance. Always phrase your requests in ways that require more than "yes" or "no" responses. They should inspire readers to forward names, e-mail addresses, phone numbers, Web sites, or other desired information. In closing, you note whether you will "patiently wait for an e-mail response" or "follow up by phone to discuss your reactions to this request."

Don't ignore the power of a brief cover note, most often an e-mail. Effective communication does not always have to be formal or lengthy. You can first briefly ask for some very specific information, and then follow up with more detailed documentation. In fact, people today may respond better at first to a number of quick e-bites, rather then one lengthy document. While it is always a good idea to attach resumes to any job-search letter, you do not have to do so with these briefer messages. Eventually, through follow-up efforts, you will send resumes to everyone you contact.

Letters of Application

A letter of application is a reactive tool used specifically to apply for a posted position. Within this letter you first state the job title (and number, when given), where you saw the posting, and your desire to interview for the position. Later in the letter, you support your request for consideration by offering an accurate assessment of your qualifications. These two or at most three subsequent paragraphs show readers that you know the field, function, and title in question and that you have thought about what it will take to succeed.

These middle sections are where you share with readers what you learned through qualifications and achievements inventories and goal-focused competencies and capabilities analyses. You are the one required to look back, then look forward, and, most importantly, share your future-focused and confident views. After review of these paragraphs, readers must sense that you are worthy of an interview.

Be prepared to reflect knowledge of the job, and use words contained in the announcement. Show readers that you have more than the minimum qualifications. Refer to "the attached resume," and expand upon the qualification summary. Definitely use phrases from your resume that reflect upon past achievements, with a preference for those that project knowledge of the future. Maintain and share your always-improving target vocabulary in letters of application. Use words from the actual job description and from Web sites and articles written about the department or agency. Through this targeted letter of application, you are applying for a particular job with a specific organization. Give them a clear sense of your focus.

Whenever possible, close letters of application with a statement like "I will call to confirm receipt of this letter and to discuss next steps." You must remember to follow up initial correspondence with phone calls and, if needed, with e-mails, then phone calls again. Do leave voice-mail messages if you don't get through when you call. Don't call too often. Be persistent, but not obnoxious.

Ⓔ Fact

At one time, all resumes were delivered by the postal service. Then FedEx and other express carriers came along. Now electronic transmission is possible and, more important, popular and convenient. As paper folded into envelopes has been replaced by e-mail messages and attachments, the world of resume writing and job search have changed.

Letters of Inquiry

A letter of inquiry is a proactive tool used to inquire regarding current opportunities and, most often, to inspire individualized consideration for future ones. In order to gain consideration, you must reinforce the sense of focus represented in your resume. In fact, the more effective you are at displaying your knowledge of the field, the more likely it is you will get an interview. Show reviewers that you have done your homework about the field, function, and department or agency. A letter of inquiry is your opportunity to state in very clear terms in what field and within what functions you are focusing your search. Ideally, you can cite some commonly used job titles, but they don't have to be specific to any particular organization. Like letters of application, the middle two or at more three paragraphs show readers that you have analyzed what it will take to succeed. You support your request for consideration by offering your summary of qualifications. You should make sure to address queries like the following:

- Why have you chosen the particular field?
- What does your background have to do with the field and the function you wish to serve?
- What are the key qualities required to serve within the desired day-to-day roles?

Answer these questions proactively, and you will have the opportunity to answer other questions reactively, on the phone or in an interview. Use phrases and vocabulary that are specific to your field.

Some letters of inquiry begin with, "I'm contacting you at the suggestion of" a specific person who is serving as an advocate or network member. A name recognizable to the reader at the very beginning of your correspondence should ensure that it will be thoroughly read and, you hope, that an interview will follow. Close all letters of inquiry with "I will call to confirm receipt." You might also wish to copy your contact person to generate some behind-the-scenes supportive communication. Don't hesitate to identify the option of "meeting to discuss current opportunities or informally discussing future options."

Networking Requests

Requests for networking assistance should be clear and concise. Not everyone shares a common definition of this term. With a letter, you can seek "information about your career biography," "advice regarding how to gain consideration within your organization," or "referrals to others who can provide information or consideration." At the pre-research (research before job search) stage, you might focus on the first and third requests. When in job-search mode, you might focus on the second and third.

When communicating with alumni, family, or friends, do not be vague in your requests. If you want the names and e-mail addresses of specific people, ask for them. If you want to know "How do I break into your field?" or whether they will forward the attached resume to the right person, ask. Regardless of your request, be appreciative in tone and in words. Be sure you say thank you. Then say it again, for good measure.

To simplify, "networking" involves clearly stating your goals, then asking for specific help of others to attain these goals. These requests can be of persons you know or of those you would like to know. They can follow or be included in letters of introduction to individuals who are at first just names gained via articles, professional association directories, or search-engine referrals. As with all communications, the impact will come from follow-up efforts.

Follow-Up Letters

Ideally, everyone you contacted would respond promptly and positively. But, sometimes, effective campaigns involve follow-up communication. While patience is a virtue in some circumstances, it is not a characteristic of a strategic job search. Your challenge is to figure out what to say next and when to say it.

Your cover letters will broadcast your intent to call and confirm receipt of your resume. Don't expect much out of this exchange. Very few of these letters will result in any kind of positive response. Most likely, you will leave a message with a receptionist or via voice mail. Do leave voice-mail messages. State your name, identify that you sent a cover letter and resume and that you wish to "confirm receipt and, ideally, set up a phone or in-person interview."

 Fact

> Whenever you make a revision in your resume, you have a good reason to send a brief follow-up letter. Whether you've changed your address, added a new course or seminar, or seen another positing on a Web site, after you've updated your resume, send it accompanied by a cover note. Refer quickly to past contacts, yet focus on what is new and directly relevant on the resume.

You should alternate your communication approaches—phone calls, e-mails, and faxes—and be sensitive to how often you are contacting potential employers. Because most resumes today are e-mailed or faxed, your initial confirmation call can take place within twenty-four hours. The old "I will call within a week" standard closing phrase is most definitely passé. If next-day calls get through, that's great. If they lead to interviews, wonderful. Most likely, they will yield a polite "please be patient." If you talk to an actual person, ask when you should call back. Then follow the suggested timeframe. If you were told next week, don't call before. In general, one contact a week for the first three weeks, then one contact a month after is a good rule of thumb.

You can follow calls with brief telegram style e-mails. A message like the following is appropriate:

"Tried to call today, but could not get through. Understand how busy you are. Just wanted to confirm receipt of resume and cover letter (below). Can we talk by phone or in person? Thank you."

For the first follow-up contact, you can include another copy of the cover letter and resume. For the following two (maximum) follow-up contacts, you can include just a copy of your resume.

Thank-You Letters

Expressing appreciation is a very effective form of job-search communication. Everyone knows to send a thank-you note after interviews, but too few communicate their gratitude before then. A thanks for confirming receipt of your resume, including an expression of continued interest and a clearly expressed wish for telephone or a face-to-face interview, is usually the first of these efforts.

A thanks for clarifying status, including an expression of continued interest, with a statement regarding when you might follow up again, is most likely the second. Too often ignored, a thank you for a rejection letter or e-mail is also appropriate. Respond to a "your background does not match" letter or e-mail with an "I remain very interested in your firm, and ideally we can discuss where my qualifications best fit" statement. Be careful of tone, but do seek continued consideration as well as some additional focus.

Appreciation should always be expressed to network members and advocates who have referred you to postings or persons. By keeping these individuals informed of your efforts you are subtly, or directly, inspiring their own follow-up efforts. Follow-up calls or e-mails by network members to their contacts, requesting "special consideration" often leads to interviews and speeds up an otherwise slow process. In many ways your follow-up networking letters are as important as those to organizations you wish to work for.

Confirmation, Acceptance, and Declining Letters

While it's usually not legally or logistically required, it is a good idea to confirm most activities and decisions in written form. Whether these expressions are transmitted via electronic means, faxed, or mailed is not important. But it is important that you communicate continually and effectively. The growing use of e-mails has made this process quicker, easier, and less awkward for most.

E ssential

Never send only a resume. Always complement this document with a brief or detailed cover page. Clearly identify your desired outcomes. In most cases this would be an interview, but sometimes it is an information conversation or a referral. No matter which, politely make your request and support it with particular entries on your resume.

You must call or e-mail a few days before each interview to confirm the time and date and to assist with your preparation for this important series of conversations. When making decisions regarding offers, you must continue to communicate enthusiastically. After you have made a decision, you will accept or decline via a brief note, either faxed or e-mailed.

These continued communications are good habits to get into, and they set the scene for future positive interactions. Pre-interview contacts facilitate critical next steps, and post-offer communications impact salary and other discussions. In many cases, they can lead to consideration and offers years from now.

Communication, Not Simply Application

If you have ever cracked open a fortune cookie and read "He who hesitates is lost," you probably understand the overly simplistic yet profound importance of continued communication. So-called "application processes" are, by nature, reactive. They inspire you to be passive. When applying to college, to graduate school, for a mortgage, or for an association membership, waiting is appropriate. When applying for employment, communication is more than desired. It is necessary if you want to succeed.

Resumes are the most common symbols of job-search communication. While they may lead most to assume that you are in job-search mode, you use supporting and continued documentation and follow-up communication to confirm your status and provide you and those you contact much-needed focus. Ironically, the most common mistake made by job seekers is overdependence on resumes. No matter how effective your resume is, it must be continually supported by your assertive and appropriate actions, reactions, and continued interactions.

E-Mail Versus Snail Mail

Today, e-mail is the most common and acceptable way to send resumes and all follow-up letters. Alternating the media you use can diminish the potential for over saturation and negative consequences. Fax, phone, express mail, and even "snail mail" can be used. "Snail mail" is the modern phrase used for the slow but sure U.S. Postal Service. At one time the only persons who delivered resumes, cover letters, and all other correspondence were the men and women in red, white, and blue. Today there are wearers of the brown (UPS), blue and orange (FedEx), and others who can guarantee delivery in one or two days. Don't ignore the impact of express delivery on specific individuals, particularly those with whom you have spoken over the phone, but remember that e-communications are now the most cost-effective, immediate, and (security-wise) safe forms of delivery.

You can follow some electronically transmitted letters with hard copies, just to be safe and traditional, but do not depend solely on paper, envelopes, and stamps as your job-search tools. When you do send items by mail, make sure you have the correct postage. Match your resume and cover letter paper, and use large mailing envelopes so you don't have to fold the contents.

E Alert

If you think recipients may be concerned about virus-carrying e-mails, copy and paste your resume straight into the text box. Do not identify it as an attachment. Remember to note the title of job desired and the words "enclosed resume" in the e-mail subject heading.

Phone and Fax

The telephone and fax machine are underused. With the increased popularity of e-mail, fewer people use phone and fax as follow-up tools. You are encouraged to use the phone whenever possible and, in order to place an actual document within someone's hands, the fax as well. While at first awkward for most, you phone skills and confidence will grow with each call. Do call to confirm receipt of documents, to identify next steps, and to make a clear "can I schedule an interview" request. Leave brief, slow, and clear voice-mail messages whenever you call. Don't appear to be a pest, but do be persistent and professional.

After you have left a message or two, fax or e-mail a note. Alternating communication techniques can be effective. Always briefly and clearly state who you are, when and how your earlier contact was made, and what you would like to happen next. Don't be afraid to state "I would like to meet with you," or more assertively, "I would appreciate an interview." Also, ask if they would like another copy of your resume to refresh their memory regarding your background. It is okay to provide one with the first two follow-up letters, particularly those that are faxed.

Chapter 20

Preparing for the Interview

In general, the resume is the key that allows you to get your foot in the door: Your resume should get you the interview, and hopefully the interview will lead to a job offer. At that point the resume has done its job and can be put away in a drawer, right? Wrong—you should also use your resume during the interview. This chapter identifies how to use resumes as both interview preparation and motivation tools.

The Resume and the Interview

Never interview without a copy of your resume in your hand. The interviewer will refer to this document to inspire questions. You can use it to inspire answers as well as attitudes. Read the following statement aloud: "as you can see on my resume." Listen to yourself saying these seven words. Do so with enthusiasm and confidence. This phrase is the verbal and strategic foundation for planning and maintaining interview communications.

E ssential

Your resume is not just for the interviewer. It is a preparation and implementation tool for you. To maximize your interview performance, use your resume before the interview to identify and link qualities and accomplishments to the job you are interviewing for. Use the resume during your interview to guide the conversation and ensure that key points are covered.

Interview preparation begins with a thorough, job-specific review of your resume. With a job title and job description clearly in mind, develop a list of qualification criteria. Highlight the most relevant experiences on your resume. Identify at least three things on your resume that you must discuss in the interview. Select the bullet points from your qualification summary, accomplishments from your experiences, or educational achievements that you must you cover. Your resume should be a psychological security blanket, nurturing confidence and diminishing anxiety, as well as a guide to the key points to cover.

Stress-Free Interviews

You avoid perspiration with preparation. By being prepared, you will skillfully facilitate conversation. Conducting pre-interview preparation builds your confidence, provides focus for communication, and enhances outcomes. Too many candidates spend hour after hour researching historical facts and obscure figures associated with an organization, increasing anxiety via off-target, yet well-intended efforts. These individuals research organizations too much and their own backgrounds and job descriptions too little. They don't review resumes, and they limit qualification criteria analysis to a quick perusal of brief, oversimplified job announcements.

≡E≡ Alert

Call a few days before any interview to confirm your meeting and, whenever possible, arrange an informal conversation with someone who knows about the job you will be interviewing for. Clarify logistics of the day, particularly for callback interviews. Know how many people you will be seeing and what to expect of your visit.

Pre-interview research does not have to be completed covertly, so specifically ask "Is there information I should be reading, or can you provide me with a very detailed job description prior to my interview?" You might also ask, "Are there particular questions I should be thinking about prior to my interviews?" Verify and be curious before, so you can be effective during any interview.

Last-Minute Tips and Strategies

You've spent hours hunting books that might help with resume writing, interviewing, and job search. Yet bookstore employees often hear from frantic customers, "I've got an interview tomorrow. What is the best book for last-minute preparation?" Here are some easy-to-follow guidelines for last-minute prepping.

Call Ahead

Two or three days before your interview, e-mail or call the employer to confirm your meeting and to request a copy of the job description and a company profile. Offer to stop by to pick up the information or ask if it can be e-mailed, faxed, or express mailed. Specifically ask this question: "Are there questions or issues I should focus on to prepare for our meeting?"

Imagine how well you can prepare if you receive a list of potential questions or critical issues to examine. You would be surprised how often interviewers will provide this information when asked. Queries can be made by phone. If you can't get through to the appropriate person(s), leave a voice-mail message, followed quickly by an e-mail or faxed note and then, later in the day, by another a call. If you start a few days before the interview, you have a greater chance of receiving a response.

Specific Research

Conduct an Internet search or visit a reference librarian, seeking information on the government agency and, most importantly, on general current-events articles on the field involved. If possible, enter a few keywords into a general search engine or into search options within the company's Web site. Don't dwell too long on researching the prospective employer. Basic and topical information on the field involved is often much more valuable. You should be able to discuss industry trends, major players, and "what's hot and what's not" within the field. Reference librarians are competent problem solvers. They thrive on the challenge of locating hard-do-find information under the pressure of a pending deadline.

Timing Is Everything

Arrive exactly one-half hour early, check in, and, if you haven't already done so, ask if you can review a copy of the job description as well as literature describing the nature of the organization and significant events of the past year. Sit down in a comfortable area and review your resume and cover letter. It's amazing that most job seekers forget this very simple preparation activity. Think about it. What do interviewers review when determining whom to meet? What do they review immediately before and during the interview? Most definitely, the answer is "your resume and cover letter." Don't forget to review these documents before your interview. Mark critical points or make notes on back. This one-page "personal note sheet" can be very effective. Have extra copies of your resume available in case you meet with someone who doesn't have one.

E ssential

Be prepared to share anecdotes of your achievements. Write down at least three times when you used specific skills to complete a project or achieve success. For each, be able to describe actions that yielded specific outcomes. You may also use the back of your resume to identify key points to make in the interview and to remember questions to ask during the two-way exchange.

Answers and Questions

Ask two questions within the first ten minutes of the interview, and bring copies of your work to show. Questions should be variations on "What are the qualities you are seeking for this position?" and "What specific expectations in terms of output and outcomes do you have for the person who holds this job?" This will allow you to gain a greater understanding of the position and reflect qualifications later in the interview. The more you learn early in the conversation, the better. Remember, an interview is simply a conversation with a purpose. Be enthusiastic, optimistic, and inquisitive.

Putting It All Together

While for some, interviews can yield the appropriate excitement and anticipatory "edge," for others it can manifest in negative ways. Sweaty palms, knotted guts, and beads of sweat are all-too-frequent physical and psychological symptoms on interview day. If you prepare and have the proper attitude, interviews can be fun. When else is it okay to brag and speak about yourself in positive ways for an hour or two? After creating and reviewing your resume, you should be very appropriately egocentric, focusing on you. You're a great candidate, or you would not have been invited to interview. Enjoy the chance to share your pride in your achievements as well as your personal visions of your future.

Your Resume As a Guide for the Interview

As qualification criteria were used to review resumes and identify whom to interview, these same qualities are the yardsticks upon which all interviewers will measure you. To determine your potential to walk the walk to success within a particular job, your interview talk will be heard and then analyzed. Those you interview with will be listening for verbal cues that reveal how strongly you match predetermined criteria. As they listen, they will process what they hear and create an overall impression of your potential to succeed within the specifics of the job.

Always keep in mind that you are interviewing for a job within a specific department, not simply with an organization. Focus your thoughts first and then your statements on roles and responsibilities of the job. Prospective employers have already identified connections between your resume and their desired and required competencies. All you now need to do is reinforce these resume-linked connections while sharing communication as well as personality style.

It is easy to use this process-oriented knowledge. Before each interview, create a list of qualification criteria for the position. What specific criteria would be associated with an ideal candidate for the position you will be interviewing for? Identify the basic qualities sought and how one would determine who possesses these traits. Most importantly, use your resume to create a carefully conceived strategy and list of discussion points.

☀ Alert

Interviews can flow as conversations, but you should figure out ahead of time what key points you want to address. You don't go into academic exams without focusing on specific topics. You don't conduct presentations without some notes or AV tools. Pre-interview resume review activities focus on topics and provide needed visual cues.

Pre-Interview Resume Review

Before each interview, complete the following exercise on the back of a resume. This will organize your thoughts, identify what last-minute information needs to be collected, and clarify what to highlight during the discussion. Using these notes, you will be focusing the interview into a target-specific conversation. Review your notes beforehand, and use them during the interview.

What, When, and Where

Answer the basic questions first. Briefly note the organization and describe the position you will be interviewing for. If you can do it in 100 words or so, you are ready to move on from this exercise. If you cannot, you have some fact-gathering or thinking to do.

If you have not yet reviewed a detailed job description, request a copy and do so. Then summarize what you have read in your own terms. Describe it as if you were speaking to the fifteen-year-old son or daughter of a close friend. In this way you will force yourself to simplify and describe actions and outcomes associated with the job in basic behavioral and functional terms.

Define Qualifications

Second, cite three key points that make you qualified for the position in question. Review your resume's qualification summary section, then identify three of those cited or define "broader connections" that clearly match qualifications for the position you are interviewing for. In general, you are completing the statements "Thinking about this job, specifically, my three key assets are . . ." or "Thinking about the job, the three key points I want to raise in the interview include . . . ." Ideally, these will match some of the phrasing used on the qualification criteria list you have already created for the job. Each of the three bulleted points should be no more than fifty words.

Illustrate Your Abilities

Third, note three anecdotes that illustrate your capabilities to succeed on the job. Stories should support the three key points cited, linking skills used when taking goal-directed actions and, ultimately, to achieve results or finish a project. Start out by very briefly noting the story. Then, identify actions, results, and tasks that were associated with your accomplishments. Last, cite the key skills used and enhanced as a result of each particular experience.

E ssential

While you should definitely prepare for interviews, identifying key points and reviewing typical questions in advance, do not memorize. Have some anecdotes to share. But don't attempt to deliver previously written soliloquies or word-for-word responses. The oxymoronic phrase "planned spontaneity" could best describe the results.

List three questions you would like to ask the interviewer. Ask one question in the first five minutes of the interview and another in the second five minutes so that you can use your interviewer's response in the discussion as it progresses. These initial inquiries should focus on day-to-day job responsibilities and on how performance will be judged. Clarifying and confirming shared expectations early in the conversation will ensure that you raise appropriate issues. Often, the answers you receive inspire immediate re-establishing of key points you wish to discuss later. If three won't do, prepare a list of additional questions to ask during and at the end of the interview session.

By writing all of the above on the back of your resume, you will have used existing printed text to create new supporting documentation. You will have a handwritten focal point containing well-conceived key points, anecdotes, and employer queries.

Two Key Phrases

Interviewers constantly use your resume as a point of reference for forming particular questions. You can and must do the same, by stating things like "as you can see on my resume," or "as my resume illustrates." Refer interviewers to key experiences or education, and use the phrase specifically in advance of anecdotal discussions. Let the interviewer's eyes focus on specific sections, and don't be surprised if they highlight text or take notes while you speak. This key phrase perks interest and invites magnified attention. Use adaptations of the key phrase, or precede it with a simple "again," but do refer to your resume regularly.

In response to questions, do state aloud or allow your internal voice to focus thoughts on the phrase "thinking about the job." Thinking or saying these four words before you make your response will inspire you to connect past achievements and related qualities to "job specific requirements." Find creative ways to restate this phrase. Creatively, you might change it to "thinking about your answers to my questions about the job," or "thinking about the job description as posted on the Net." Or, you might refer to your past answers by stating, "thinking about job-specific issues I addressed earlier." This is a very effective technique.

You will be amazed at how powerful these two simple phrases can be and how using them in various forms can improve your interview skills. At first, practice with role-play interviews. Have someone ask you typical interview questions, and then respond aloud, as you would in an actual interview. This is perhaps the best way to complete final preparation efforts. While the person asking the questions will be playing the role of interviewer, you will remain yourself and answer as you would in a real interview. Be yourself! Don't be the person you think the interviewer wants you to be. Sincerity during the interview will yield honesty-based relationships as well as the personality and capability required for on-the-job success.

⚡ Alert

Don't practice too much, and don't overanalyze and dissect each role-play or actual interview. You don't want to become stiff or appear too rehearsed. Preparation is meant to relax you and provide stimuli for normal interactions.

Common Questions

Interviewers use very special questions and answers to determine whether you have the potential to succeed. Because potential can be very difficult to measure, much of the interview process is subjective. No matter how difficult it is to predict, it is a process that is easy to prepare for. You just have to translate past actions into words and, using an appropriate tone, project confidence as well as your knowledge of self and your knowledge of job-specific qualifications.

Your past actions and accomplishments are cited on your resume. Your ability to connect your past to the future and to your desired goal will be the basis upon which your interview skills will be judged. In fact, a popular interviewing trend these days is called "behavioral interviews." This technique allows interviewers to quantify and objectify a traditionally subjective process. It is based a upon a principle stating that past behavior is the best predictor of future performance. Moreover, more recent behavior is a better predictor of future performance than older behavior, and trends in behavior are better predictors than isolated incidents.

Interviewers present "what did you do when" scenarios or ask you to identify past incidents when you used certain behaviors to reach a goal. Before the interview, a behavioral interviewer determines the behaviors that are desired. Basically, the interviewer arrives with an established checklist for determining if you have the qualities associated with success in a particular job. Be prepared for this, and don't get rattled by any open-ended questions.

 Fact

Note-taking by the interviewer is not unusual, so don't interpret it as negative or positive. Interviewers may seek clarification or contrary evidence of your statements by continually probing, so don't become rattled or express frustration.

No matter the style, whether it's conversational, traditional, or behavioral, a review of common questions is extremely helpful. Attempting to memorize answers can do more harm than good, so please use the list to stimulate thoughts and inspire you to share ideas effectively during interviews. You might ask a friend, family member, or peer to select five and ask them aloud, initiating a role-play interview. Hearing the questions as well as your answers, rather than just thinking about responses, is valuable.

Traditional Interview Questions

Conduct a practice session, having a friend or family member ask you these questions. Remember, there are no right answers to particular questions. Responses during an interview must seem well conceived, yet spontaneous. Think of this interaction as a conversation, not an inquisition. It is best to complete this exercise aloud, even if you are doing so alone. To maximize your use of this list, after you review the general as well as behavioral queries, identify a "top five" list of questions that related to a specific job matching your goals:

- Why are you interested in this particular field of employment?
- What academic or career achievements are you most proud of?
- Why did you choose your major, and how does it relate to your goals?
- What classes did you find most stimulating, and did they nurture job-connected skills?
- What would you like to be doing in five years?
- What are your greatest strengths and weaknesses?
- How would you describe yourself, and how would others describe you?
- How would you characterize career-related success?
- What are your three most significant employment or school-related achievements?
- When did you use persuasive skills or sales talents?
- Why should we hire you?
- What are your long-term career goals?
- How have your academic experiences to date prepared you for a career, and what are your future academic goals?
- What would you do differently with regard to academic or career experiences?
- What was your most difficult decision to date, and how did you go about making it?
- Why did you attend your alma mater?
- What do you think it takes to succeed in the job you are being interviewed for?
- What lessons have you learned from your "failures" or "mistakes"?
- What are your geographic preferences, and are you willing to relocate?
- What concerns do you have with regard to this job and our organization?
- How would you describe this opportunity to friends and family members?
- What additional information do you need to determine if this is the "right" opportunity for you?
- What motivated you to first contact us?

Behavioral Interview Questions

Behavioral questions, and those that might be used during what some might call a traditional interview, include the following:

- Describe when you faced problems at work that tested your coping skills. What did you do?
- Give an example of a time when you could not participate in a discussion or could not finish a task because you did not have enough information.
- Give an example of a time when you had to be relatively quick in coming to a decision.
- Tell me about when you used communication skills in order to get an important point across.
- Tell me about a job experience when you had to speak up and tell others what you thought or felt.
- Give me an example of when you felt you were able to motivate coworkers or subordinates.
- Tell me about an occasion when you conformed to a policy even though you did not agree with it.
- Describe a situation in which it was necessary to be very attentive and vigilant to your environment.
- Give me an example of a time when you used your fact-finding skills to gain information needed to solve a problem; then tell me how you analyzed the information and came to a decision.
- Tell me about an important goal you've set and tell me about your progress toward reaching this goal.
- Describe the most significant written document, report, or presentation you've completed.
- Give me an example of a time when you had to go "above and beyond" to get a job done.
- Give me an example of a time when you were able to communicate successfully with another person, even when the individual may not have personally liked you.

- Describe a situation in which you were able to read another person effectively and guide your actions by your understanding of his/her individual needs or values.
- Specifically, what did you do in your last job in order to plan effectively and stay organized?
- Describe the most creative work-related project you have completed.
- Give me an example of a time when you had to analyze another person or a situation in order to be effective in guiding your action or decision.
- What did you do in your last job to contribute toward a teamwork environment? Be specific.
- Give an example of a problem you faced on the job and how you solved it.
- Describe a situation when you positively influenced the actions of others in a desired direction.
- Tell me about a situation in the past year when you dealt with a very upset customer or coworker.
- Describe a situation in which others within your organization depended on you.
- Describe your most recent group effort.
- Describe the most challenging person you've interacted with and how you dealt with him or her.

Questions You Can Ask Potential Employers

Questions you might ask potential employers during an employment interview or during a pre-interview information conversation include the following:

- How would you describe the job in terms of day-to-day roles and responsibilities?
- What qualities are you seeking in a candidate?
- What type of person would most likely succeed in these roles?
- What advice would you give someone who would seek to achieve success as quickly as possible?

- What should I expect of myself over the first few months on the job?
- How will my performance be judged, and by whom?
- Whom should I use as a role model for this position and would it be appropriate to contact this person?
- What characteristics does it take to succeed within this organization and within this position?
- What are the best things about the job and the most challenging requirements of the position?
- Who would have the highest expectations of me, or be the one(s) who would be most difficult to impress?
- What is the typical career path and time frame associated with career development?
- How will I be trained, and how can I appropriately seek skills enhancement?
- Who last served in this position, and what is he/she doing now?
- What goals do you have for the person who will serve in this job?
- What project would you expect to be completed first, and what would be involved?

Conversations, Not Cross-Examinations

Each interviewer has a personal style, but most interviews can be identified using a few common labels. Many interviews will be conversational or "traditional," in which interviewers chat with candidates and ask fairly typical interview questions. Some are behavioral, in which interviewers ask about past achievements, seek details regarding behaviors (and skills) that contributed to these undertakings, and ask candidates "what would you do in this situation" questions. Occasionally, particularly for consulting firms, interviews are case studies, in which interviewers ask candidates to analyze specific situational cases and problems; revealing how candidates "think on their seats" in response to specific analysis-driven cases.

No matter the label used, resumes are tools for you to use during any interview. Interviewers review these documents during your conversation with a particular purpose, so you should do so too. Bring the resume with you to the interview. To prepare, review typical questions. Identify three key points and three anecdotes associated with academic and experiential achievements. Don't memorize the answers to any questions, but be prepared to expand upon the key points and anecdotes you identified as illustrating qualifications. Bring a resume with you to every interview.

≈ E ≈ Alert

Remember, interviews are not simply a series of questions and answers. They are conversations with a common purpose for you and the interviewer. During the exchange, the more verbally inspired images of success that are sent and received, the more likely an offer will be made.

Don't be shy! Talk about your achievements with pride. Interviewers have limited time to get to know the real you. Don't think there are right answers. When asked a technical question, if you don't know the exact answer, talk the interviewer through how you would find the correct information. Don't wait to do so, but always ask questions when invited.

Don't overanalyze or dissect your performance after each interview. Decision-making is very subjective. The process changes from initial screening through call-back stages and, ultimately, through selection interviews. If your style and strategies remain sincere, no matter the interviewer's style, technique, or temperament, you will find a good fit. If you don't receive an offer, never stop to ask why. Instead you should, via follow-up contacts, seek "consideration for the next available similar opportunity." Remain confident and enthusiastic. More often than you think, you can transform someone who rejected you into a strong advocate and network member who might interview you again very soon.

Ultimately, you will communicate motivations and, most importantly, qualifications successfully via phone and in-person interviews. Have confidence in your abilities to project qualifications and capabilities. Always check in advance regarding how many people you will be interviewing with and how long the entire process might take. Specifically ask, "Are there any materials you recommend I read prior to my interview?"

What to Wear to the Interview

Make sure to inquire about the appropriate mode of dress. Some situations and organizations go "business casual," when neatly pressed slacks and an ironed shirt and a tie (with sport coat optional) would be appropriate for men, and slacks or skirt, ironed shirt, or sweater would be appropriate for women. Others are "business formal," when suits, ironed shirts, polished shoes and ties are a must for men, and suits are required for women.

What was once known as casual Friday, has become "confusing Monday-through-Friday" for contemporary candidates. Old-fashioned rules regarding power suits, colors, and ties may not seem to apply today. But because what you wear may impact what you say, and how others perceive your professionalism, in truth, they still do. Your interview image, revealed by your attire, is a projection of common sense rather than fashion sense. As with the font you choose for your resume, it's always recommended that you remain conservative and traditional with the clothing you select for interview days.

E ssential

Bring extra resumes with you in case you unexpectedly meet additional interviewers. You might also wish to bring supporting materials to serve as illustrations of your work. Some fields, specifically publishing, public relations, and journalism, require writing samples or portfolios. Be ready to detail what samples you have included and why they demonstrate specific talents.

Ties can be loosened, jackets removed, and sleeves can be rolled up. It's easy to transform business formal into something more casual, but the opposite is not possible. Unless specifically told otherwise, and the circumstances of the interview confirm that casual is the only appropriate attire, dress more formally. Suits are always appropriate and required for banking, financial services, consulting, and conservative fields. For other settings, blue blazers, gray or khaki slacks or skirts, crisply ironed shirts, and appropriate neckwear may seem like prep school uniforms, but these basics are always good bets for interviews.

Chapter 21

Testing One, Two, Three

You have perused the pages of this book and now have an idea about what kind of government job would be most appropriate and interesting for you. You know how to write an effective cover letter and how to tailor your resume to catch the eye of your prospective employer. You're ready to ace that interview! Now on to the next step. It's time to go back to the classroom to take a test.

Civil Service Tests

As you have learned throughout this book, government jobs exist at the federal, state, county, city, and local level. In many cases, part of the application process is sitting for a written test. There are also other tests, depending on the kind of job. Notification about the results of civil service tests is posted in a variety of places. There is an opening date and a closing date for applications to take the test, and you have to file within that time frame. There is often a nonrefundable fee to take the test.

Job bulletins or announcements are posted at government offices, sometimes published in newspapers, and almost always posted on the Internet. For local government jobs, you may often find posters in local stores. For example, announcements for upcoming New York City police and fire department tests are advertised on city buses and subways. And New York City has a weekly newspaper called *The Chief* that prints nothing but civil service tests listings.

You should call the government agencies in your area. You can find many of these agencies in the telephone book and on the Internet. If you find a job opportunity, and the agency is not taking applications at this time, you can ask to be notified when applications will be taken by filling out a request. Many agencies provide e-mail notification.

Every state has its own Web site of civil service job listings. Use the Internet to find the one for your state. For an example, here is the site for the state of Louisiana. It is typical of the other forty-nine: *www.dscs.state.la.us/examining/info/civilservicetests.htm.*

Government jobs are listed as either "open," "promotional," or "exempt." Open jobs are open to non-civil service employees. Promotional jobs are opportunities for civil service employees within the agency announcing the job. Exempt positions are exempt from civil service protection. These positions are usually for limited, part-time positions or for executive positions where the jobholder serves at the discretion of a top executive, council, or board. However, almost all government jobs are filled by establishing a list of eligible candidates through an examination.

 Fact

There is no single database that includes all federal, state and local government job openings. In addition to *USAJOBS.com*, you can also find listings of federal jobs and civil service test guides online at *www.pse-net.com/joblistings/joblistingFederalJobs.htm.*

Different kinds of tests are given for different types of jobs. An examination may consist of more than one test. Different types of civil service tests include written tests, in-basket exercises, essay tests, performance tests, tests that assess physical abilities, psychological tests, and interviews. The test date and location will be provided by the agency after your application has been submitted.

Eligibility lists are established by ranking candidates based on their overall scores in the examination. Candidates must be successful on each test of the examination. Lists are effective for a given period, as determined by each agency. When the period expires, a new examination is given. If you are not hired during the life of the list, you must take the examination again to qualify for a job.

Vacancies are usually filled through a selection from among the highest scores on the eligible list. If you are selected from the list you will be notified about appearing for an interview. You must not only do well on the examination but also on all subsequent interviews to receive a job offer. Candidates who score high on the test but are not selected to proceed with the next hiring phase usually remain on the employment list and will be evaluated for other vacancies as they occur.

E ssential

You're probably familiar with most of the tests that you will encounter, but you may not have heard of an "in-basket exercise." These tests simulate the conditions of the job for which you're applying. You're given enough information to make decisions and then assessed on your ability to deal with simulated daily tasks and emergencies.

Depending on the position, agencies may also require a medical examination, drug screening, and a probationary period. Probationary periods are usually six to twelve months.

There are several types of tests that you may encounter:

- Multiple choice test: In these tests, you choose the single best answer or choose the most likely and least likely answers.
- Assessment center, essay, and in-basket: These tests are used for professional and executive jobs such as administrative and management positions. Law-enforcement promotional exams may also use assessment centers. The assessment center simulates the typical duties of a position. The in-basket tests your ability to handle typical assignments that might cross the desk of the position for which you are applying.
- Performance test: This test is usually used for skilled craft jobs. It requires you to demonstrate your skills in one or more physical tasks that the job entails.

- Physical ability test: These are required for public-safety positions such as law enforcement and firefighting.
- Psychological test: These tests are also required for public-safety positions such as law enforcement and firefighting to determine if you can maintain good judgment in high pressure/stressful situations.

You also will be interviewed at least once. The interview might count as a part of the exam score. You will also be interviewed again if you score high in the test and are called in. You can score high on a written test, but if you do poorly in either a scored interview or the interview for the job offer, you will not be offered the job.

Study Techniques

First of all, you should pick up a study guide. Just as you can find test prep books for the SAT, GRE, LSAT, and MCAT, it's easy to find test prep books for civil service exams. Check out your local bookstore or search the Internet. There are many study guides available online for free. If you do not find an exact match, you are likely to find a test guide for a similar position.

 Fact

You can find a comprehensive list of civil service test guides at: *www.911hotjobs.com/bookstore/civilservicebooks.htm*. Review the free sample tests from various agencies. Be aware that the sample tests online are not as comprehensive as the study guides you can buy.

There are many ways to prepare for a test. A key element is to minimize your stress and anxiety level. Stress can do you in even if you have a firm grasp of the material. Here are a few ways to reduce stress before an exam:

- Create a quiet, neat study area. Distractions and clutter interfere with studying. Select a quiet spot where you are unlikely to be interrupted, and organize it so that you can study efficiently. If space is cramped at home, use a corner of the local library or other suitable spots.
- Study from good notes. Your study sessions will be productive only if you are studying from a legible and complete set of notes. If your notes are incomplete, see if your teacher has a loaner set of master class notes that you can review to get the missing information. Or ask a classmate who takes thorough notes if you can borrow them.
- Take advantage of your peak energy levels. Pick the time of day when you tend to have the most energy and try to schedule your study sessions at this time. Also, study your most difficult or challenging material first, while you are still fresh. When you study at the same time each day, you will also find that studying begins to turn into a habit!
- Create a study group. Gather together classmates to form a study group. Groups can make studying more fun. Another advantage of groups is that its members can consult multiple sets of notes whenever a course concept is unclear.
- Recite information aloud. One study trick is to recite important information aloud. As you say the information, you also hear yourself saying it. Using both speaking and hearing will help to embed the information in your memory.
- Avoid cramming. Pulling all-night study sessions only tires you out and leaves you exhausted on the day of the test. Break your study up into short periods and study more frequently. Also, start studying early in the course, well before the first test, to give yourself a head start in learning the material.
- Get plenty of rest the night before.
- Minimize or eliminate caffeine, tobacco, alcohol, and other stimulants and depressants.
- Reward yourself. Select an activity that you enjoy. Promise yourself to complete a set amount of studying. If you have

met your short-term study goal at the end of the study period, give yourself the reward.

- Engage in positive self-talk. Replace irrational negative thinking with positive self-talk. Adopt an upbeat but realistic attitude.

You may also want to engage in moderate physical activity or exercise prior to taking the test to reduce body tension. A student who gets a full night's sleep, goes for a jog, and eats a balanced breakfast prior to the test will improve the odds of doing his best on an examination.

Here are some relaxation exercises to help you handle test anxiety:

- Tense and hold muscles throughout body for ten seconds. Relax and repeat.
- Take a deep breath and hold it for ten seconds. Breathe through your nose and exhale through your mouth. Repeat.
- Take a deep breath, hold for ten seconds, and squeeze both hands into tight fists at the same time. Exhale and relax. Repeat.
- Tense the muscles in your feet for ten seconds. Relax and repeat.
- Repeat positive affirmations to yourself. Corny as this may sound, it works.

Stretching and breathing exercises are excellent ways to reduce stress. These simple little activities do not take much time or effort yet can do wonders for your performance at exam time.

Before the Test

On test day, you are understandably a little nervous. You really want this job and want to score well on the test. There are a few basic things you can to do help things go smoothly.

Allow extra time to find the testing site or to counter potential delays due to traffic, parking problems, or bad weather. Give yourself at least an extra half hour to get to the testing site. You want to arrive on time and in a calm state of mind. The wheels of bureaucracy grind slowly, but they have no pity. If you arrive late at the testing site, you may not be permitted to take the test.

When seated, listen carefully to all testing instructions. The more information you have about the examination process, the more confident you will feel. Listen carefully for instructions on how to fill in your answer sheet. If you fill in information incorrectly, the computer will not read your form correctly, and this may render your test invalid. If you do not follow the directions precisely, the computer may have difficulty reading your answers.

E ssential

Check the Internet for the latest news in your profession. You can use the Web site ✍www.job-interview.net. The free mock interviews include civil service jobs. You can match the key duties and key skills that you have to possible interview questions.

Pay heed to instructions about how much time you will be given to complete the examination and what to do when you are finished. Ask the proctor any questions about the exam. He or she is there to help to you.

Strategies for Success

Always bring more than one sharpened No. 2 pencil to the test site. Answer the easy questions first, then go back to the more difficult ones. If possible, try to save some time at the end of the examination to review your answers to the hard questions and to check your answer sheet to be sure you have not missed any questions.

Become familiar with the test that you are about to take, and have a mental plan for how you will spend your time most productively during the examination. If you follow a positive plan of action as you take the test, you will be less likely to feel helpless or to be preoccupied with anxious thoughts.

At the Starting Line

Listen carefully to directions. Make a point to listen closely to any test directions that are read aloud. Read through written directions at least twice before starting on a test section to ensure that you do not misinterpret them. If you are confused or unsure of the test directions, ask the teacher or test proctor to explain or clarify them. It is better to seek help to clear up any confusion that you may have than to run the risk of misunderstanding the directions and completing test items incorrectly.

Perform a "brain dump." At the start of the test, write down on a sheet of scrap paper any facts or key information that you are afraid you might forget. This "brain dump" will help you to feel less anxious about forgetting important content. Plus, you can consult this sheet of information as a convenient reference during the test.

Preview the test. Look over the sections of the test. Think about the total amount of time that you have to complete the test. Look at the point values that you can earn on each section of the examination. Budget your total time wisely so that you don't spend too much time on test sections that contribute few points to your score.

Multiple-Choice Questions

Don't get sidetracked looking for patterns of answers. Some people claim that students can do better on multiple-choice tests if they look for patterns in the answers. Most likely, there are no patterns, and looking for them will be counterproductive.

Remember not to rush. On multiple-choice items, force yourself to read each possible choice carefully before selecting an answer. Remember, some choices appear correct at first glance but turn out to be wrong when you take a closer look.

Essay Questions

Underline key terms. Before writing your essay, it is a good idea to underline important terms that appear in the test question as a check on your understanding. Words such as "compare," "contrast," "discuss," and "summarize" will give you clear direction on the form that your essay should take and the content that it should include.

Outline your answer before you write it. No teacher wants to read a rambling essay that fails to answer the test question. You can improve the quality of your essay by first organizing your thoughts into a brief outline on scrap paper before you write it. Even a few short minutes of planning time can significantly improve the readability and organization of your essays.

Nearing the Finish Line

Skip difficult items until last. On timed tests, you should avoid getting bogged down on difficult items that can cause you to use up all of your time. Instead, when you find yourself stumped on a tough test item, skip it and go on to other problems. After you have finished all of the easiest test items, you can return to any skipped questions and try to answer them.

If you finish a test early, use the remaining time to check your answers. On multiple choice items, check to see that you answered all questions. Reread each written response to make sure that it makes sense, uses correct grammar, and fully answers the question.

Web Sites and Contact Information

Many local governments, including states, counties, and cities, have their own Web sites on which they list job openings, along with other information. There are also several Web sites dedicated to local government employment.

General Government Job Web Sites

USAJOBS

This is the official job search Web site of the United States government. All vacancies in every federal government agency are listed here. You can do a basic search by keyword, job category, and location. You can also search for jobs within specific agencies or by Occupational Series (all federal jobs are assigned a series number). Additionally, you can specify a salary range when you search for a job. To create an online resume you must become a My USAJOBS member. Membership also allows you to apply for jobs online. As you can with the other job-search sites, you can create automated job alerts.

✎ *www.usajobs.com*

GovtJobs.com

At this site you can search through job categories, or you can use the search box to specify a job title. Use it to find jobs with local governments, including states, counties, cities, and towns.

✎ *www.govtjobs.com*

Careers In Government
At this site, you can search for jobs by selecting a job category, organization type, location, and salary.

✍ *www.careersingovernment.com*

U.S. Department of Labor
Bureau of Labor Statistics
Occupational Outlook Handbook
This web site provides a listing of the job requirements, salary, and employment outlook for hundreds of jobs, along with job search tips and information on the job market in each state.

✍ *www.bls.gov/oco*

Federal Government Agency Contact Information

Drug Enforcement Administration
2401 Jefferson Davis Highway
Alexandria, VA 22301
(800) 332-4288

Federal Communications Commission
445 12th Street, SW
Washington, D.C. 20554
(888) 225-5322
✍ *www.fcc.gov*

Government Accountability Office
441 G Street, NW
Washington, D.C. 20548
(202) 512-3000
✍ *www.gao.gov*

Internal Revenue Service
1111 Constitution Avenue, NW
Washington, D.C. 20224
(800) 829-1040
✍ *www.irs.gov*

National Aeronautics and Space Administration
Suite 1M32
Washington, D.C. 20546-0001
(202) 358-0001
✍ *www.nasa.gov*

The Nature Conservancy
4245 North Fairfax Drive,
Suite 100
Arlington, VA 22203-1606
(703) 841-5300
✐ *www.nature.org*

Security and Exchange Commission
100 F Street, NE
Washington, D.C. 20549
(202) 551-6551
✐ *www.sec.gov*

Social Security Administration
Windsor Park Building
6401 Security Boulevard
Baltimore, MD 21235
(800) 772-1213
✐ *www.ssa.gov*

U.S. Department of Agriculture
1400 Independence Avenue, SW
Washington, D.C. 20250
(202) 264-8600
✐ *www.usda.gov*

U.S. Department of Commerce
1401 Constitution Avenue, NW
Washington, D.C. 20230
(202) 482-2000
✐ *www.commerce.gov*

U.S. Department of Education
400 Maryland Avenue, SW
Washington, D.C. 20202
(800) 437-0833
✐ *www.ed.gov*

U.S. Department of Energy
1000 Independence Avenue, SW
Washington, D.C. 20585
(800) 344-5363
✐ *www.energy.gov*

*U.S. Department of Health and
Human Services*
200 Independence Avenue, SW
Washington, D.C. 20201
(202) 619-0257
✐ *www.hhs.gov*

*U.S. Department of Homeland
Security*
Washington, D.C. 20528
(202) 282-8000
✐ *www.dhs.gov/dhspublic*

*U.S. Department of Housing and
Urban Development*
451 7th Street, SW
Washington, D.C. 20410
(202) 708-1112
✐ *www.hud.gov*

U.S. Department of the Interior
1849 C Street, NW
Washington, D.C. 20240
(202) 208-3100
✐ *www.doi.gov*

U.S. Department of Justice
950 Pennsylvania Avenue, NW
Washington, D.C. 20530-0001
(202) 514-2000
✐ *www.usdoj.gov*

U.S. Department of Labor
2 Massachusetts Avenue, NW
Washington, D.C. 20001
(202) 216-9058
✑ *www.dol.gov*

U.S. Department of State
2201 C Street, NW
Washington, D.C. 20520
(202) 647-4000
✑ *www.state.gov*

U.S. Department of Transportation
2100 2nd Street, SW
Washington, D.C. 20593
(202) 646-5095
✑ *www.dot.gov*

U.S. Department of the Treasury
1500 Pennsylvania Avenue, NW
Washington, D.C. 20220
(202) 622-2000
✑ *www.ustreas.gov*

U.S. Environmental Protection Agency
Ariel Rios Building
1200 Pennsylvania Avenue, NW
Washington, D.C. 20460
(202) 564-0300
✑ *www.epa.gov*

U.S. Food and Drug Administration
5600 Fishers Lane
Rockville, MD 20857-0001
(888) 463-6332
✑ *www.fda.gov*

United States Postal Service
Office of Personnel
Management
P.O. Box 961
Washington, D.C. 20044-0961
(800) 275-8777
✑ *www.usps.com*

Human Resources Departments: A State by State Guide

State of Alabama Personnel Department
300 Folsom Administrative Building
64 North Union Street
Montgomery, AL 36130-4100
(334) 242-3389
✑ *www.alabama.gov*

Alaska Department of Administration, Division of Personnel
P.O. Box 110201
Juneau, AK 99811-0201
(907) 465-4095
✑ *www.jobs.state.ak.us*

Arizona Human Resources
(602) 417-4678
✍ https://secure.azstatejobs
.gov

California State Personnel Board
801 Capitol Mall
Sacramento, CA 95814
(916) 653-1705
✍ www.spb.ca.gov

Colorado Department of Personnel
and Administration
633 17th Street, Suite 1600
Denver, CO 80202
(303) 866-3000
✍ www.colorado.gov

State of Connecticut Department of
Administrative Services
165 Capitol Avenue
Hartford, CT 016106
(860) 713-5115
✍ www.das.state.ct.us

Delaware Human Resource
Management
Carvel State Office Building
820 N. French Street
Wilmington, DE 19801
(302) 577-8977
✍ www.delawarepersonnel
.com

Florida: People First!
✍ https://peoplefirst.myflorida
.com

Georgia Department of Labor
✍ www.dol.state.ga.us

Hawaii Department of Resources
Development
✍ www.hawaii.gov

Idaho Division of Human Resources
P.O. Box 83720
Boise, ID 83720-0066
(208) 334-2263
✍ www.dhr.idaho.gov

State of Illinois Job Opportunities
✍ www.illinois.gov

Indiana State Personnel Department
✍ www.in.gov

Iowa Department of Administrative
Services
Hoover State Office Building
1305 E. Walnut Street
Des Moines, IA 50319
(515) 281-3087
✍ http://das.hre.iowa.gov

Kansas Civil Service Jobs
(785) 296-4278
✍ http://da.state.ks.us

Kentucky Personnel Cabinet
200 Fair Oaks Lane, Fifth Floor
Frankfort, KY 40601
(502) 564-8030
✎ *http://personnel.ky.gov*

*Louisiana Department of State Civil
Service*
1201 North Third Street, Suite
3-280
Baton Rouge, LA 70802
✎ *www.dscs.state.la.us*

Maine Bureau of Human Resources
#4 State House Station
Augusta, ME 04333-0004
(207) 624-7761
✎ *www.maine.gov/statejobs/*

*Maryland Department of Budget and
Management*
45 Calvert Street
Annapolis, MD 21401
(800) 705-3493
✎ *www.dbm.maryland.gov*

*Massachusetts Human Resources
Division*
Commonwealth Employment
Opportunities (CEO)
✎ *http://ceo.hrd.state.ma.us*

State of Michigan (click on job links)
✎ *www.michigan.gov*

*Minnesota Department of Human
Relations*
(651) 296-2616
✎ *www.doer.state.mn.us/
employment.htm*

*State of Mississippi (click on job
links)*
✎ *www.mississippi.gov*

Missouri Office of Administration
Harry S. Truman Building
301 West High Street, Room 760
Jefferson City, MO 65101
(573) 751-0929
✎ *www.oa.mo.gov*

*State of Montana Employment
Information*
✎ *http://mt.gov/statejobs/state
jobs.asp*

State of Nebraska State Personnel
(404) 471-2075
✎ *www.das.state.ne.us*

Nevada Department of Personnel
555 East Washington Avenue,
Suite 1400
Las Vegas, NV 89101-1046
(702) 486-2900
✎ *http://dop.nv.gov*

New Hampshire Human Resources
25 Capitol Street
Concord, NH 03301-6313
(603) 271-3262
&www.nh.gov/hr/employ
mentlisting.html

New Jersey Department of Personnel
&www.state.nj.us/personnel/
jobs/index.htm

New Mexico State Personnel Office
&www.state.nm.us

New York State Department of Civil
Service
Alfred E. Smith State Office
Building
Albany, NY 12239
(518) 457-2487
&www.cs.state.ny.us

State of North Carolina
&www.ncgov.com

North Dakota Human Resource
Management Services
600 E. Boulevard Avenue,
Dept. 113
Bismarck, ND 58505-0120
(701) 328-3293
&www.nd.gov

State of Ohio Job Search
&http://statejobs.ohio.gov

Oklahoma Office of Personnel
Management
Jim Thorpe Building
2101 North Lincoln Boulevard
Oklahoma City, OK 73105
(405) 521-2177
&www.ok.gov

State of Oregon Jobs Page
155 Cottage Street, NE U-30
Salem, OR 97301-3967
(503) 378-8344
&www.oregonjobs.org

Pennsylvania State Civil Service
Commission
&www.scsc.state.pa.us

Rhode Island Department of Labor
and Training
Center General Complex
1511 Pontiac Avenue
Cranston, RI 02920
(401) 462-8000
&www.dlt.state.ri.us

South Carolina Office of Human
Resources
SouthTrust Building
1201 Main Street, Suite 800
Columbia, SC 29201
(803) 737-0900
&http://ohrweb.ohr.state.sc.us

South Dakota Bureau of Personnel
Capitol Building
500 East Capitol Avenue
Pierre, SD 57501-5070
(605) 773-3148
✍ *www.state.sd.us*

Tennessee Department of Personnel
James K. Polk Building
Nashville, TN 37243-0001
(615) 741-2958
✍ *www.state.tn.us/personnel*

Texas Workforce Commission
✍ *www.twc.state.tx.us*

Utah Department of Workforce Services
P.O. Box 45249
Salt Lake City, UT 84145-0249
(801) 526-9675
✍ *http://jobs.utah.gov*

Vermont Department of Human Resources
103 South Main Street
Waterbury, VT 05671-2801
(802) 241-1119
✍ *www.vermontpersonnel.org*

Washington State Department of Personnel
P.O. Box 47500
Olympia, WA 98504-7500
(360) 664-1960
✍ *www.dop.wa.gov*

West Virginia Division of Personnel
✍ *www.state.wv.us/ admin/personnel/jobs/*

Wisconsin Office of State Employment Relations
101 East Wilson Street
P.O. Box 7855
Madison, WI 53707
✍ *http://wiscjobs.state.wi.us*

Wyoming Human Resources Division
✍ *http://personnel.state.wy.us*

Federal Salary Ranges and Pay Grades

Federal Government General Schedule Pay Rates for 2005

The salaries of most government jobs are based on a pay grade list called GS-grade salaries. The list can also be found at: *www.usa-jobs.opm.gov/B5A.asp*

GS Level Entrance Salary Levels	
GS Level	Salary Range
GS 1	$16,016 to $20,036
GS 2	$18,007 to $22,660
GS 3	$19,647 to $25,542
GS 4	$22,056 to $28,671
GS 5	$24,677 to $32,084
GS 6	$27,507 to $35,760
GS 7	$30,567 to $39,738
GS 8	$33,852 to $44,004
GS 9	$37,390 to $48,604
GS 10	$41,175 to $53,532
GS 11	$45,239 to $58,811
GS 12	$54,221 to $70,484
GS 13	64,478 to 83,819
GS 14	$76,193 to $99,053
GS 15	$89,625 to $116,517

Average Annual Salary Range for Selected Federal Government Jobs

Federal Job	Salary Range
Accounting Technician, Bureau of Prisons	$37,000 to $54,000
Administrative Assistant, Office of the Comptroller of the Currency	$33,000 to $56,000
Aerospace Engineer, Defense Technology Security Administration	$77,000 to $140,000
Agent, Customs and Border Protection	$35,000 to $40,000
Agricultural Engineer, Natural Resources Conservation Service	$41,000 to $61,000
Associate Administrator, Department of Agriculture	$110,000 to $165,000
Bank Examiner, Office of the Comptroller of the Currency	$91,000 to $170,000
Biologist, National Institutes of Health	$54,000 to $71,000
Biomedical Engineer, Defense Logistics Agency	$33,000 to $62,000
Carpenter, National Park Service	$42,000 to $46,000
Chemical Engineer, U.S. Navy	$26,000 to $51,000
Chemist, Food and Drug Administration	$77,000 to $101,000
Chief Information Officer, National Institutes of Health	$110,000 to $165,000
Child Development Director, Air Force Personnel Center	$46,000 to $60,000
Civil Engineer, Army Corps of Engineers	$65,000 to $85,000
Clinical Psychologist, Veterans Health Administration	$64,000 to $99,000
Computer Scientist, Air Force Materiel Command	$63,000 to $81,000
Correctional Officer, Bureau of Indian Affairs	$27,000 to $43,000

Average Annual Salary Range for Selected Federal Government Jobs

Federal Job	Salary Range
Counseling Psychologist, Army Installation Management Agency	$46,000 to $60,000
Court Clerk, Court Services	$24,000 to $26,000
Court Reporter, U.S. Courts	$67,000 to $80,000
Customer Service Representative, Forest Service	$27,000 to $39,000
Database Administrator, U.S. Court System	$50,000 to $81,000
Data Entry Clerk, U.S. Court System	$31,000 to $38,000
Detention and Removal Assistant, Immigrations and Customs Enforcement Bureau	$28,000 to $46,000
Drug Abuse Treatment Specialist, Drug Enforcement Administration	$44,000 to $57,000
Electrical Engineer, Army Corps of Engineers	$65,000 to $85,000
Electrician, Department of Energy	$48,000 to $67,000
Emergency Management Specialist, Federal Emergency Management Agency	$54,000 to $84,000
Environmental Engineer, Army Corps of Engineers	$63,000 to $81,000
Equal Employment Opportunity Specialist, Natural Resources Conservation Service	$91,000 to $119,000
Fish and Wildlife Biologist, U.S. Fish and Wildlife Service	$43,000 to $56,000
Human Resources Assistant, Bureau of Land Management	$27,000 to $39,000
Human Resources Specialist, Employee Benefits, U.S. Army	$35,000 to $56,000

Average Annual Salary Range for Selected Federal Government Jobs

Federal Job	Salary Range
Human Resources Specialist, Employee and Labor Relations, District of Columbia Government	$63,000 to $82,000
Immigration Information Officer, Citizenship and Immigration Services	$28,000 to $50,000
Industrial Engineer, Naval Sea Systems Command	$26,000 to $51,000
Intelligence Analyst, Federal Bureau of Investigation	$35,000 to $66,000
Intelligence Specialist, Central Intelligence Agency	$55,000 to $86,000
Internal Revenue Agent, Internal Revenue Service	$52,000 to $70,000
Investigative Analyst, Bureau of Alcohol, Tobacco, and Firearms	$35,000 to $56,000
IT Specialist, Veterans Health Administration	$55,000 to $72,000
Laborer, Army Corps of Engineers	$29,000 to $33,000
Landscape Architect, Army Corps of Engineers	$65,000 to $85,000
Lifeguard, Air Force Personnel Center	$21,000 to $26,000
Maintenance Mechanic, Army Aviation and Missile Command	$37,000 to $42,000
Mechanical Engineer, United States Marine Corps	$52,000 to $66,000
Microbiologist, Environmental Protection Agency	$54,000 to $85,000
Motor Vehicle Operator, National Park Service	$40,000 to $42,000
Painter, United States Coast Guard	$35,000 to $42,000

Average Annual Salary Range for Selected Federal Government Jobs	
Federal Job	**Salary Range**
Park Ranger, National Park Service	$40,000 to $57,000
Public Affairs Specialist, Army Operations Support Command	$55,000 to $72,000
Revenue Officer, Internal Revenue Service	$35,000 to $40,000
Safety Engineer, Occupational Safety and Health Administration	$41,000 to $66,000
Social Worker, Veterans Health Administration	$53,000 to $69,000
Special Officer, U.S. Secret Service	$37,000 to $53,000
Tax Compliance Officer, Internal Revenue Service	$28,000 to $35,000
Technical Writer, Nuclear Regulatory Commission	$91,000 to $119,000
Transportation Security Officer, Transportation Security Administration	$24,000 to $35,000
Transportation Specialist, Transportation Safety Administration	$25,000 to $41,000
Utility Worker, Architect of the Capitol	$31,000 to $51,000
Vocational Development Specialist, Bureau of Reclamation	$35,000 to $42,000
Writer-Editor, Forest Service	$31,000 to $49,000

Index

compensation/benefits
  management, 162–63
computer-audit specialists, 216–17
computer programmers, 187–89
computer scientists, 185–87
construction trade, 193–95, 202–4
copywriting, 113–14, 119
corrections officers, 178–82
court clerks, 172
court officers, 171–72
court reporters, 173–77
court system. *See* judicial system
cover letters, 248–49
creative directors, 119
credit checks, 42, 240–42
customer service positions, 158–61
Customs and Border
  Protection (CBP), 28
customs inspectors, 79

D
database administrators, 185–87
data entry positions, 189–91
day care centers, 134–36
Defense Department. *See*
  Department of Defense (DOD)
Department of Agriculture
  (DOA), 17
Department of Commerce, 17
Department of Defense (DOD), 16
Department of Diplomatic
  Security, 78
Department of Education,
  18, 228–29
Department of Energy (DOE), 17
Department of Health and
  Human Services, 17
Department of Homeland Security
  (DHS), 16, 27–29, 56, 57
  See also specific departments
Department of Housing and Urban
  Development (HUD), 17, 223–24

Department of Justice
  (DOJ), 16, 33–34
Department of Labor, 17
Department of Motor Vehicles
  (DMV), 231–32
Department of the
  Interior, 17, 224–28
Department of the
  Treasury, 16, 219–21
Department of Transportation, 17
Department of Veterans
  Affairs (VA), 16, 144–52
  application process, 149–52
  national cemeteries, 147–48
  outlook and benefits, 148–49
  science jobs with, 146–47
  services provided by, 145–46
detectives, 62–63
diversity, 21–22
Drug Enforcement Agency
  (DEA), 34–37
drug tests, 237–39

E
editors, 114–15, 116–17
Education Department. *See*
  Department of Education
elderly, social services for, 124, 128
Electoral College, 3–7
electrical engineers, 95
electricians, 195–98
e-mail communication, 257–58
emergency medical services
  (EMS), 70–72
employee-benefits
  management, 162–63
employee-relations
  specialists, 162, 164
employment-tax specialists, 216
Energy Department. *See*
  Department of Energy (DOE)
energy resources, 227